'THIS IS WAR!'

'THIS IS WAR!'

The Diaries and Journalism of ANTHONY COTTERELL 1940–1944

JENNIE GRAY

Cotterell was emphatic that our first publication should be called *WAR* because it afforded the opportunity to answer the telephone with the words 'This is *WAR*', which are susceptible of a variety of dramatic enunciations.

Stephen Watts, *Moonlight on a Lake in Bond Street*

Front cover: Anthony in the *WAR* office. (Geoffrey Cotterell)

First published 2013
by Spellmount, an imprint of The History Press
The Mill, Brimscombe Port
Stroud, Gloucestershire, GL5 2QG
www.thehistorypress.co.uk

British Library Cataloguing in Publication Data.
A catalogue record for this book is available from the British Library.

ISBN 978 0 7524 9309 1

Typesetting and origination by The History Press
Printed in Great Britain

CONTENTS

ANTHONY COTTERELL, WAR REPORTER

Anthony Cotterell wrote a unique form of war journalism, witty, sharp, engaging, and so vivid that at times it was almost cinematic. His style was deceptively stripped down and simple, seemingly very easy to imitate. However, its powerful effect was due to a masterly skill in choosing the right materials. The telling anecdote, the brief but evocative description, the perfect choice of dialogue between his fellow servicemen – these are some of the things which gave his work its inimitable quality.

There are two main reasons why his name has not been widely remembered. Firstly, it was the radio journalists of the Second World War who have attained iconic status in history, such men as Quentin Reynolds, Stanley Maxted and Richard Dimbleby. War reporters whose medium was the printed word, such as Alan Morehead, Alexander Clifford, and Anthony himself, have fared less well in historical memory. Secondly, much of Anthony's most successful writing was about the Army, and as such did not have a permanent interest for the wider public although its value is now being rediscovered by historians.

Anthony reported not just on the blood and thunder stuff, the stirring and thrilling campaigns, but the minutiae of everyday life in the Services, being in a unique position to do this as a serving officer. The picture which he gives of fighting men is very far from gung-ho heroics; he spotlights real people and uses the actual words which they speak, thus giving his work a high degree of realism. Above all, he has the ability to make his readers feel that they are actually there with him at the scene. To take one example, his account of the battle of Fontenay-le-Pesnel – this is surely the nearest that a modern reader will ever get to experiencing what it was like to be in the thick of a Normandy tank battle.

Anthony's reports of D-Day and the Normandy campaign were the summit of his reporting career. Less than three months later, he went to Arnhem with 1st Parachute Brigade, and was amongst the small force which got to the bridge. As is well-known, Arnhem was a colossal military disaster, and it was in the chaotic aftermath of the battle that Anthony somehow lost his life. After the battle was over, he and several other British officers at the bridge were captured by the enemy. On 23 September 1944, they began the long journey to imprisonment in Germany. Along the road, in the Dutch village of Brummen, two of the British officers escaped from the truck in which the party was being transported. This precipitated a terrible incident in which two members of the SS shot up the remaining unarmed prisoners in the truck. Three were killed outright, and three were seriously wounded, including Anthony. He was treated in a German dressing-station in Zutphen in Holland, but subsequently disappeared without trace, the only one of his party to do so. To this day his fate remains a mystery. The full story of what happened can be read in my book, *Major Cotterell and Arnhem: A War Crime and a Mystery*. Had he lived, Anthony's account of Arnhem would have been a masterpiece, and the definitive story of what happened at Arnhem bridge.

Anthony was not a career soldier. When reluctantly conscripted in March 1940, he was a twenty-three year old staff reporter on the *Daily Express*, at that period the most dynamic and lively of British newspapers, with the world's highest daily circulation. Anthony had won his staff post at the early age of seventeen and was all set for a high-flying career in journalism when the war intervened. He saw conscription as a levelling process, in which the distinctions one had earned in civilian life were brutally stripped away and everyone was reduced to the same lowly, slave-like status. Then, slowly and painfully – if one was lucky and had a talent which the Army could use – one worked one's way back up again. In Anthony's case, it took fifteen months before the Army recognised his brilliance as a witty and engaging commentator on military matters and gave him what amounted to a plum job, together with considerable latitude to pursue his journalistic career. However, he always remained to a large extent a cynical and sharp-eyed outsider, albeit one who acquired the most tremendous respect and admiration for fighting men. In his Army diaries and journalism, he would always bear in mind the harried private, then the even more harried junior officer that he once had been; this gave his writing an immense humanity, and was one of the reasons why he became such a successful commentator on Army affairs.

The diaries and extracts included in this book fall into two distinct parts. The first part relates to Anthony's first fifteen months in the Army, which were frequently very unhappy; the second part to his three-year attachment to the War Office, where in a department called ABCA (the Army Bureau of Current Affairs) he at last found himself the perfect Army niche.

Part One begins with Anthony's life as a new conscript. The first four extracts come from his book *What! No Morning Tea?*, which was based upon a diary which he kept from March to May 1940. The original version of the diary has been lost and what survives has been tailored for public consumption. Anthony always edited his diaries when he used them for published work, and in this case the entries have a buoyant, positive tone which disguises the true painfulness of his experiences. As always with Anthony, the result is entertaining and informative, but the private man has disappeared behind the jaunty self-portrait necessary to make the book a commercial success.

The same is true – though rather less true – of his accounts of his training as a signaller and then as an officer. The extracts used here come from his October 1944 book *An Apple for the Sergeant*, which was also based upon a contemporary diary. By the time that *An Apple for the Sergeant* was published, Anthony had established his role in the Army so securely that he could pretty much say anything he wanted. He thus freely admitted several of his past military delinquencies without the slightest shame or any fear of the consequences. His service persona was always a key part of his writing, and in these particular accounts he makes his laziness, disenchantment, and complete uselessness as a conventional soldier part of the comedy and absurdity of military life.

The longest text in Part One is the diary which has been entitled here 'Defending the Realm'. It is for the most part taken from the typed transcript of the original diary and, therefore, is much closer to what Anthony really thought. It concerns the period when he was a very junior officer in an infantry battalion, and extremely unhappy and discontented. Being in the Army had become something to endure, a prison sentence which had no known end, and the fact that the Army was not actually doing any fighting meant that the sacrifice of his personal freedom had come to seem extremely pointless. His journey from the raw conscript of March 1940, who had tackled his seismic change of lifestyle with considerable wit and courage, to the resentful officer of early 1941 could almost be said to be a sort of 'Conscript's Progress', paralleled in the experience of hundreds of thousands of other Army conscripts at this particular stage of the war.

The progress of the war had had a severe effect upon Army morale. Very briefly summarised, the quiet period known as the Phoney War had ended during Anthony's first weeks in the Army. From April 1940 onwards, events on the Continent moved with lightening speed to a catastrophic conclusion. Denmark, Norway, the Netherlands, Belgium, and Luxembourg all fell under Nazi control. On 22 June the so-called Armistice was concluded by the Germans with the Pétain government in France, and Britain's war strategy lay in ruins.

Much of the British Expeditionary Force had come home from Dunkirk, but this was the last fighting that the bulk of the Army was to see for years. Instead, the war took to the sea and the air. As the only role that the bulk of the Army was likely to have for the immediate future was a defensive one, boredom, demoralisation, and numerous tiny rebellions against military authority became endemic features of military life, a reaction to the lack of purpose and the ceaseless, apparently pointless training. As Anthony wrote:

Military training is one long charade. You have to be able to pretend that live men are dead and dead ammunition is alive and take the consequent military problems to heart.[1]

---

1   Anthony Cotterell, *An Apple for the Sergeant* (Hutchinson and Co, London, 1944), p.32.

'Defending the Realm' gives a fascinating insight into a side of Britain's war which is rarely covered – the disenchantment, shading perilously close to demoralisation, of many conscript soldiers at this period. Men whose normal peacetime lives had been violently torn apart could stand that disruption if they felt that their presence in the Army was vital. What undermined them was that nothing seemed to be happening, not even the threatened German invasion.

Their discontentment did not pass unnoticed – the top brass were becoming increasingly concerned that the troops' morale, commitment and effectiveness were being eroded by the lack of any purposeful activity. One of the ways in which they planned to remedy this was through Army education, and, in fact, it was for exactly that area that Anthony would be hand-picked in June 1941. He had, of course, no idea that this would happen when he was writing 'Defending the Realm' between January and March of that same year.

What changed everything was his book, *What! No Morning Tea?*, which was published in January 1941. Its tale of how an incompetent conscript became a passable soldier was a huge success. Despite saying many things which were anathema to conventional military types, the book's message – that soldiers were human and that conscripts should be treated as rational, sentient beings – chimed perfectly with the concerns of early 1941. Within two months of its publication, the book had become recommended reading for Army officers. Within five months it had come to the notice of the big guns in Army welfare and education, who then arranged for Anthony's transfer to the War Office. In June 1941, Anthony became part of what was soon to be christened ABCA and his role in the Army was radically transformed.

Part Two of this book covers the reporting which he did whilst at ABCA. Working for ABCA enabled him to take a panoramic view of the war and brought him into a close acquaintance with the cream of the British armed forces. As Britain's fortunes in the war gradually changed, it was ABCA which gave him the pass into various fields of action, culminating in the world-changing events of D-Day and the Normandy campaign. Finally, it led to him parachuting into Arnhem with 1st Parachute Brigade in September 1944.

Throughout his time at ABCA, Anthony worked on the fortnightly bulletin, *WAR*, a small pamphlet-sized publication with a glaring red cover which supplied raw material to education officers. The idea was that by using *WAR* these officers could give a lecture, then chair a discussion and generally get the troops motivated by the key issues behind the war. As a top general told Anthony just before he joined ABCA, the bulletin had the approval of the highest military authorities – 'We want to get rid of this pernicious idea of we can take it. Stop being passive and turn aggressive.'[2]

---

2   The top general was the Director-General of Welfare and Education, Major-General Harry Willans. Anthony Cotterell, *An Apple for the Sergeant*, p.93.

WAR's claim that it was written 'by soldiers for soldiers' was entirely true. Mindful that pedantry would not impress the troops, the authorities deliberately selected two ex-journalist soldiers who had worked in the popular press to write for *WAR*, the first being Anthony, the second being Stephen Watts from the *Sunday Express*. Their first issue was published on 20 September 1941 under the subtitle 'News-Facts for Fighting Men'. All the articles in the first two issues were anonymous, and the overall style of the publication was brisk, soldierly, and no-nonsense. Even so, the two ex-journalists were incapable of writing a completely dull piece. Parts of the editorial were written in a deliberately informal, modern, personal style, with short sentences which had no verbs or which commenced with 'But' and 'And', this being one of the dominant styles at the *Express*.[3] Although their names did not appear, Anthony and Stephen referred to themselves as 'we' rather than writing in the third-person or indeed no identifiable person at all. They made their promise to the readers and sided with them.

> A word about the campaign stories. They are not dispatches hot from the battlefront. *WAR* is not competing with the newspapers. But what we can and will do is to give you a complete picture of the campaign. And that is possible only when all the information has been received, collated and edited. That takes time.[4]

Tracking the editorial (or, as it came to be named, 'Lines of Thought') through the ninety-seven issues of *WAR* is a quick and easy way of identifying the publication's change of tone. Initially it could be rather admonitory, speaking with the official voice and in the official language of ABCA's formation. However, over the course of three years *WAR* changed dramatically. By the D-Day issue, the no-nonsense briskness had gone, and to a large extent so had the official justification for *WAR*'s existence, i.e. the provision of material for group discussions. The D-Day issue was unashamedly a news issue, with virtually no attempt to turn Anthony's account into discussion material. As he wrote in the very short accompanying editorial piece:

> The 6th June, 1944, is a date that will live in history with Trafalgar, Waterloo, and the Dardanelles landings. These accounts of what happened then are of interest if they are simply related to your men as straightforward narratives.[5]

WAR had, in fact, gradually acquired something of the nature of a small magazine, with varied and interesting content, much of it relating to various exciting campaigns rather

---

3   'It has been said, only half in jest, that in a Beaverbrook paper a paragraph consists of no more than six lines – it always begins with "and" or "but".' R. Allen with John Frost, *Voice of Britain, The Inside Story of the* Daily Express (Patrick Stephens, Cambridge, 1983), p.70.

4   'Lines of Thought' (Editorial), *WAR*, issue 1, 20 September 1941 (ABCA, The War Office), p.2.

5   'Lines of Thought' (Editorial), *WAR*, issue 74, 8 July 1944, p.2.

than the humdrum practical stuff. From the end of 1943, it was carrying increasingly lengthy and frequent articles by Anthony, all of which appeared under his own name; his report on the D-Day landing, for example, ran for nine small-type pages, almost the entire issue. Anthony had become the star reporter as well as the editor of *WAR*, and he had modified the original ABCA official brief to suit himself. He went where he wanted, wrote what he wanted, and only later tacked on a small amount of ABCA window-dressing.

Ernest Watkins, who was Stephen Watts's successor, gives a very clear picture of how Anthony had made *WAR* his personal fiefdom.

By 1943 Anthony was in complete control of *WAR*. Nominally the two sections of ABCA responsible for publications were in charge of a lieutenant-colonel answerable to Williams and through him upwards to the Director of Army Education and on to the Adjutant-General himself.[6] In this respect, the Adjutant-General resembled a Fleet Street press baron […]. He had the power of instant dismissal. But he did not interfere with *WAR*. Nobody did. There was no editorial board, not even an advisory commit-tee. Anthony decided what went into each issue, how it was handled and what lessons were to be learnt from it. For a military publication in wartime, it had a most unusual degree of independence.[7]

During the course of four short years, Anthony changed from an embittered (and fre-quently almost intolerably depressed) conscript who thought he had lost his journalistic career forever to a highly successful writer on Army affairs who brilliantly exploited all his opportunities. In working for *WAR*, he also worked for himself, collecting far more material than could ever be used in that publication and reserving it for the books which he wrote or planned to write.

His superb journalism was widely acknowledged. Stephen Watts greatly admired Anthony's gift for capturing a scene – 'Anthony's eye and ear for the significant line or moment were deadly'.[8] Ernest Watkins wrote that what made Anthony's writing so distinctive and memorable was 'the occasional unexpected flickers of his own personal-ity. I thought of them as eddies on the surface of a swift flowing river, indications of its depth, its third dimension.'[9]

---

6   Williams – William Emrys Williams, a civilian, had been taken on at ABCA because of his flair and expertise in educational matters; he was one of the most distinguished of a number of educational spe-cialists who had been drafted into the War Office for the duration.

7   Ernest Watkins, 'It Is Dangerous to Lean Out', Ernest Watkins papers, Special Collections, University of Calgary, file 5.1–5.2, Accession Number: 469/90.9, p.159.

8   Stephen Watts, *Moonlight on a Lake in Bond Street* (The Bodley Head, London, 1961), p.112.

9   Ernest Watkins, 'It Is Dangerous to Lean Out', p.167.

That Anthony's very individual style of writing was considered an essential part of *WAR*'s success was summarized by the man ultimately in charge of *WAR*, the Adjutant-General, General Sir Ronald Adam, one of Britain's top soldiers. Adam wrote in his farewell message to *WAR* in June 1945:

> I should not like to conclude this message without some reference to Major Anthony Cotterell. [...] He believed that you could best describe a thing only after you had done it yourself, and it was to give you the best account that he flew with the USAAF, landed in Normandy on D-Day, and qualified as a parachutist. Many gallant men have lost their lives in this war, and I think this is the right place to mention this one.[10]

10   General Sir Ronald Forbes Adam, 'The End of *WAR*, a farewell message from the Adjutant-General', *WAR*, issue 97, entitled 'Swan Song', 23 June 1945, p.2.

ABOUT THE TEXTS

After his death, Anthony's unpublished papers were preserved by his younger brother, Geoffrey Cotterell, who had been extremely fond of his brother and was devastated by his loss. Geoffrey dedicated an immense amount of effort in the immediate post-war years to finding Anthony; a very considerable amount of help was given by the Dutch, and a parallel search was conducted by the British War Crimes Group for North-West Europe. Sadly, Anthony's disappearance remained a mystery. Geoffrey carried a lifelong burden because of the entirely forgivable failure to find his brother's body or to discover what had happened to him. He kept Anthony's papers almost as an act of piety, a connection with the much-loved past. He also preserved them because, as a writer himself, he might one day want to use them as raw literary material.

Nonetheless, Anthony's papers clearly have large gaps in them. By the time I met Geoffrey in 2008, he was living in a shambles, in a very untidy and disorganised flat in Eastbourne where everything was unkempt and covered in dust. His health had been poor and he had recently had a hip replacement – keeping things immaculate was not exactly a priority. As he was then in his late eighties, Social Services had become involved, and it seems that in one of their bouts of tidying up they disposed of various dusty papers, to their mind valueless, which had been left lying around. At one stage there was a cuttings book of Anthony's newspaper articles, but by the time I asked to borrow it, it had disappeared. Geoffrey was very contrite, apologising for 'such monumental carelessness'. Thankfully, before that particular purge he had given me a huge box of Anthony's papers, amongst which was the D-Day and Normandy material in this book, together with the drafts for 'Defending the Realm'.

It is impossible to know now how much material was disposed of by Anthony himself, by his family, or by accident in later years. Clearly the material was severely edited at some stage, because the only surviving personal letters (apart from one to Anthony's old journalistic mentor, George Edinger) are a handful from Anthony's first year in the Army.

Because Anthony disappeared after the battle of Arnhem, his papers were left in a very disorganised state and became even more so over the next sixty-four years. The Normandy papers, in particular, were in a confused mess, in multiple drafts with no page numbers or titles; the only aids to making sense of them were the very rusty paper-clips which fastened some together.

Jumbled up in the mess of papers was the only surviving fragment of the extensive handwritten diaries upon which Anthony based his books and articles. Written in 1941, just before he joined ABCA, it gives a unique insight into the type of diary entries which Anthony wrote before he began the filtering, reshaping, and writing-up process which resulted in a finished piece of work. The ruled pages are very small and covered with neat writing in blue ink which fortunately has not faded like the yellowing paper. Each page has punched holes to fit Anthony's tiny trouser-pocket file, the method of diary-keeping which he used throughout his Army career.

When composing books and articles from his diaries, Anthony had a distinctive working method. He extracted what he wanted from the source diary and then discarded it as if by itself it had no intrinsic value. Apparently he also did not keep the typed transcripts of the diaries which were part of the working-up process. However, in the case of *An Apple for the Sergeant*, published in October 1944, some of these diary drafts still exist, possibly because he did not have time to dispose of them before he went to Arnhem, or possibly because these drafts alone survived the vagaries of the next sixty-four years.

Although the way in which Anthony worked up the material often added new, very interesting details, it also frequently destroyed the immediacy and freshness of the original writing which, in my view, is of the greater interest today. I have, therefore, always used the earliest version of any text, although I have often added in sections from the later versions. The loss of spontaneity is particularly marked in cases where the end result was an article in *WAR*. Because of the need to condense and to sound authoritative, much which was of great interest was deleted as being unsuitable for the publication. For example, Anthony usually removed men's names and called them by their role or their rank instead, e.g. Brigade Major, Corporal, Flight Lieutenant, and so on. He took out the worst swearing, thus rather taming the way that soldiers speak, and understandably he also cut out anything which might be too revealing of military secrets. Lastly, he removed his most amusingly sarcastic and militarily unacceptable opinions, being cool-headed enough to know that at *WAR* he was in a highly privileged and responsible position.

The *WAR* article which was based on a section of the Normandy material is a good example of this editing process. The article was called, 'Tiger, Tiger, Burning Bright' – a typical Anthony play on words, referring to the much-feared German Tiger tanks and the way in which the tank war often ended in conflagration.[1] The original typescript has a lot more information and is far more exciting and direct than the *WAR* article. However, there are also a number of errors or blank spaces in the typescript where Anthony was temporarily lost for a word or did not know some piece of military terminology.

---

[1]   'Tiger, Tiger, Burning Bright', *WAR*, issues 76 and 77, 19 August and 2 September 1944.

Where possible the two texts have been cross-referenced, and gaps or omissions filled in. I have also done this for other texts where more than one version exists.

Further to the unpublished D-Day and Normandy material, in several places it is obvious that Anthony was reading his notes out to someone who later typed them up. There are a number of small errors where the wrong word is used but one which sounds extremely like the right one. Anthony would shortly tell an interviewer, John Paddy Carstairs, that he was 'cultivating dictation', and that this helped 'to solve the equation between mental activity and physical translation on to paper'.[2] The method must have helped in getting the text down quickly, but it is clear from the various mistakes that there was no time to check it properly before Anthony went to Arnhem. In particular, whoever was taking down the text often made mistakes with military terminology. For example, 'sometimes tracer would drift in our direction' became meaningless when the word 'paper' was substituted for 'tracer'. In another place, where Anthony clearly meant 'Tiger', the German tank, the typescript reads 'fighter'. I have corrected such mistakes wherever they are obvious.

In early drafts where words are missing, I have guessed when the meaning is clear. Otherwise, I have omitted the gap altogether, or in the most impossible cases used a '—' to indicate the space. Other editorial decisions taken were not to use square brackets or '…' in places where the text has been cut, and not to footnote the different versions used. These decisions have been made in the interests of readability, because with multiple versions being used, the text would soon end up looking like Spaghetti Junction. I have added paragraph breaks where necessary to clarify the meaning. I have standardised the capitalisation of military ranks and written out the full version of Army acronyms in most cases, or occasionally footnoted them.

An Apple for the Sergeant, from which several texts have been taken, bears many signs of having been put together in something of a hurry and not very scrupulously edited. In particular, tenses sometimes go astray. Anthony usually wrote in the present tense in moments of high drama like the bombing trips, so I have tidied up incidences where he uses the past tense in the middle of an otherwise present tense section.

In all this I have tried to keep as close to the original text as possible but the one place where I have been forced to take a slightly more laissez-faire approach is in the Normandy texts. I have always used the earliest version as the template and inserted chunks of the later versions where they are necessary to complete the story.

Jennie Gray, Editor

---

2   John Paddy Carstairs, *Hadn't We the Gaiety?* (Hurst and Blackett, 1945), p.34.

PART ONE

THE RELUCTANT SOLDIER, MARCH 1940 – JUNE 1941

THE RELUCTANT SOLDIER

*I*n March 1940, Anthony was conscripted into the British Army. He did not want to be a soldier but faced it reasonably stoically as inevitable.

The book which he wrote about his first eight weeks in the Army, *What! No Morning Tea?*, begins at the exact point when he received his call-up letter, which had been anticipated for many weeks.

> I was just putting the lead on the dog when our maid Daisy gave me the letter.
>
> I took one look and knew. This was it. And it was.
>
> A railway voucher, a postal orders for 4s, and some orders.
>
> For the first time since I left school someone was giving me orders which I couldn't walk out on or argue about.
>
> I really laughed. The whole thing was so awful, it was funny. Everything you had ever worked for was sent up in smoke by that halfpenny circular. Every hope, every plan.
>
> Not that I had anything in particular against the Army. But I was comfortable and I didn't want to be disturbed. An unconscientious objector.[1]

The one bright spot, as Anthony saw it, in his forcible induction into the Army was that he was in the first group to be called up under the National Service Act. As an Army colleague later commented, this gave Anthony a great deal of satisfaction: 'The Government was giving him the chance to cover at first hand an event of the greatest interest to the public, and this he was prepared to exploit to the full.'[2] As soon as Anthony received the call-up letter, he began to keep a diary, and it was this diary which would form the basis of his best-selling book on conscript life, *What! No Morning Tea?*

---

1   Anthony Cotterell, *What! No Morning Tea?* (Victor Gollanz, London, 1941), pp.9–10.

2   The colleague was Ernest Watkins, who worked with Anthony at ABCA. From his unpublished autobiography, 'It is Dangerous to Lean Out', p.158.

The call-up letter arrived on 9 March 1940. This was a Saturday, and he had only six days to put his affairs in order. On Friday 15 March, he left the life which he had lived for the previous six years to travel down to a barracks at Dorchester and his new life as an infantry private.

WHAT! NO MORNING TEA?

'First Week, Friday: Off the Deep End'

I caught the 8.30 a.m. from Waterloo.

The train was packed with young men all carrying attaché cases and mostly hatless. Like football teams and with the same aura of nervous anticipation.

The general standard of dress and appearance was extremely good. Shoes had been shone, faces scrubbed, trousers pressed, hair slicked back. You couldn't see who had been a clerk and who had been a navvy.

I got a corner seat. There were four other conscripts in the compartment, and an old lady going to stay with her married sister in Portland.

There was very little seeing off, and it was very restrained. 'Good luck, boy.' 'Look after yourself, lad.' One man in our compartment had his father, mother and sister on the platform. There was no sign of the wrench except the death-house intensity of the mother's last-minute kiss, and the father's 'Write and let us know 'ow you get on, son.'

It was a perfect spring morning, but the country scenes racing past the windows were not appreciated. 'All fields, ain't it?' and 'Couldn't ever stand it; nothing to do.' We were all desperately anxious to be friendly. It was 'After you' and 'Have a fag' all the time. There was a lot of conversation; bewailing our fate fervently but not bitterly. And all those jokes about the Sergeant-Major.

They talked of the parties they had had. 'Twenty-three in the room. I spent thirty bob and there were others spending. Had to carry the bottles from the pub in baskets.' And the quantities of beer they were going to drink. Presently they went out for a drink and came back half an hour later with a sinister customer called Danny. They started playing solo.

I didn't feel like drinking. I had a flask of brandy but didn't want to face the problem of whether or not to share it. I ate a plum, a pear, an apple for breakfast. I felt melancholy rather than miserable; but not very much of either: and surprisingly no physical excitement.

We got there about 12.30. About 200 got out of the train. We were led off by an NCO, shambling down a subway like convicts, and watched by other passengers with the same fascinated horror that people watch convicts. Our first sight of the place was not particularly attractive, though of course it isn't fair to judge a town by its station yard.

The main feature of the view through the coal trucks was Messrs Eldridge and Pope's neat but not breath-taking brewery. We walked down the station yard, past a small and empty market, and up a villa-lined hill.

After about ten minutes' march we arrived in sight of the barracks; the entrance was impressively medieval. A turreted grey stone heap with an archway entrance through which we could see a giant quadrangle lined with red-brick barrack buildings. We queued up under the archway to have our names ticked off on a list. We straggled sheepishly across to an ominously well-equipped but well-heated gymnasium where we queued up to be sorted into batches under whatever sergeant God had in store. It was getting on for 2 p.m.

Our sergeant turned out to be a very pleasant, soft-spoken, stocky West Country man. He marched us along one side of the barrack square, out the other side, down along a road and turned right down a hill lined with big barrack huts on one side and miscellaneous buildings and tall trees on the other. About three-quarters down the hill the Sergeant led us off the road, up a little path to our barrack hut.

There are fourteen huts in a line down the hill. They are about 60 feet long, 20 feet wide, and 20 feet high. They are stained various shades of brown, and about 15 feet apart. The entrance is half-way down one of the 60 foot sides. There is a wooden porch and a green door. Just inside the door there are three fire buckets of water and one of sand.

There is accommodation for twenty-four men. There is a large locker supported on wooden brackets above each bed. They provide plenty of room for anything you are likely to have. Underneath each locker there are four hat and coat hooks, but these are used for military equipment. There is a towel rail on the side of the locker and a hook for the greatcoat.

The beds are iron frame affairs which you pull out for the night. They have a good but hard mattress and an under-sized cylindrical pillow. The general atmosphere of the hut is roomy and airy. It is heated by hot-water pipes. On the corporal's advice I took a corner bed just by the door.[1] I forgot to see if it was properly lighted, and it wasn't, but it did at least provide a certain illusion of privacy.

Each room has a corporal who sleeps in one corner. Sergeants sleep elsewhere, sharing rooms of their own. Our corporal was a slim, rather solemn-looking young man who looked about thirty. Like everyone else he was very concerned to see us comfortable, very eager to answer questions, several times assuring us that if we played the game by him he would play the game with us.

---

1   Anthony may have been slightly disingenuous in saying that the Corporal had recommended he take the corner bed; he was perfectly capable of grabbing himself the best spot. In his first letter home on 17 March 1940, he advised his brother Geoffrey, who was also just about to be conscripted, 'I have a corner bed. (When you are led to the huts, Shubbles, get in front of the herd so you can get one too.)' Shubbles was Geoffrey's pet-name.
      Anthony Cotterell to Graham and Mintie Cotterell, letter, 17 March 1940. Cotterell family archives.

We were marched up to the stores hut to get four blankets, a large china mug, a knife, fork and spoon. Then back across the barrack square into a two-storey red-brick building and up the stone stairs to lunch. Two from each table went to collect the food. The food is served in tins. You queue up at a counter and it is slammed across at you by noticeably well-fed warriors. You take it back to your table and dish it out; and those who dish it out never go hungry.

On this occasion it was stewed meat, potatoes and beans; followed by stewed apples in gelatinous custard.

It was no worse, no better than I expected. I ate it greedily. In the face of this dramatic change of life, normal critical standards are almost completely suspended. The fact that the bread is piled on the table and passed by a series of hands doesn't mean a thing. Someone else's spoon being used to serve the stewed apples doesn't seem distasteful at all.

After lunch we washed knife, spoon, fork and mug and went back to the gymnasium where we had to strip to the waist and queue up for a medical inspection. Then we went to be fitted with clothes. We queued up outside a hut and went in ten at a time. We had to line up and take off coats and waistcoats. ATS girls fitted us with battledress blouses (they have to be loose fitting) and trousers, then the same outfit in dungarees.[2] Three pairs of socks, two pairs of long pants or drawers, woollen as we later learned to call them, a long pullover, three shirts, greatcoat, hat, pair of boots, pair of brown plimsolls, pair of braces and a kit bag.

We signed for these and retired to the hut to put it all on. I hadn't been so thoroughly dressed for some time. You wear a khaki shirt next to the skin, then a pullover, then the battle dress. Down below you have your long paints, narrow trousers, thick Army socks, and outsize Army boots.

But the thing that bothers you most is the side cap. You walk like a juggler every minute afraid it will fall off. It takes weeks to get the knack of wearing it at the proper angle: you have to 'walk beside it'.

We went to tea, feeling considerably superior to anyone we passed not yet in uniform.

For tea we had bread, butter and a hunk of fish. No decadent dickering with plates however. There were no plates. I ate my hunk crushed into a monster sandwich.

After tea we made our beds and were free until 11.15 p.m. (but lights out by 10.15 p.m.).

I walked down round the town and went into the YMCA where there were half a dozen playing billiards. At the bar you could buy tea, coffee, cocoa, cigarettes, chocolates, sandwiches and buns. Prices negligible. The two women helpers were willing but vague; they couldn't work the urn and they weren't very strong on the prices. They would have been more at home in a cathedral-shadowed tea-shoppe. But then so would I.

I slept well. The bed was hard but tolerable. The lack of sheets didn't bother me. I woke once or twice. The snoring was something awful, and one or two were talking

---

2   ATS – Auxiliary Territorial Service, the women's branch of the Army.

in their sleep. 'It's raining, it's raining,' one of them said. Fortunately these manifestations died down after the first few nervous nights.

Easter Sunday

As I write we are hanging around waiting for a cobbler to come and stud our boots. Odd job for Easter Sunday morning.

Everyone is lying on his bed.

Two have been wrestling, but you don't get much physical ebullience. So far most of them have spent most of the holiday in the hut on their beds. They can't afford to do anything else, poor devils. Money is the big complaint. There is also a good deal of homesickness. Bred no doubt by lying about in bed.

This is the second weekend. Everything seems to have been going on for a long time. We are beginning to know where to go and what to do. Some have even learned to stand to attention when speaking to an NCO.

Everyone swears a lot in the Army. Just one word. I don't quite know how not to say it. It starts with the sixth letter of the alphabet.

When we first came the old soldiers intensified their swearing to show us recruits that they were old soldiers. And after two days no one swore harder than the recruits. The non-stop use of this adjective definitely slowed up conversation.

(Self-Summary after Ten Days.)
I am much tidier, I put everything back and do everything up. I fold things, I shut doors, I look for the ashtray.

It's funny to have to think about money. Not that I have ever had much to spare. But I always had plenty for the way I lived. Now I am trying to live the same way in my spare time without the same money. Trying to fill a quart pot with a half a pint. It involves those unpleasant division sums.

My income has been divided by eight, but so have my opportunities for spending it.[3] I can live comfortably on what I have got providing I don't go near London. And get keen on walking.

Odd how quickly I have got reconciled to relatively rough living and having no money. To me earned income was the main criterion of merit. I wonder how long this new Gandhi attitude will last. Most people have been even more philosophical. They

---

3   In his 17 March 1940 letter home to his parents, Anthony told them after making some comments on Army food, 'Fortunately there are plenty of places to eat out in Dorchester. I am writing this at the place where I had lunch. A good lunch, the bill for two with half a bottle of wine being about ten shillings. Ten shillings being easily one week's pay. (The other 4s are saved for you presumably to provide for the purchase of a wreath.)' Anthony Cotterell to Graham and Mintie Cotterell, letter, 17 March 1940.

hadn't so much to lose but they lost more of what they had. It was pathetic to hear them say things like, 'Well, no more Player's Woodbines after today'.[4]

'Fourth Week, Tuesday: Oh, Bad Shot'

My shooting form took a disastrous turn to the normal this morning. We went out to the small range for snap-shooting. You stand in a trench, crouch down to load the rifle, then the Sergeant shouts 'Up'. You come up into the aim and fire before he says 'Down' a few seconds later.

I didn't concentrate properly. I concentrated on concentrating instead of on shooting properly. I didn't hit the target at all. Not once. My score was nothing. I was the only one who didn't. When I'm bad I'm very bad.

Rumours all day about the Germans invading Holland, Denmark and Norway. But hardly the slightest interest in the hut. The morning papers had nothing and there aren't many radios.

But after lunch – just now – Padbury came running in to say that Hitler had gone into Denmark and Holland and was at war with Norway.[5] The atmosphere electrified for several minutes.

Comments: 'It won't be long now.'

'I'm going on the bottle tonight.'

'No more Maginot now; it'll be you or him.'

'I don't bloody well care.'

'I'll buy a paper tonight to have a look.'

But a few minutes later it had completely dropped out of the conversation. There were nineteen in the room; four were reading papers, three were writing letters, two were singing 'I'll pray for you', the rest were sleeping or cleaning their buttons.

'Sixth Week, Monday: So Many Men'

I have just had a set-back. Tonight after remedial exercises in the new gymnasium there was a passing out test. Each man had to stand on his bare feet, full knees bend and up on the toes. I was quietly confident. I stood at the back cleaning my feet to help create a good impression. My turn came. Firmly, even proudly, I stood before the Sergeant.

---

4   Player's Woodbines – cigarettes.

5   This was Tuesday 9 April 1940, although Anthony does not give the date in the book. Eventually the news was confirmed that that it was only Norway and Denmark which had been attacked. It would be another month before Germany invaded Holland.

'What was your job in civvy street?' he asked. My heart sank.[6]

'I was a journalist, Sergeant.'

'Did you flamp everywhere?'

I didn't get this, but taking my cue from the sniggers around me, I sniggered too and said, 'Well, yes and no.'

He put his pencil on the floor. 'Try and pick it up as if you were a parrot,' he said. I tried and failed.

'You want to take care of your feet,' he said 'You haven't used them enough. They aren't very flat now, but they will be if you don't work on them.'

Professor A.L. Rowse, the left-wing pillar whom I met at a Liberal Summer School five years ago, has been staying at the hotel in Dorchester over the weekend with a very pleasant history professor, now attached to the Chatham House foreign press investigators.[7] He was saying that the Government are likely to embark on a big campaign for giving lectures to the troops. On the theory that the troops must be hungry for enlightenment. Personally I have noticed no evidence of hunger for higher learning.

The idea of these lectures would be to banish boredom. As far as I am concerned, they would definitely produce it. Especially when you think of the bores and charlatans who would inevitably work their way into such a scheme. I don't think people would want to go to lectures, but once they got there, I think that most people would be interested. Just as they don't want to to go to church or learn to fold blankets properly, but once they are marched along to it, they take an interest. Which immediately subsides on the command 'Dismiss'.

After giving my advice on keeping the Army happy I had to fly back to the camp for our first night operations. The start was rather glamorous, with night falling fast and a whispered peptalk from the Corporal on the virtue and necessity of silence at night, for a careless laugh may mean ambush and death.

We marched off in platoons to a barrage of caustic comments from soldiers leaning on doors and out of windows. 'Oh, you lucky people.' 'Have a nice time.' 'Does mother know you'll be out late?' 'Look, dear, soldiers.'

On through the gates at the bottom of the hill and up through the half-made roads and huts of the new camp. A good many of the huts are completed. They are occupied by the last intake of recruits. They were singing to a banjo in one of them. We might have been back on the old plantation.

---

6   By now, Anthony had become accustomed to being belittled by sergeants and gym instructors for his former profession – journalists were considered to be self-indulgent and unfit.

7   The hotel was The Antelope in Dorchester, to which Anthony regularly escaped from Army life. He had probably gone there for a meal or a bath, and then got into conversation with Professor Rowse and the history professor. At this stage Anthony had no inkling that he himself, just over a year later, would be involved in the immense project to educate the troops.

It's an adventurous feeling to march along in silence at night. There's a pleasant atmosphere of daring purpose about things. Heightened by the drum-like thud of hundreds of feet coming to the ground at once. We must have marched about a mile out over the common.

We were halted and the whole company was bunched together on ground sloping sharply down to the river and the railway. The Sergeant-Major cleared his throat and started as usual. 'Now listen here a minute …' when a train came along the line destroying the silence. In daytime no train would have stood a chance, but now the Sergeant-Major had to stop and wait until it passed. Amazing how much louder the same sound seems at night.

That was the point of our coming out. For a demonstration of how far a cigarette glows in the dark, how loud a laugh sounds, how far talking carries.

We all had to turn about while various numbers of men marched along the road at the top of the hill. We had to guess how many there were. It was difficult to hear them. For one thing there was rarely silence. A dog barked, some ducks quacked, a car stopped and started, and an engine shunted away on the other side of the town. Each sound in turn seemed to fill the world.

And our own people coughed, despite previous orders to stop it with a rag. The Company Sergeant-Major blew his whistle again, and somewhere in the distance men laughed to order. You could hear them telescopically well.

THE SIGNALLER

*A*fter eight weeks in initial training, Anthony began a signallers course lasting three months, having applied for this course on the grounds that it was 'easier on the feet'. The following exert is from a chapter in *An Apple For the Sergeant*, published in October 1944; now established as a highly successful commentator on Army affairs, Anthony is looking back on his time as a signaller some three and a half years earlier, basing his account on the diary which he had written at the time.

★★★

I sometimes wondered whether I wasn't a fool to waste what little spare time I had in writing something which, apart from its literary demerits, looked like being profoundly outdated by the Fall of France, which was now taking ominous shape.[1] Not that we were particularly aware of this.

We were more interested in our progress in the Morse code. It was quite extraordinary how interested we became. To my surprise and complacency I picked it up very quickly. It is the only military activity for which I have shown more than mediocre aptitude. You become a sort of mental athlete with off-days and on-days so far as your speed and accuracy in sending and receiving Morse is concerned. Your whole life is permeated with de-de-de-da-de. After a day devoted to arms drill or weapon training you have no particular conviction of progress nor often any means of assessing it. But here we spent the day with the Sergeant reading us blocks of letters or news stories from the *Daily Mirror* in Morse dots and dashes. We had to write them down, then hand them in to be marked. You could see how you were getting on.

Most of the time we spent in the stable doing this or listening to lectures. Every day we would march out in a little crocodile, armed with our pencils and notebooks, and stand in pairs reading a lamp which one of the corporals was operating several fields away. The great attraction was that it occupied your mind and made the time pass very quickly.

---

1   Anthony was working on *What! No Morning Tea?* in May–June 1940; on 22 June the Armistice was concluded by the victorious Germans with the Pétain government in France.

You had to learn to send Morse ten words a minute WT and eight words a minute with the lamp.[2] Your whole life was devoted to obtaining this proficiency. It is a tangible skill, with a pleasant sense of expertness attached to it and most people get interested in it.

I think the reason why sailors seem to be on the whole more content with their work than soldiers is simply that their jobs have more of this satisfying sense of expertness about them. Some time ago I ventured a little from the shore in a destroyer.[3] The living conditions were violently overcrowded. Those who didn't sleep in hammocks slept on lockers or on the floor, on the pitching, heaving, devilishly vibrating floor.

Guarding convoys up and down the North Sea is sometimes very exciting, often very monotonous, but at least it is a vital job. In the mere business of sailing, let along fighting, every man is well occupied. When at dusk they go to Action Stations there is a very good chance that there will be some action. It is much more exciting than manning a Bofors gun on land, guarding an area which the Germans have never attacked and don't apparently intend to.[4] You may have been there two years without anything happening, but all the time you must behave as if it is going to happen any minute. It is much easier to be interested in cleaning a gun if you think you are going to use it, that if such an event is improbable. That is, and always has been, the main problem in keeping an Army eager – the fact that you have to train and live most of the time in an atmosphere of make-believe and rehearsal.

As the weeks went by our course became more complicated. Sometimes our training was interrupted by such irrelevancies as trench-digging. There were beginning to be quite a few air raids in the neighbourhood and we had to dig trenches to shelter in and – what was worse – we had to shelter in them. Whenever the siren went we were all marched out to stand there in six inches of water with no conviction of improved security whatsoever.

I didn't enjoy digging the trenches. It wasn't that I didn't approach these jobs in the right spirit. I approached digging as constructively as I could, working industriously and trying to appreciate the pleasures of straightforward manual work in the open air. As I dug I kept thinking how creditable it was that, after a life of almost total physical inactivity, I was able to dig with the best of them. The trouble was that I couldn't dig with the best of them for very long. It wasn't only the weariness which assailed me, it was the dullness. Daly, on the other hand, was uninterested from the start.[5] He didn't even try to be interested. He simply stood there leaning on his spade, keeping an eye cocked for our many superintendents. There must have been 200 of us doing this dig-

---

2   WT – wireless transmitter; the lamp – a specialised Aldis Lamp.

3   The full account of this trip on a destroyer which was published in *WAR* is given in Part Two, 'And What Did They See?'.

4   Anthony is referring to his brother Geoffrey's work as an officer in the anti-aircraft batteries.

5   Daly was a distant relative and the nearest thing to a friend that Anthony had in the Army at this period.

ging. One did twenty minutes with a pick and then rested while the others did twenty minutes with a shovel. Life was certainly much easier with a pick and it was even easier when we hit on the formula of resting when our picks were resting and joining another resting groups of picks when our lot went back into the trenches. Then I separated the head of my pick from the handle and, carrying it in a purposeful way, as if on my way to have it repaired, walked off along the road across the barrack square into the NAAFI, where I had a cup of tea along with several other men of initiative and resource. No one ever thinks to question a man who is carrying something if he looks as if he has been ordered to carry it. I think the secret is to look resentful, as if you didn't want to go where you were being sent.

I had been invited to dinner at Upwey, down near Weymouth, about eight miles away. It was a perfectly delightful house, with all the comforts which are totally lacking in a camp. The properly furnished bathroom, the books and bottles, the gramophone records and manicured hands, the scent and the voice were very welcome. Women are a great idea. You don't realise how arid a barrack room is until you are reminded that the other kind of life still goes on.

OFFICER TRAINING

*I*n June 1941, before he had finished his signallers course, Anthony was posted to Officer Corps Training Unit (OCTU). Ever since being conscripted in March, he had held great hopes for a better life as an officer, but in the event he was to find it in some ways even more painful than being a private. Living conditions would be markedly better, but his inaptitude for military life would become even more humiliatingly apparent.

168 OCTU was at Aldershot, a place with several cinemas and many shops, pubs and restaurants. But, as Anthony wrote, it was all fiendishly overcrowded; 'everywhere was thick with troops'. He took an immediate dislike to the place because it was so saturated with military life. In a letter to his brother Geoffrey he wrote, 'Gone to Aldershot, the town with the lowest collective IQ on earth'.[1]

The opening address by the 'subsequently famous' (as Anthony called him mischievously) Lieutenant-Colonel R.C. Bingham, Commanding Officer of 168 OCTU, set the tone for much that was to come.[2] The exert is from *An Apple for the Sergeant*.

***

We were marched down to a big wooden lecture hall to hear an opening address by our Company Commander, who was tall, broad and fearsomely military. There is nothing more forbidding than a face hidden behind a fine military moustache; it makes it so difficult to detect any sign of human sympathy. The Company Commander told us that we were no longer ordinary private soldiers; we were now potential officers, and perfection must therefore be our standard, particularly when walking out after duty.

---

1   Anthony Cotterell to Geoffrey Cotterell, letter undated but June 1940. Cotterell family archives.

2   In January 1941, Bingham had a letter published in *The Times*, which stated that officer shortcomings were directly due to commissioning men who did not have 'the old school tie' instincts for leadership and for taking responsibility for their troops. He was referring to middle- and lower-class men whom, he considered, did not have the instinctive *noblesse oblige* which the public schools bred. His comments sparked off such an immense furore that Bingham lost his post. Jeremy A. Crang, *The British Army and the People's War 1939–1945* (Manchester University Press, Manchester, 2000), p.62.

There must be no familiarity with other ranks, though, of course, it would be advisable not to carry this to any ridiculous lengths. However, we were subject to the same discipline as the ordinary private soldier, and in fact this would be even more rigorously applied. We should find that there were bars set aside for officers and cadets and we were advised to keep to these particular bars.

He also warned us that there were women in Aldershot, some of whom were not above reproach. Personally he couldn't understand any man who had the chance to hold the King's Commission losing his head over women; but there it was. There were also a large number of tailors' representatives in the town who would attempt to lure our custom with specious promises and beer. There were cases of men who had ordered their uniforms on the strength of their outfitting allowance and had then failed the course. You couldn't, in fact, be too careful.

'Four grades of cadets are turned out here,' said the Company Commander: 'Grade A, first-class chaps, above the average – any Battalion proud to have them; Grade B, good chaps and good value for anybody – any Battalion very pleased to have them; Grade C, good fellows, men you could trust, but perhaps not quite so quick as the others; nothing against them, of course, probably tried very hard but they hadn't quite got that little extra. Yes, all those three grades are very good chaps. And then,' he said, with a tinge of disgust, 'there's Grade D.'

I was sorry he didn't say much about Grade D, because I had the feeling, rightly as it transpired, that that is what I would turn out to be.[3] I was the only one in our Company.

We soon settled down to our new life, and a pretty horrible one it was. There is something about the process of qualification for commissioned rank which brings out the worst in most people. Careerism rears its ugly head. An OCTU is the perfect playground for the fancy notebook character, the man who loves to spend his evening writing up notes on the lectures he has heard during the day and illustrating his usually wooden, inaccurate reports of what the lecturer said with multi-coloured diagrams. We had a number of young men who really enjoyed this kind of thing. They sat in the front rows at the lectures asking questions designed to demonstrate their grasp of the subject, laughing like drains at any attempted joke by the lecturer, scribbling notes as furiously as any woman undergraduate, and being generally appalling.

But probably these rather bitter feelings were prompted by jealousy, for personally I am no good at drawing diagrams. They used to take us out and station us in front of a piece of landscape and tell us to draw a panorama sketch map of it. While all the others were deftly summarising the topographical features I would laboriously, with dropped, hopeless jaw, produce the kind of thing I could have done equally well at the age of six.

---

3   Although Anthony makes a joke of this, it must have been very humiliating for a man who had won scholarships to King's School, Rochester, and to Guy's Hospital.

The general routine of the OCTU was that during the first weeks we learned the elements of foot drill and rifle drill and gradually worked up to tactical problems, with a strong background of lectures and demonstrations. We started right at the beginning. The first day on the square we were taught to stand to attention. We were a little puzzled by this, seeing that we would never have been sent to the OCTU if we hadn't been able to stand to attention satisfactorily. We also had that well-worn lecture which starts 'This is the rifle …' We were standing in a circle round the Sergeant and opposite me was a cadet who had been in the Army ten years. He had just come back from France.[4] I well recall the expression on his face when the Sergeant said, 'This is the rifle …'

It was all very much like a hotted-up version of our recruit training, but with the added nervous strain of living up to much higher standards. There was none of the old slap-happy approach. Everything was grim and dutiful and humourless. Of course, this can't last long in any situation. You find your level in the back row of the squad and adjust yourself.

I was coming back from a bath one evening when I came across a queue of men in civilian clothes. They were the last remnants of the direct commissioning system, come straight to OCTU from civilian life. Halfway down the queue there were two familiar faces – Geoffrey Cox and John Grime, both from the *Daily Express*. Come to think of it, Geoffrey wasn't in civilian clothes, he had already been a few days in the New Zealand Army, He had covered several wars and won a great name for himself as a war correspondent, but he didn't look like a man with a great name at the moment. John Grime had been the dramatic critic. They were both pathetically pleased to see a familiar face, and treated me with more than usual respect, perhaps afraid that I might twist their arm or report them to the prefects. Also in the queue I noticed a man who is quite noted as a divorce lawyer. Standing in the queue he looked quite incapable of conducting his own affairs, let alone anyone else's.

The man who slept in the bed opposite to me was an absolutely champion lead-swinger; he was a plausible talker with unlimited confidence and he fixed things for himself to a quite extraordinary degree, sent himself telegrams asking for himself to be sent on leave for business reasons, wrote himself letters on his firm's notepaper, and I don't know what – and got away with everything.

We spent a lot of time out on the training ground studying the general principles of attack, defence, advance and withdrawal, each process being remarkably like the other. We selected lines of advance and studied stalking and the use of cover. We walked miles and miles over the undulating, gorse-infested countryside around Aldershot. We attacked and advanced on each other from every possible angle and at all hours of

---

4   The cadet would have been with the British Expeditionary Force, which was evacuated under very heavy fire from Dunkirk in May–June 1940.

the day and night. We also spent a lot of time digging a tank ditch and constructing wire fences as part of the Bingham Line, so called after our Commanding Officer, which was designed against the currently expected German invasion. We also had an operational role, which was to defend the neighbourhood against attack. One of our concerns about the German attack was that if they were going to do it they should do it quickly and enable us to leave the OCTU. We had to man road blocks. My usual role was to stand in a pillbox with my rifle pointed up a railway line. We had to do this for an hour just before and about dawn, as the Germans were expected to land on these shores at that time. The only flaw in the arrangement that I could detect was that by the time they came thundering up the Aldershot road we should have gone home to breakfast.

OH! IT'S NICE TO BE IN THE ARMY!

Anthony just scraped through his OCTU course, which ended on 12 October. On 19 October, he began life as a subaltern with the Royal Fusiliers, his first posting being at Tenby in South Wales.

Over the coming months, having completed *What! No Morning Tea?*, he worked on another book, a sort of compendium of interviews and accounts of soldier's experiences, together with his suggestions for making the lot of the troops easier. It would be called by his publishers, *Oh! It's Nice to be in the Army!*, a title which Anthony said appalled him because it made it difficult to take the book seriously. However, he himself had favoured some fairly awful titles, such as *Let Them Eat Coke* and *Sir is the Password*.

Although Anthony wrote the book with a buoyant positive tone, his real view of conscription and the Army was very much darker. In one place, he was for a moment remarkably frank about what he really thought, although he concealed his highly controversial opinion by pretending it was part of a film scenario:

> The Army: A social experiment of monstrous extent. Not just a trade or another way of making a living, but the birth of a nation within a nation. Four million men jerked away from everything and everyone they ever had and lived for – jerked away and marched into a new world.[1]

'Why Does He Shout So Loud?'

One day a man is a Sergeant, authoritative, yes, commanding instant obedience from the men certainly, and treated with considerable civility by the officers, no doubt of that. But withal human, capable of unbending, known to make mistakes. Then one night there is a notice in Part II Orders and the Sergeant becomes the Company Sergeant-Major and never makes a mistake again, or if he does hardly anyone dares to point it out. From that day on he is addressed as 'Sir'. Most of the men are mildly frightened of him, the officers are terrified.

---

1   *Oh! It's Nice to be in the Army!* (Victor Gollancz, London, 1941), p.132.

If a subaltern is late with a return, say the names of men from his platoon whom he wants to recommend for a stripe, the Sergeant-Major says icily, 'You won't be late with them again will you, SIR?' and the subaltern stumbles apologies, while the Sergeant-Major salutes him with a thunderbolt precision which is a reproof in itself. Sergeant-Majors are tremendously correct in everything they do. Everything about them is spotlessly well kept, their boots never need repairing and are apparently proof against splashes of mud. They always know where everything is and where everyone should be. They never get excited except when at frequent intervals they lose their tempers, but even then you feel that they have read how to do it in an Army training manual.

Their attitude to young officers is that of a rich uncle to a pleasant but rather stupid nephew. In milder moments they often address other ranks as 'Now lad,' but their milder moments aren't usually very mild. They don't get much time away from their responsibilities. They can't walk many yards in daylight without seeing something someone has done wrongly or not at all.

Their authority is tremendous. If they get to be Regimental Sergeant-Major, i.e. roughly speaking Head Sergeant-Major to a battalion, it is unspeakable. It is strange and consoling to think that men who exercise such power so wisely over hundreds of fighting men often end up hailing cabs outside rich women's dress shops.[2]

They are responsible for the enforcement of discipline The officers give the orders and the Sergeant-Major sees that they are carried out with proper speed and thoroughness.

'Life is Very Different as an Officer ...'

Life is very different as an officer. They wake you up with a cup of tea. The food and beds are better, often they are very good indeed. No one shouts at you. Instead of trying to find your faults, the Sergeant-Major tries to hide them, for just as the customer is always right the officer must never be wrong. The transformation from barrack room to Officers' Mess is nearly as complete as the original one from over the wall to inside. You wear a collar and tie again and the first few days you fumble inexpertly with the stud. You wear shoes and they feel like plimsolls after the Army boots. The trousers feel soft as peach skin. You let your hair grow, and you manicure your nails. Instead of having to do everything for yourself you don't have to do anything. In the ranks you spend a large part of your spare time getting ready for tomorrow, every little errand, every little chore, you have to do yourself. But now someone else scrapes the mud off your boots, someone else takes the letter to the post, someone else books the trunk call, someone

---

2   Anthony means that once they retired from the Army, this was the sort of work sergeant-majors might end up with – as front-of-house porters to smart shops or hotels.

else does the laundry. And as you are walking up the road, the Army car pulls up and the driver asks if he can give you a lift.

Until the fighting starts being an officer is a good game for the rich young men and the best job they ever had for the poor ones.

'DEFENDING THE REALM', DIARY, JANUARY – MARCH 1941

'**D**efending the Realm' is not Anthony's title for this diary, although it is one which he might quite possibly have chosen given his fondness for titles with ironic or punning overtones. There are no dates, only days of the week, on the typescript pages, but one date is given on an enclosed military form – 1 March 1941. This is enough to place the diary as having been written between January and March 1941. It covers Anthony's life as a very junior officer, serving as a platoon commander in an infantry battalion in a deserted seaside area. Anthony does not give the exact location, but various clues point to it being on the vast expanse of Chichester Harbour, probably between West Itchenor and West Wittering. Chichester Harbour and nearby Portsmouth, Southampton, and the Isle of Wight were all critical defensive positions in the event of a possible German invasion. Britain was going through one of its frequent invasion scares, and Anthony and his platoon had been posted to beef up the frontline of national defence.

This is a long and detailed diary for which Anthony clearly had a lot of time, not only because of the isolation of the posting but also because he was going through a phase of intense resentment against conscription and the Army and needed to let off steam somewhere. The diary contains some of his very best writing on the Army as well as some of his most jaundiced views about it.

The diary records the troops' flippancy, cynicism, and perpetual love of grumbling, but it also notes many instances of the ordinary soldier's resigned endurance of service life, a stoicism which Anthony found almost impossible to emulate. The professional soldiers are the only ones who come across as fully committed to their role, probably because they had chosen the military life as a career whereas the conscripts had not. The key professional soldier in the diary is Anthony's commanding officer, whom he simply refers to as 'the Major'. Anthony had originally been under the command of the Major at Tenby. He then characterised him as 'very upright, very military, rather shy, complete with an Army moustache and a prominent sense of integrity'. Much of the fun of this diary, viewed from this safe distance of years, is the contrast between the Major's keen professionalism and Anthony's lackadaisical and disenchanted attitude.

The diary begins in Malvern as Anthony's unit is preparing to move to the seaside posting.

Defending the Realm

I came back from leave on the Friday night: I was naturally feeling very happy.[1] Our Mess, which had been a private house, looked rather barer than usual, though it could never be called over-furnished. It was a house of attics, each with a different wallpaper more horrible than the last, and the kind of truckle beds which collapse if you approach them the wrong way.

I went up to my room; most of my things and the other man's were packed up on the floor. (So we were moving again, there had been rumours before I went on leave.) I unpacked a bit and went downstairs to the ante-room. All the furniture was gone except half a dozen Army chairs and a card table. Philip was sitting there as usual, spectacled and quizzical.

'Hullo,' he said, 'You back. Have a good leave?'

'Yes, fine.'

'Have a drink.' He poured me out a glass of beer.

'I see we're moving then,' I said.

'So nothing escapes you,' he said. 'It's going to be hell where we're going. Company messes, stand-tos all day and night.'

'Nearer London though isn't it?'

He laughed at that, and said that we wouldn't be allowed out of the company lines for more than about an hour at a time. 'We've had it coming mind you. We haven't done so badly and now we've got it.'

George came in, he used to be a bookie and he had been out with a girl.

'Hullo,' he said. 'Have a good leave?'

'Yes, how's the girl?'

'Fine,' he said.

I went upstairs to bed: there was a man I had never seen before asleep in the bed opposite mine. I was just getting off to sleep when Lawson came in, a little loudly, 'Hullo,' he said. 'Had a good leave?'

He woke me up, but it was not unpleasant to have people taking an interest, it dilutes the gloom of coming back from leave. The miserable feeling of being sucked back into circumstances quite out of control and mostly uncomfortable.

The Army. What a game! Always waiting, and thinking about the past. Waiting in the cold dark outside call boxes.

Extraordinary comfort of primitive beds. Hours spent standing in fields; hours subtracted from any part of the twenty-four, perhaps around dawn, perhaps about

---

1   Anthony's conscript book, *What! No Morning Tea?*, which was about to be published, had just been bought by the *Daily Express* for serialisation. The *Daily Express* had an enormous circulation, and this virtually guaranteed that the book would be a success.

midnight, perhaps all the appalling day. Just standing in a field waiting for some unfor-
tunates to advance over a hill. Waiting for the RAF to give a demonstration, in the
almost certain knowledge that it would be cancelled at the last minute. Then the long
march back, the long way round. Dragging agony of equipment becoming progressively heavier and deader.

As I lay in bed I couldn't say I was particularly pleased with the prospects. During my
leave I had been seeing a good deal of the American and British newspaper people.
They were all full of plans to go here and go there. I had been staying part of the time in
the same house as Mr Quentin Reynolds, then approaching the zenith of his *Postscript*
renown.[2] I thought about Mr Reynolds as I lay in bed. No doubt at this moment he
would be sitting happily having a quiet drink in some congenial restaurant. Thousands
of people were doing that all over the world. Why not me? I didn't like my evenings
and week-ends being out of control. Still, there you are, and what can you do about it?
I went to sleep. Sleep is no mean standby.

I didn't get up until ten past eight; the first person I met downstairs was the Major
who used to be my Company Commander. He told me that from today he was going to
be my Company Commander again and that I was to have No. 14 Platoon. After breakfast I went up to the Company Office and got one of the corporals to show me the
platoon billets. There was no one in them. They were all out on fatigues so I went back
to the Company Office and asked if there was anything to do; as there wasn't I went for
a walk up round the town and back again to the Mess, where I read the papers which
were very excited about British parachutists having landed in Italy.[3] Other people kept
drifting in and out of the Mess, all disgruntled by the moving. One or two were staying
behind for a day or two on the rear party and they were trying to fix up a party to go
out to the roadhouse near Tewkesbury. John, the one with the goatee moustache, asked
me to come up to the Foley for a drink, but on the way up a man brought a message
that I was to check the Company ammunition. This meant standing watching it loaded
on to a truck.

---

2   Quentin Reynolds was a famous American journalist with a marvellous gravelly voice. *Postscript* was a
     very popular radio programme on topical issues, which featured well-known speakers like Reynolds
     and J.B. Priestley. The house in which Reynolds and Anthony were staying was almost certainly Cop-
     pins, the Kent farm which belonged to Sidney Bernstein, the Deputy Director of the Film Division
     of the Ministry of Information, and his wife Zoe Farmer, a great friend of Anthony's. It was a meeting
     place for highly talented media people. Reynolds spoke the commentary for Bernstein's 1940 docu-
     mentary film about the Blitz, 'London Can Take It'.

3   This somewhat cynical remark about the British airborne forces belies the intense interest which
     Anthony would develop in them once he was working on *WAR*. The Italian operation was Operation
     Colossus, 10 February 1941; it was almost a test-run for later operations. All of the force was captured,
     but one of their number, Anthony Deane-Drummond, would escape back to England, rejoin the
     airborne forces, and would be a prisoner in the same house as Anthony after the battle of Arnhem in
     September 1944.

After lunch I sat around watching the batman pack my things.[4] I walked up to the town and bought some books for the journey and a gramophone record. I went to the Priory tearooms where I have been for tea most days since we have been here, I am sitting there now as I write; I wonder how long it will be before the faces of the people who run it will be unrecognisable again; life nowadays is nothing but reshuffle, one long goodbye.

I walked back to the Mess and back up to the town, back to the Mess again and back to the town. We had soup, cold meat and tinned pineapple for supper. I went to bed soon after. When they said we were going to the south coast I had visions of Sunday trips to town, but the RASC Captain who is staying with us to superintend the move showed us where we are going on the map; it might as well be BugBug.[5]

Reveille was at 2 a.m., breakfast at 2.30 a.m.

We are now on a high ridge with a high wind blowing through the broken windows of the coach. It is 9.20 a.m., on a Sunday morning. We have been on the move five hours and sitting in the coach for six. I managed to doze a bit but very twisted and cramped. Some have been sleeping all through, they could sleep on a clothes line. The others have been swearing at each other, cursing every aspect of the journey. It was like all Army journeys, unexplained delays and apparently endless. It was cold before day-light. I wrapped myself in blankets like a squaw and the driver lent me a bit of sacking as a substitute window pane.

After daylight the men became less abusive; the man behind me launched out on an account of what we would be doing on Sunday morning at home. Others argued whether or not West Ham were the best little football team in London.

About ten o'clock we stopped for about forty minutes on the edge of a market town. No one knew what it was called because no one knew where we were, or cared.

The street we stopped in was no Rue de la Paix, aspidistra-ridden Victorian houses and pin-money general shops but of the kind that stay open on Sundays. We couldn't buy any food but I got a glass of milk at a dairy and a cottager gave me a cup of coffee which was however horrible. I was then cheered up a great deal by buying the Sunday papers and finding my book advertised in them.[6] We moved on, nearly everyone falling asleep, I read the papers. An hour later we had to get out and push the bus up a hill. We didn't stop for dinner but I didn't feel hungry; one gets very inured to these journeys, the nice thing about them is that you aren't called on to do anything. We drove straight on until 3.40 p.m., when we arrived in a lane leading past a farm. We were ordered to debus, men are very sluggish after such a long journey, and marched into the farm.

---

4 The batman was Barter, whom Anthony characterised in a letter home as acting like Kenneth Kove, an actor in the famous Aldwych farces such as 'Rookery Nook'. Kove was a light comedian, ideal for playing a clueless curate.

5 RASC – Royal Army Service Corps. In the published version of this text in *An Apple for the Sergeant*, Anthony substitutes Teheran for the slightly more contentious Bug-Bug.

6 The book was *What! No Morning Tea?*

The men were billeted in barns. We were greeted by some Royal Engineers who were there as staff to look after the billets which for the current ten days of mass-moving were being used by different convoys every night.

'Will there be any food tonight, sir?' the RASC driver asked me with the unconcern of one used to the answer being no.

'Everything alright?' I asked the platoon when they were all lying round the hay-carpeted barn floor. One man said 'Well it's a bit rough like, sir,' but otherwise the response was not overwhelming.

'One thing I can't stand is blasted farmyards,' said the Company Sergeant-Major. 'Always such a bloody mess they are.'

Having attended to the discomfort of the men we went to find our own quarters; these were a couple of rooms in the farmhouse, nothing special but certainly nothing to grumble about. The Major drove off to find an Officers' Mess cook who had been abducted by another Company. I was sent to get some bread for the Mess.

Dinner wasn't so bad. Soup, steak, rice, and a savoury, and a couple of bottles of beer each. There were three of us, the Major, another subaltern and I. There are two other officers in the Company, one has gone on ahead, the other is left behind. We talked about what Hitler will do next and also what we were going to do next ourselves. The dining room was large, cold and cluttered with the typical farmhouse miscellany of mail order acquisitions. They had an extraordinary large number of books including one room devoted to them. 'Three tons of books, I've got sons you see,' the farmer told me.

I am writing this sitting on a wooden stool with my notebook resting on a low stone ledge in an empty seaside bungalow just behind the Sussex seafront.[7] It is getting dark and we haven't been able to draw bulbs. I feel really very tired, exactly as I felt yesterday after dinner in the farmhouse. After dinner the Major took us to the farmyard to hear him talk to the six bad men of the company. The Sergeant-Major ranged them in a semi-circle in front of the Major and then stood with us two subalterns behind him.

'None of you are habitual Army criminals as I used to know them in the old days,' the Major said to them, 'Otherwise I wouldn't bother with you. But there's nothing really bad in any of you. The things you have done when you've fallen foul of us, well you know the result. Well now we are going into the front line and when you are in the front line things – little things like you have done in the past – are treated much more seriously than they are in a place like we have just come from. So now is your chance to show what you're really made of.

'If you let the Company down where we're going you will be in real trouble, But you've got your chance and I know you'll take it. This isn't a threat but a warning and

---

7   Anthony was actually writing this section in the afternoon of the following day, Monday, but this is
where it appears in the typescript because it is the conclusion of the previous day.

that is why I am giving it to you in front of your Platoon Commanders so that we can all see how you get on.'

It was still awfully early; when you get up at 2.30 a.m. it makes a nice long day. I went to bed at 8.30 p.m.

MONDAY

It's a funny thing but here am I a professional writer, successful anyway to the extent that since taking it up as a living I haven't missed a meal, yet I can't describe anything connected with nature. I look at it and nothing comes into my head, whereas if I look at a man my brain immediately registers some combination of words to describe him. We drove through very beautiful country today and it would help this story if I could describe it with a bit of Henry Williamson intensity but what's the good of trying?[8] It isn't that I haven't got any feeling for that kind of thing, but I certainly haven't got much, nor have the rest of the platoon. They didn't take the slightest notice of the country they were going through, only the cinemas whose appearance and current programmes they criticised interestedly, and the people, not only girls but men.

We didn't start passing people in any numbers until about nine when we were going through the outskirts of Reading or some such place. It is surprising how far you can travel through the English countryside without seeing more than one or two people if any at all.

At one time there was a rumour that we would have to debus and march some twenty miles. 'I want to report sick, sir. I've got galloping standstill,' said one man.

'He can't get his stomach used to the rich food, sir,' said his neighbour.

'Nice bit of stuff coming along here.'

'For Christ's sake don't touch her.'

Terrific whistles and hoots broke out as we passed the girl. The old argument broke out between Londoners and provincials as to whether or not London girls are better-looking.

The man next to me was reading yesterday's *Empire News* which I had given him. There was an article in it called 'The Army of Today's All Right'.

'Bloke that wrote that works for the Labour Exchange then,' said the man behind.

By this time we had been sitting down far too long, we had that dull obsessive ache at the points where the thigh bones articulate with the rest of the skeleton; I didn't study anatomy for two years for nothing.[9]

At 10.20 we stopped; there was a certain amount of comment about the stopping place which was apparently miles from anywhere as usual. John, the other subaltern, and

8   Henry Williamson of *Tarka the Otter* fame (published 1927).

9   Anthony had been a medical and dental student at Guy's Hospital in London before he became a journalist.

I walked off down the road and found an admirable olde worlde teashop where we had a boiled egg, read the papers, and bought some sandwiches for lunch. We came back in great humour and walked up to the Major. 'We've been doing very well, sir,' I said.

He looked bayonets at us.

'Were you given permission to leave this column?' he demanded in an iced voice.

'No, sir.'

'Then will you kindly see that this does not happen again. Whatever are you thinking of, leaving the line of march? I've been over half the countryside where your men have been wandering. Will you kindly control them in future. That is your job, not mine.' And he strode off down the road.

We got back into the coaches feeling rather bedraggled, but Somerset Maugham was right when he said that if you write it all down it soon stops bothering you.[10]

We began to get near the place about three o'clock; it was very flat country and inclined to marshiness, a typical seaside bungalow landscape punctuated with rock and postcard shops. The bungalows and houses were mostly pretty new and relatively well built. Speculation about what the new billets would be like was pessimistically rife. The Major had said they would be 'fairly good' and he described last night's billets in the barn as 'good'.

'A fucking field I suppose he means.'

'I wish it was huts like we had at Lowestoft.'

'Work all the bloody time at Lowestoft.'

'I don't mind work so long as you get comfort.'

We passed a bashed-in cowhouse.

'There's a likely place,' said the men behind me.

'Luke at the nawtice, 'acks for 'ire.[11] It'll do nicely when we get a bit of time off.'

'I wish he'd get a move on. Git on driver, let the fucking thing go. Throw the bloody wheel away.'

The driver, an RASC man who had been driving and sleeping in this same bus for three months, did not abandon his technician's aura of aloofness and responsibility. He ignored whatever was said to him or about him.

The last three or four miles were alarmingly unpopulated, just marshy fields. We finally pulled up in a road of suburban-looking little houses like you get on the Southend Road. There was the usual wait on arrival. John and I went up and stood around while the Major talked to the Captain he was taking over from and to our own Company Second-in-Command who had come on ahead, a week ago.

---

10   Anthony left this sentence out of the published version of the diary in *An Apple for the Sergeant*, probably on the grounds that it was a bit too outspoken, even for him, in his current position at *WAR*.

11   That is, hacks for hire, riding ponies. This was typical other ranks sarcasm; it was the last thing any of them would be doing.

Each platoon was given a guide and we drove off down the road round the corner along a muddy track between planlessly situated bungalows. We stopped near a row of small houses. Our platoon were allotted three houses and a bungalow, marvellous accommodation of course. We have a house for each section and the bungalow for Platoon Headquarters. The men can practically have a room each.

Although a lot of people are still living in the neighbourhood, many of the houses are empty and a high proportion have been left unfurnished. The billets are extraordinary in that you keep finding things like primus stoves and bicycles, and coal in the cellars and even flour. The troops we took over from just couldn't be bothered to take it away.

This and the empty houses all round make it seem like occupying abandoned enemy territory. We found a wireless set in my bungalow and all sorts of kettles and crockery, not to mention a motorboat in the garage.

As dark fell it started raining. My room is quite pleasant with French windows, though a deplorable outlook onto a grass patch and the back door of another bungalow. Subalterns sleep with their platoons, the Major and the Second-in-Command at the Officers' Mess which is about 200 yards of mud away. It is quite reasonably comfortable.

After dinner I came back and worked in my room, it has a rather pleasant open red-brick fireplace. My bed was made up on the floor but with a mattress so perfectly comfortable. I rather enjoy the business of making oneself comfortable in new quarters, it's the sort of petty adventure I like, when successful of course.

TUESDAY

Up at 5.45 a.m. for the stand-to. They fall in along the dark potholed road outside, dressed as for battle. After inspecting them they go back to their billets and get shaved; they are not allowed to take off their equipment though.[12]

I worked in my room, it makes rather a good opportunity to work.

After breakfast there was a Platoon Commanders' conference in the Company Office, which like all Army offices is a bleak uncarpeted room with trestle tables and forms for sitting on and filling in. There were seven of us: the Company Commander, the Second-in-Command, the Company Sergeant-Major, the Company Quartermaster-Sergeant, the other subaltern and the Sergeant who is deputising for the absent subaltern, and myself.

The Major is a regular soldier of pretty orthodox mould, who after an almost lifelong connection with the Army, has begun to develop a vaguely military flavour. He does not say much, and at first sight seems rather formidable. There is nothing ragtime about his approach. He likes everything to be in its proper place and is persistent to have it so. On

---

12   The platoon was on high alert for a German invasion.

extra-curricular subjects he is a sometimes rather naive inquirer, but on the business of running a Company office he knows how to get what he wants.

'This is a Platoon Commanders' show, so there will be considerable decentralisation and all sorts of administrative problems,' said the Major. 'The CO is coming round this morning. Show him if the posts are mutually supporting with fire plans interlocking. Have posts got overhead cover?'

'Some have, some haven't,' said John, the other subaltern.

'Ammunition must be kept dry,' said the Major, 'Do you know how many latrine buckets you have got, Anthony?'

'Six, sir,' I said smartly, without having the vaguest idea.

'Don't leave vehicles in the open together. I want your opinion on whether we cook as a company or by platoons.'

We said by platoons.

He went on to make the following points:

1. No inside latrines to be used except by officers and full rank NCOs.

2. Action stations to be manned at once.

3. All meter readings to be taken.

4. No mattresses will be used.

5. Rations for tomorrow, collect from Q5 about 1800, Newark Farm, Shipton Green.

6. Blackout is bad.

7. No man allowed on beach.

'Minefields will be marked. There will be a bicycle for each Platoon Commander. Warn your truck driver on the state of roads. Nothing a truck driver likes more in my experience than bucketing along over potholes to see how high he can bounce. Any man seen doing this must be charged.'

The conference went on for about an hour.

We drew our bicycles; they were in a terrible condition. I decided to make my first ride my last. I went back to the platoon billets and inspected them properly for the first time. Some of them were in a pretty bad state from their previous owners – cigarette ends and old food in the stoves, rubbish in the cupboards, baths that needed scouring. The men were already at work on them. I went round with the Lance Corporal in charge of each billet, deciding such problems as where to put the latrine bucket and what room to use as a drying room. It is going to be difficult to keep men dry here. I sent six men off to unload our stores from the baggage train which had brought them from Malvern. Then I told the batman where to store my own things. I then asked the Corporal to suggest two men to be cook and mess orderly. He suggested two names and I summoned them to my room which now has a garden chair by the fireside. They were reassuringly clean and intelligent-looking. Both of them had cooked for their families, being married men. No, they didn't think they would be incapacitated by having to cook for a large number. Yes, they would take an interest in the job.

We went round to the kitchen. It is an ordinary small house kitchen with a coal-burning stove and an electric one. They hadn't cooked by electricity before but they supposed it would be all right. After some further remarks on the virtue of cleanliness I left them to meet the Sergeant-Major, who had arrived on a truck with gum boots and leather jerkins for the platoon. We counted them and started issuing them out.

I am now sitting in my room while the batman cleans my greatcoat: it is 1.10 p.m.

'When is dinner coming, sir?' asked Barter.

'I don't know, they have got ten miles to go to 15 Platoon and back. Was breakfast hot all right?'

'Yes the porridge was nice and hot, sir. Tell you what though, sir, the fried bread was hard as nails, came off your teeth like bullets.'

WEDNESDAY

Being Duty Officer I slept in the Company Office. The idea is to have an officer ready to set the machinery going if anything happens.[13] You sleep near the telephone which only rang once during the night. It was the Adjutant checking up that the phone was answered quickly.

I was reading the *Strand Magazine* at breakfast when the Major came in from an early morning tour of inspection. 'What are your platoon doing this morning, Anthony?' he asked. He had me there. 'I didn't know what plans you had for us, sir.'

'Well in that case you should have asked me. A leg stretcher I think, yes, go for a leg stretcher from ten to half past twelve.'

'Yes, sir. Sir, about this question of cooking, when do we draw the rations?'

'They'll be ready any time from half past nine.'

I walked over to the billets and sent Sergeant to organise a truck. I went to see the cooks, they were entertaining some friends to a nice cup of tea. 'No coal, sir, no food,' they said. We waited round for twenty minutes until Sergeant came back in a truck with half a ton of coal and said the food was on its way. Then we marched off they knew not where and nor did I. They started singing immediately all the usual songs about I didn't want to join the Army, I don't want to go to war, I'd rather hang around Piccadilly underground, but soon merging as usual into word-perfect and heartfelt versions of sophisticated sentimental songs. Some had been to a dance last night; the NCO walking close behind me is a Romeo. 'Lovely little dame I found last night, twenty-two she is, smashing she is.' They went on to the usual anecdotes about NCOs like the time when halfway through a drill parade the Sergeant-Major suddenly inexplicably threw his hands to his head and shouted, 'All I ask is a hundred yards of road to train a million men. Don't grudge me that.'

---

13   i.e. if the invasion started.

All this time we were marching through absolutely flat country with nothing on the skyline but clusters of weekend houses. They are mostly empty and rather pathetic when you pass them close by. Many of them are attractive and no doubt nearly all of them represented the ultimate achievement in comfort of someone's working life. You feel sorry for the estate agents whose prosperity used to seem so wickedly easy; their offices are sprinkled all over these 'private roads' and 'garden estates', and if they are open the only business they ever do is with the War Office man who deals with damage done by troops billeted in their properties. One wonders how long it will be before the tennis and cocktail and weekend parties come again. These emptied areas are ideal for soldiers, there is so much accommodation.

We stopped for a break at a WVS canteen, very comfortably fixed up in a small modern house with a properly equipped kitchen.[14]

We went on again over a circuit about seven miles long. I don't want to flaunt my great physical strength but it seems I set rather a pace. It's very much a mental thing this business of endurance; it is far easier to keep on without feeling tired when you are leading than when you are irresponsibly following.

As we marched up the road towards the billet a depressing smell of burning came from the cookhouse. Everyone was delighted. 'Not only get no dinner, 'ave to put the fucking fire out.' I dismissed them and made for the cookhouse but surprisingly all was well, an extra cook had been sent by HQ and the meal was ready. Only the rice was underdone because it had arrived late.

After dinner they had a lecture on map-reading and I offered 50 Players for the best essay on 'What I did on my last leave and what I would like to do on my next'.[15] One man who couldn't write was given a job in the cookhouse.

We had an officers' conference about the defence of the place after tea and then went for a drink to a well-equipped but otherwise unpatronised club down the road. We played ping-pong.

We had a most varied conversation at dinner, everything from night-clubs to Moses, newspapers to working conditions in Ford factories. The Major stood up as the champion of the Ten Commandments and a glass of port to your dinner as the basis of a sound life. He maintains, as professional soldiers will, that in the Army one is out to look after one's fellow men, or rather one's men, and in civilian life purely oneself.

This is a line of thought not without foundation. Most professional soldiers I have met have a pronounced quality of selflessness and integrity on a far more practical plane than a lot of the people who sit round the W.1. grills denouncing blimps — and red tape.[16]

---

14   WVS – Women's Voluntary Service.

15   Players – a type of cigarette. Fifty Players was quite a generous bribe. Anthony was using the material which he gathered this way for his next book, *Oh! It's Nice to be in the Army!*

16   The reference to W.1. grills and to people denouncing blimps (pompous and antiquated military types) seems to refer to some recent incident in London which had annoyed Anthony.

It is 10.45 p.m. I am back in my bungalow writing this by the fire over a cup of tea. Very cosy these old wives' pleasures. I like being in a small Mess, for a while at least; there are fewer people to sit around talking to, which may be pleasant but doesn't write books.

THURSDAY

Up before 6 a.m. to stand-to, the wind was blowing like mad, it seemed unlikely for the stars and moon to be standing still.

Under a new and more comfortable system, the men stand-to to be inspected in their rooms. I do hope I looked a little less unattractive than some of them did this morning.

The cooks complained rather temperamentally that the men had shouted to them because tea was late yesterday. It wasn't their fault they said, someone had switched off the electric kettle. For breakfast there was some watery porridge, a slice of bacon, one slice of bread and margarine, and a mug of tea. No wonder if they laugh a little acidly at the current agitation to reduce soldiers' rations. It may sound splendid to get more meat than the civilian allowance but you need it if the only other attraction is a slice of bread.

Somebody ought to tell John Steinbeck about this place, it has a fascinating atmosphere of decay.[17] I walked down along the front this morning. The beach huts are tumbling to ruin, their doors swing in the wind and inside you find a chaos of old paraffin lamps and broken furniture. I took an inventory of one. There was a smashed-up table, a banjo case, faded cotton curtains flapping through the broken windows, and on the floor a record of 'Body and Soul'.[18] I sat on the little railing outside, there was a board nailed to it with the name of the hut: 'Wy-Wurry'. Sitting on the railing I couldn't see the sea – the concrete and barbed-wire defence works came in the way. All along the beach in either direction there were soldiers sitting with Bren guns in little emplacements. How now Sunny South Sam?[19]

Further along the coast there was a hotel. I walked into the bar, it was a big bar glittering with bottles and chromium. One of those bars where the people running it aren't quite sure whether they want it to be a pub or a cocktail bar. There was a big open fire blazing, but the milk and *The Times* hadn't been taken in from the step outside. An old woman washing a glass scampered away and fetched out a full-bodied, red-lipped, red-haired woman who looked absolutely in character. Her excitement at getting a customer died down when I said I didn't want a drink. I was just looking around. She started

---

17　John Steinbeck, the American writer best-known for his novel of the Depression, *The Grapes of Wrath*.

18　'Body and Soul', a popular jazz-type song recorded in 1941, sung by Dinah Shore.

19　Sunny South Sam, a fictional railway man of enormous helpfulness who featured on Southern Railway advertising posters during the 1930s, usually with a slogan like 'The sun shines more on the southern coast'.

going through an account book. 'Yes it is a bit quietish here during the week, but it livens up weekends, the evacuees usually have their husbands down. 'Course it used to be awfully jolly here, in summer get a jolly crowd you know, and we had a lot of fun. I say, if you don't want a drink would you like a cup of tea?'

That made the seventh cup today.

Just down the road there were two other bars, the usual drinking club bars born to Seagers Gin out of the Kingston By-pass, but clean and stocked up with drinks, carpet on the floor and red leather chairs round the same red-brick open fireplaces; not a soul in them of course. Nearly all the houses round were empty. It looked quite mad.

I spent most of the morning superintending my platoon working on the defence works on the beach, and the afternoon too. We were told to look out for the CO flying over the Battalion area (in a plane) but didn't see him.

There was a Battalion dance tonight. I decided to look in before dinner and if it was good go back after. It was in W-Company's dining room and this turned out rather further away then it sounded. Two men showed me the way, they told me how their company had had to march the last eight miles here starting at midnight after travelling all day. 'The usual business, sir, "Only another few hundred yards" all the time.'

'It must have been most popular.'

'It was nearly a fatal mistake, sir.'

The first dance in a new situation is naturally full of emotional significance and rarely justified optimism. The men were already standing in groups watching the local girls arrive. It was held in a holiday camp dining room, quite a large wooden bungalow hall with a radiogram booming. The cook Sergeant, that other Astaire, was already tango-ing like a mad thing with a little dark girl just like the girl he used to swoop round the Winter Gardens floor at Malvern, he might have brought her here in his kit bag.[20]

I went down the road to the club we went to last night. 'Ah you've got it all to yourself this time,' said the man behind the bar. It was as empty as the pub was this morning. After dinner continuing my round of gaiety I went to another club. There were five people here, three of them engaged in owning or running the place and a gunner officer who had brought his landlady in from next door. They were playing bridge. They were very apologetic about this. I kept saying it was quite alright, I was perfectly happy. I only wanted a quiet drink, but they wouldn't have it. 'We don't often play bridge,' they said. 'We haven't played for ages.' They felt guilty at not being found drinking or dancing.

'Next time you come we'll have a game of darts,' said one woman.

'Oh good,' I said, horrified.

---

20   'That other Astaire', meaning Fred Astaire, the famous film actor, singer and dancer.

FRIDAY

They were late at standing-to this morning. I asked the last man to arrive why he was late.

'I'm sorry I'm late down, sir,' he said handsomely.

'We're all sorry,' I said. 'Very sorry indeed. What we are interested in is why.'

'I lost my voice, sir. I couldn't 'ardly speak.'

'Now will you tell us all what bearing that has on your not being dressed in time?'

'Well if you lose your voice, sir, you can't 'ardly move. I'm very sorry, sir.'

Breakfast was half an hour late and not ready then. The electric stove went wrong at 6.50 and wasn't repaired until 7.40 am. There were sausages for breakfast — two sausages each, a slice of bread and margarine, and porridge. The sausages had to be cooked in batches on the fire and the porridge couldn't be started until the stove was repaired. In future they must half-cook the porridge the night before.

The men arrived at 7.30 and were told to get cleaned up instead. As so often happens the man who arrived with the most cookhouse experience is a passenger, he must be replaced.

'How many sausages are there?' asked the Sergeant.

'Sixty-two', said the cook.

'Thirty-three men, there ought to be sixty-six.'

'Only sixty-four issued, Sergeant.'

'How d'you make sixty-two then?'

'I had two last night.'

'You don't have two this morning then.'

'Don't want any, Sergeant.'

Apparently cooks rarely eat breakfast and very little lunch, the constant smell and sight of food anaesthetises them against hunger, but they have constant cups of tea and usually an evening meal.

Apparently last night's dance livened up considerably in the end. The band didn't arrive until 9 as some were on duty and all the instruments were locked in the Quartermaster's stores.

The meat for dinner went bad suddenly and thoroughly. We buried it in the garden. It was disappointing because this dinner was meant to be the best meal we have produced, actually it still was. Sergeant managed to get some bacon from the Quartermaster, there were also carrots, cabbage and potatoes. I wanted the potatoes to be roasted to bridge the rather odd combination of bacon and cabbage, but we hadn't enough oven accommodation to roast more than one per man, making up the roast with mash. There was steamed sultana pudding to follow and together it made a very presentable meal. A touch of style was lent by having tables to eat it off. These were issued this morning, a pity the legs aren't the same length.

Pay parade in the afternoon – it was held in the dining room. The Corporal sits by my side selling National Savings Stamps, the thirty-three men bought 12 shillings worth.[21]

The Padre came to tea in my room. He volunteered to go abroad, and he is waiting to go but he finds this place so amusing he wishes he could put it off for a month or two. He gave me quite a proprietorial feeling to see him out of our front door to his car. I have never been a householder before.

One way and another I feel quite a family man, arranging how the meals are to be done and the coal and the bath water and so on. Perhaps after the war I shall join the Boy Scouts. At dinner the Major said 'I always say that any fool can make himself uncomfortable but it takes a man of character and vision to make himself comfortable in difficult conditions. Pass the port, Anthony.'

A man came up to ask my advice on a somewhat ticklish matter. He had gone home on leave and found that his girl had gone off with another man. I said I was sorry to hear it, but if she was likely to do that kind of thing perhaps it was just as well he had found out so soon. But it wasn't sympathy he was after, it was legal advice. He had bought the girl a ring on the instalment plan, and as she had still got the ring he wanted to transfer responsibility for the rest of the payments to her. I told him I didn't fancy his chances and advised him to write to the girl to get the ring back and hold it for use for some future occasion.

SATURDAY

We had another conference at 9.30 a.m. with one of the local gunner officers present. There are a lot of changes to be made in the Company defence system. We were each given our areas to reconnoitre. I took the Sergeant and the Corporal and we walked up and down our platoon front, working out where to put who and what.

The difficulty in making tactical plans is that no one can say whether they are right or wrong, and, when inexperienced, you feel a certain diffidence about saying which is the right position for the gun, especially when you realise that on your right decision may rest the lives of your whole platoon including as it does, mark you, yourself.

After lunch the Padre drove me into Chichester which seemed like New York. It made you realise what an isolated countrified life we are leading. I felt like a country-man coming to London for the first time or as if I had been out East. It was pleasant to see pretty women and the other amenities of civilisation. We had tea in a rather unusual marble hall café, very big with a stone-walled balcony all round, very slick waitresses and a radiogram. I had to come right back as I was Duty Officer. Nothing much happened. I had to pay a man who had got overlooked on pay parade; a man reported

---

21 National Savings Stamps were one of the ways in which the government raised money for the war effort, thus buying a stamp was patriotic.

back from leave. The Adjutant rang to say there would be a Company Commander's conference on Sunday at 9.30 am. There was a message asking if any of our trucks were out between 2130 hrs Thursday and 0600 hrs Friday, stating routes followed, probably in connection with the ATS girl who was found dead by the road.

The Major and Stephen came in from duck shooting, unfortunately without having shot any ducks.

SUNDAY

There was a slight discussion at the breakfast table among the more junior officers on how to take rockets. Rocket is officer slang for a formal reproof. Personally I believe in the straightforward confession of full responsibility, say it was all your fault even if it wasn't, try not to point to extenuating circumstances, on no account try to pass the buck to someone else. This is not only despicable but usually unpractical; you can't help being favourably impressed with a man who takes full responsibility and if after taking it and not using the obvious excuses, he then draws your attention casually to the circum-stances which explain, albeit do not excuse, his conduct, then the probability is that you feel more lenient towards him than to a man who stands there whining excuses.

At least that is my experience not only in giving punishment but in getting it. If I get in trouble and I often do, it is usually through forgetting to do things. For instance, a few weeks ago I went on weekend leave. I asked my Company Commander's permis-sion and put my name down in the officers' leave book. That was on the Wednesday and I went off on the Friday without looking in the leave book to make sure that the Colonel had initialled his permission. They wanted me over the weekend, I was wired for and didn't get the wire, so when I got back Sunday night the news was not good. I went round to the Orderly Room on the Monday morning. The CO was away so I was arraigned before the Second-in-Command and the Adjutant. It is remarkable how effective this kind of telling-off is for, looking at the thing from a completely unscrupu-lous point of view, you know before you start that there is nothing much they can do to you. They aren't going to cashier you for an offence of this kind. They might make you Duty Officer for fourteen days running. This would be inconvenient but by no means insufferable. But in point of fact I felt just as anxious as I did on similar occasions at school when there was the immediate probability of being bent over a chair.[22] Officers' discipline in the small offences is based on making a man feel that he has played a pretty poor trick and let down people who trusted him, with the background point that he is making things worse for his brother officers. Then there is the embarrassment of living in the same house with a man who has just told you of these things. Altogether it is a very effective system.

---

22   King's School, Rochester.

Geoffrey rang up this morning, he is on weekend leave from the OCTU.[23]

It is a marvellously sunny Sunday morning. I am sitting in the Mess listening to the German radio band, waiting to go round my platoon posts with the Second-in-Command, but he hasn't come back from fixing up a football field. The men are mostly punting a ball around on waste ground at the back of the billets. They all wear scarves, leather jerkins and wellington boots.

News in German has just come on; the mess waiter who is cleaning the room hurries to adjust the radio, he twiddles in a quite anxious quest for jazz. Unhesitatingly he jumps the needle away from a symphony concert, a piano recital, a voice talking Spanish, and a cinema orchestra giving 'In a Monastery Garden'. I should have thought that hackneyed light music would be more popular than it is, but Sonya is out and Hutch is in.[24]

Swedes were one of the dinner vegetables, hardly anyone would touch them though they always seem a very acceptable vegetable to me. The kitchen is being kept very clean. There were two slices of bread per man at breakfast and ten weren't used. The solution is to cut the bread giving each man what he wants, but in practice to avoid a service bottleneck it is necessary to cut it beforehand. In future they will cut fifty slices in advance and the rest as required.

We were talking about how to preach a sermon so that it is remembered at lunch. I said the Church ought to go in more for solving human problems, how to get on with your mother-in-law, that kind of thing. The Major is a great admirer of W.H. Elliott; he used to make a point of staying in to hear his mid-week service, and one day three years ago, on his way home from the Cavalry Club where he seems to have spent an awful lot of his time, he dropped in at W.H. Elliott's church.[25] He could remember a lot of the sermon word for word, which is no bad tribute to Reverend Elliott's personality.

There was a company football match against the Royal Artillery after lunch.

We have started an allotment. The ground is so completely mud that it didn't seem likely to me that anything would grow; but one of the men who used to have an allotment was very keen. He ruled out a plot behind the billets and started digging. Seeds have been provided by some obscure official process.

---

23 Geoffrey – Anthony's brother, who was training to be an AA officer at Shrivenham, near Swindon.

24 A somewhat impenetrable topical reference but 'Hutch' almost certainly refers to Leslie 'Hutch' Hutchinson, a much loved wartime singer and entertainer who was often on the radio.

25 Another very topical reference. The Reverend W.H. Elliott was Vicar of St Michael's Church, Chester Square, Belgravia, between 1930 and 1941. He was known as the 'Radio Chaplain' because of his broadcasts on the BBC. Alyson Wilson, *St Michael's, Chester Square, Church History and Guide*.

MONDAY

Liver for breakfast, it never seems natural.

The Divisional Commander was inspecting the defences but as we are in reserve he didn't come near us. I sounded the gas alarm which consists of running up and down the road beating an old petrol tin. It was reassuringly successful, everyone recognised it and put their respirators on. They were having a lecture on field-engineering, they are going to have plenty of field-engineering these coming weeks. Then they had a lecture on security.

At this point the Corporal came running to tell me that two men from the electricity company were taking away the electric stove. I said to the men, 'Here, what about the dinner?' in tones calculated to mingle reasonableness with authority. They said they couldn't help it, they had their orders. I told them to drive round to the Company Office but when we got there the Major was out. The Company Sergeant-Major let go at them. 'You got your orders, blast your bloody orders, how dare you come trespassing on military property, breaking and entering that's what it is.'

'They shouldn't have let us in then,' said the van man. The Sergeant-Major could hardly contain himself, he isn't used to being contradicted.

The loss of the stove made dinner an hour late. The Adjutant came to lunch; we had a couple of ducks shot by the Major, rather tough and overcooked.

I spent the afternoon on the beach discussing new wiring and weapon position arrangements. It was a lovely afternoon and the tide was out; it is true that the Army gets you into good scenery as well as bad, including the shot-down German bomber which you can see on the beach at low tide. This business of fixing on how to defend a place can be an interminable business. One difficulty is that you have to be very diffident about knocking down private property in order to get a clear field of view. Stephen and John had an awfully long conversation.

'Personally I think the worse thing we have to fear is attack by parachutists from the rear.'

'I'd like to get the Vickers on that roof.'

'You must curb this itch of yours to get off the ground. It's the sure route to being blown to pieces.'

'If we have it there we shall be swamped by the tides, remember the spring tides are coming.'

And so on until teatime.

In the evening there was a social for the troops at the WVS canteen. There was dancing to a piano played by one of our men, refreshments and card tricks by a gunner sergeant. I talked to Mrs Bloxham the extremely nice woman who did most of the organising. Her husband is an advertising man, now in the Ministry of Information. She told me how some of the local WVS workers had been somehow rather shocked to find that she had invited the local girls though the results were unexceptionably decorous.

'Are we wanted here then?' some of the helpers had acidly asked. 'They can't seem to get the human touch,' Mrs Bloxham said. 'They get to look on it as a money-making thing, not for themselves mind you. But they try to run it as a machine instead of a home.

'I love looking after these boys don't you? Yours are a very lively lot, the last lot were like turnips. You know I sometimes think the girls they marry and go after don't realise how decent they are. They're so pleased to get a nice letter and so miserable when it's not. You see them when the mail comes in, they're so excited and if it's a good letter they're different beings, and if it isn't their faces go down.'

TUESDAY

I was woken at 6.30 a.m. and meant to get up but I felt too sluggishly comfortable. I lay there rationalising how it wouldn't be any loss of time if I didn't get up, that it would be all the simpler and more logical to make up for it later. I had a second cup of tea and listened to Crosby and the bath running in.[26] I had ordered the bath to give me a pleasant purpose in getting up and I must say it gives an aura of civilisation.

Leave is starting again having been stopped while we were moving. One man from the platoon is allowed forty-eight hours' weekend leave when approved by me. Applications have to be submitted to the Company Office by lunchtime Wednesday. There were four applications on my table after breakfast. Three in the conventional terms:

To Officer Commanding Y Company
From Private -----
Sir,
I wish to submit this my application for weekend leave.
Hoping this meets with your approval.
I have the honour to be, sir
Your Obedient Servant,
Smith, Private.

The other one from the Corporal went on to say 'My reason for requesting this leave is that having been in the Service for sixteen months I have only had two periods of seven days (the second three months ago) and have not had a weekend leave since March 1940.'

In granting leave you usually have to choose between several cases like this, men whose brothers are being drafted abroad, men who want to get engaged, men who want to fight the man who took their girl.

---

26   Probably Bing Crosby, the highly popular American entertainer – Anthony is once again listening to the radio.

At 9 a.m. sharp I arrived on the beach at the place where the platoon was to be working. I was keyed to walk round giving out encouragement here and a useful tip there, and many a kindly good morning. I also intended to show my right spirit by joining in one of the simpler tasks myself. 'Here, I think I'll have a go,' I was going to say, rather in the same spirit as royalty planting a tree. The only thing was that I found an empty beach. With a rising sense of indignation I walked up to the other end of the position. I was still alone. My mental rehearsal switched to another mood. 'What the devil do you mean by this, Sergeant? This isn't good enough you know,' I was saying. When I got back, of course, the explanation as usual was that the tools hadn't arrived. Sergeant had gone down to the Company Office to see about the barbed wire, and the 250 sandbags we had trustingly stored in No. 13 Platoon's billet had been used by them, mostly as door mats.

I sent the men off to see what they could do with their bare hands.

I decided to institute a new system of time off for good work. Every man gets a half hour break during the morning. It will be taken staggered, two men at a time to eliminate the time lost in starting after a mass break – you lose continuity, work is much better done in a smooth flow than in jerks. The new system would be to award an extra twenty minutes to any man who worked specially hard.

At lunch the Major demanded an investigation into officers' rations, were we getting more than the men? If so it must stop at once.

There was another conference after lunch: our defence plan and orders were read out. We were asked what our fire-fighting arrangements were. I hadn't one. We have to fix up targets on the beach to fire at some time next week. The CO has noticed many local girls wearing our regimental cap badges. 'He doesn't object to this and personally I'm all for it,' said the Major, 'but in future new ones will cost 9d. Impress on the men that there won't be any replacements except by payment.'

WEDNESDAY

Corporal to the Mess Orderly: 'You're looking cleaner this morning, cleaner than yesterday.'

Mess Orderly: 'Thank you kindly, Corporal, very civil.'

One of the better Lance Corporals has been drafted off as a permanent guard at Divisional Headquarters just as he was getting very good at running the kitchen. The amazing thing about him was that he was willing to be up at 5 a.m.

I had a slight passage of words with the Sergeant on the subject of whether leave should be a reward for work well done or an automatic amenity. This arose because I had told one of the corporals that how long before he had leave depended to some extent on whether we get our new positions well under construction quickly. There is of course a lot to be said for the security of automatic amenities and emoluments unaffected by the results of one's work. But I have always been used to a business where if you didn't get on you were got out and pretty quick.[27] It may be unfair and uncomfortable (for those who weren't very competent) but it gets things done.

I spent the morning reconnoitring the beach up to the next position. Stephen was there interviewing the cooks who were complaining of short rations. They said the daily ration of porridge was only enough to provide a small portion every other day. They thought other platoons were drawing more at their expense.

'I'll see that this platoon gets its exact ration from now on if there has been any unfairness, but that's all I can do. I can't tell the Government to alter the ration.'

'Supposing the men complain then, sir, send them to you, sir?'

'Send them to go to hell.'

We walked along to examine the two houses I have my eye on for billets for the platoon. After spending some time on billeting, Stephen is developing a house-agent-cum-Quartermaster-Sergeant or only-a-stone's-throw-from-the-sea technique.

'Now that's a fine billet for eight men,' he says, pointing lyrically at some disused rat-run.

I saw two rabbits running along the beach. I never thought rabbits were at all maritime.

It is really extremely difficult to tell when men are working reasonably well at these miscellaneous labouring jobs when one is not experienced enough to know how much to expect of them. It is so difficult to tell whether a man is having five minutes rest after twenty minutes work or twenty minutes rest before five minutes work.

I am Duty Officer tonight. The Sergeant-Major has been sitting in the Company Office with me. 'The days I don't mind, it's the nights I can't stand. I'd get drunk but me wife's got all me money.'

I have hired a typist to type out the book on comfort in the Army which I am just finishing. She is evacuated with her parents to a bungalow — nay, villa — just across the road from our billets. I still don't know what to call the book, I hesitate between *The Land of Sir* and *Sir is the Password*.[28]

The Sergeant Major has just come in again. 'I've just finished my fifteenth letter since I've been here. The last marriage telegram, telegrams we got when we got married. I hate writing but I better I guess, otherwise she'll be suspecting something even though I am pure.' He's a wag, our Sergeant-Major.

Durrant's sent me the cutting of a review of my last book by L.A.G. Strong in *The Spectator*.[29] It is bracketed with Alex Dixon's book *Tinned Soldier* and Mr Strong says 'Mr Dixon is a proved writer, and Mr Cotterell has a few years' experience as a journalist on our liveliest daily paper'. Discounting as much as possible the hurt pride

---

27   Anthony is referring to life as a journalist at the cutting edge of the newspaper industry.

28   Eventually published as *Oh! It's Nice to be in the Army!*

29   Anthony's last book was *What! No Morning Tea?*

element, that is the kind of statement that makes me good and mad. It seems to me an echo of the attitude that attaches more importance to a statement in a book than the same statement in a newspaper; and more importance if a statement is in the cliché and stock-market report style of the unpopular press than if it is written so that anyone can understand it. If the meaning is obscured by muddled expression it is good writing; if you can understand it at a glance it is superficial. Three cheers for William Saroyan.[30]

THURSDAY

Woke up to find a wind and rain storm had sprung up over night. Work had to be suspended for the morning, anyway only one third of the men were available as the others were resting after being on guard all night relieving the other two platoons.

The cook has had a cyst developing in his eye. I sent him to the doctor who is probably sending him to hospital; he didn't get back until 11.30 a.m., when we suddenly realised that the dinner hadn't been started as the Company Office hadn't sent the relief cook as arranged. Dinner therefore delayed until 1.45 p.m.

I walked along the front with Sergeant, the sea was lashing in white horses as far as you could see which wasn't far. The coast is being eaten up at about a foot a week and the spring tides will be starting soon. The Bren gun post we have been building looks like being pulled in, but if you put it far enough inland to allow for a few months' erosion you lose your field of vision. Wavell and I are faced by some ticklish problems. The sea-wall in front of us caved in a few months ago except for a big right-angle of high concrete wall. It blocks one of our aims of fire and we have been trying to undermine this by digging; we made one small hole and the sea is doing the rest frighteningly fast. When you consider how long it takes a gang of man to dig the same effect, the power of the water is depressing.

This girl I have typing for me is a great little knitter. I keep on going over to her bungalow to ask how she is getting on. 'How many thousand words have you done today?' I said.

'Well I don't know. I didn't really count.'

'Think now, dear,' her mother said.

'I should think about four.'

'Do you think you could do more than that tomorrow?'

'Well I could have done more but you see I had some knitting to do.'

'When you finish with me you ought to start a commercial college,' I said, but I don't think she noticed anything.

---

30 Saroyan's stories celebrated energy and positive thinking in the midst of the trials and tribulations of the American Depression; his exaggerated prose style spawned its own adjective, 'Saroyanesque'.

It was my big afternoon this afternoon, the Major and Stephen had gone off to a conference with the Home Guard. 'I leave you in command then,' said the Major. 'Look after this new officer when he arrives.' We are expecting a new subaltern today. I left word at the Mess for them to send over for me when he came, but when he did I was just drying off after getting soaked through all afternoon, so I didn't go over — I felt guilty though; fundamentally I have a lovely nature.

When I finally met him at dinner he seemed very pleasant, full of course of the new subaltern's anxiety to please. You know how when you are nervous you feel clumsy? I had always thought this was largely imagination, but I watched this new man carefully and it isn't. His hands were a bit tense with excitement so he did act clumsily with his food and so on.

Stephen and the Major had been discussing arrangements for a Home Guard exercise which they are refereeing and how to fit it in with the platoon firing practice.

'When you are used to having everything worked out for you I suppose it must seem rather a headache to have to start fitting them in for yourself,' said the Major to Mr Cross, the new officer.

'Rather a headache and rather a bore I should think, sir.'

This was not well received.

'I must say I never find it that,' said the Major, 'If one did, one might as well throw one's hand in.'

'Oh I didn't mean it that way, sir,' said Mr Cross hastily.

I went along to the W-Company dance, held in the same holiday camp as last week but much more successfully. As I was wearing gum boots I didn't dance, not that I ever do very much. I met for the first time one of the sergeants who used to be a sub-editor on the *Daily Mirror*. We wondered how Hugh Cudlip, the *Sunday Pictorial* editor, was getting on in the Army, we discussed the capabilities of Stuart Campbell his successor. We said what a funny coincidence it was that Peter Wilson had been on this stretch of coast with the unit we took over from, and how strange that he, the Sergeant, had never met Conrad Phillips, man of letters and about town.[31]

I had a couple of drinks but no more. I no longer drink except with meals. I have a glass of sherry at lunch, and one at dinner and a glass of port. Lately I have been having two glasses of port but I don't think it is agreeing with me; I think it makes me sluggish next morning. I lie in bed wondering whether I would have got up already if I hadn't had that second glass. Sometimes I think I am going porty.

---

31   Peter Wilson — a celebrated sportswriter, who had a short spell on the *Daily Express* but was mostly associated with the *Daily Mirror*; Conrad Phillips — probably the actor. Once again we see how Anthony was preoccupied with what media figures were doing in wartime.

FRIDAY

The new subaltern was down early to breakfast

'I know just how you'll be feeling these next few days,' I said. 'You'll feel you ought to be doing something all the time. Well don't worry, you aren't. There won't be anything for you to do these next few days, they'll just leave you alone. It may sound screwy but that's what'll happen. You want to walk around a bit and get some good book to read.'

After breakfast I took him for a walk round. I spent most of the morning walking up and down our platoon front with the Major, having a further discussion on the huts we are building. All people living in houses a certain radius from our posts are to be ordered to leave. I feel rather conscience-stricken when they wish me good morning as I am more or less responsible for deciding who is to go and who isn't, subject to about fourteen other authorities of course.

I watched the Yorkshire pudding cooking, there were air bubbles popping up through it. 'It's all the eggs in it sir,' said the cook sarcastically, no, ironically.

The dining room now has table cloths; one of the men found some old curtains, washed them and sowed them together.

After lunch the officers had to collect pay for this platoon from the Company Office. This took half an hour because they had forgotten to get the National Savings Stamps which are sold on pay parade and someone had to go to the Post Office and get them. There is something faintly ridiculous about the hitching-on of revolvers and the salute which precede and follow on these essentially civilian expeditions.

I was also given three scraps of paper.

1. To: Company Commander   No. 14 Platoon
From: No. 14 Platoon Commander   1/3/41
Sir
This is to certify that all men in my platoon have had a bath and changed their under-clothes for week ending 1/3/41.

      .... Second Lieutenant

2. Sir
All arms and ammunition of my platoon have been checked and found to be correct with exception of the following:

      .... Sergeant

and 3. What is the religion of Corporal Marchant?

The coal supply has run out and no more can be got until they find out who is responsible for its supply. All the local civil and military authorities have been approached and all say it is nothing to do with them. The one household problem I don't have is what shall we have for dinner today; the answer to that is it arrives in a truck the night before.

Sergeant brought me a letter one of the men had had, the usual pathetic mixture of tragedy and absurdity, ghastly news in the pleased-to-meet-you idiom.

SATURDAY

I heard this morning that I am going on a Motor Liaison Officer course at Brasenose College, Oxford.[32]

I spent from 9 till 10.15 trying to get the petty cash in order. When I handed over to the Major I was 24s down. I only had 4s to give him and I should have had 28s representing 1s stopped from each man's pay for barrack damages, sports fund etc, this being a weekly affair. On investigation it turned out that I had had an extra man to pay so that accounted for 14s except that I had only given him 13s, having stopped 1s from his pay like the rest. This left 10s, unaccounted for; it finally turned out that I had paid one man 17s instead of 7s, the mistake arising because Sergeant mistook the flourish on the 7 for an extra figure 1. I went down to the beach to get the 10s back and of course he hadn't got 10s left, only 8s 8d. I took 7s.6d. and kicked in 2s 6d. which I borrowed from the Sergeant-Major.

At dinner the Major was extremely irritating about newspaper ethics and methods in writing about Army matters. I often feel very critical myself, but I resent criticism from outsiders.

SUNDAY

I finished the book today. Am thinking of calling it *Let Them Eat Coke*, after Marie Antoinette's suggestion. I worked all day and finished about 4.30 p.m. It was pleasant to sit down and read without feeling I ought to be writing.

Like every other unit, we have a great following of stray dogs, five or six living on this platoon alone. I was sitting watching Barter trying to raise a bit of a fire when a man came in, very concerned, to say that one of the dogs had blown itself up on a land mine. I shouldn't have thought it would have been heavy enough, but when we got there the poor animal had certainly been blown up by something, more probably run over. It was in a very bad way, so we shot it.

This was no sooner done than, out of a house nearby, a woman came running, shouting and carrying on.

---

32 Anthony had already done the preliminary course and this was the last step before he would cease being an infantry officer and become a motor contact officer liaising between units.

'Call yourself a man?' she screamed – well, almost screamed – at me. 'You fancy yourself, donchew? Shooting a poor little animal. Great coward, you. You make me sick. Don't half fancy yourself, donchew?'

It always takes me a minute or two to find my tongue on these occasions, but once I have summoned up my little stock of self-assertion I think it pays to be aggressive. 'Back to your kitchen, you silly trollop,' I said firmly; and immediately regretted it, thinking perhaps I had gone too far. But it worked. She stopped in mid-sentence, looked at me uncertainly, and withdrew.

While we were burying the dog one of the men said to me, 'That's the only way to talk to women, sir; only way they understand.'

When we were on another part of the coast a golfer wandered on to a minefield and was blown up, all that came down were his boots.

'Serve him right for playing golf in boots,' as one of our officers remarked.

I was Duty Officer. The local Home Guard commander brought in a water-logged camera found on the beach, 'suspiciously near a bomb crater'.

The Major who is going on leave came in to the office to clear up things. I was listening to J.B. Priestley's 'Postscript'.[33]

'D'you mind turning that man off, Anthony. He's such a bore.'

I said I had been reading an article by Beverley Baxter making just that criticism.[34]

'Oh really I can quite believe it. I was in the Cavalry Club one night and he came on and everyone shouted for him to be turned off.'

There have been great activities working on the new positions down at the beach.

There was a minor air raid during the night. A bomb dropped near the Company Office and injured a horse which we had to shoot.

---

33 J.B. Priestley, the famous writer and broadcaster, who had a distinctive slow northern voice which some people found very irritating. However, it is more likely that the Major disliked Priestley's politics, which were considered by some to be too left-wing. Priestley's Postscript broadcasts had an audience of many millions.

34 Beverley Baxter had been the Editor of the *Daily Express* before Arthur Christiansen took over. Christiansen was the Editor whilst Anthony worked on the paper. Anthony is being a bit know-it-all with the Major.

MOTOR LIAISON OFFICER

Before he moved to the Chichester Harbour posting, Anthony had taken the preliminary course for training as a Liaison or Motor Contact Officer (MCO). Shortly after he had joined the Royal Fusiliers, he had met a young officer who had chosen this specialisation and Anthony had decided that it would be just the thing for himself. The MCO's job was to liaise with units which had been cut off by battle or other untoward circumstances; he carried orders to the isolated units, found out what was happening there, and reported back to HQ. Anthony wrote:

> Potentially a job of frightening responsibility in battle, it was not at all bad at other times. First of all you were relatively your own master. Secondly [...] you had to spend a lot of time going round units in the pleasantly irresponsible and relatively entertaining capacity of visiting officer from a higher formation.[1]

In early March 1941, notification came through that he was to begin on the full MCO course, and so, without much repining, Anthony said farewell to his Royal Fusiliers infantry battalion and the men of his platoon.

The course was based at Oxford, and ran from March to April. Anthony's typescript diary concerning the course has no dates, only days of the week. It begins with what appears to be some leave he took prior to starting the course – inevitably, because he loved London so much, this is where he headed. *An Apple for the Sergeant* also contains material on the course and is the source of the second and third extracts in this chapter.

---

1   *An Apple for the Sergeant*, pp.74–75.

Diary, March–April 1941

I went to lunch at Victor's, the very French restaurant in Wardour Street. John Gielgud was shown to the seat opposite me.[2] He said:–

> That playing for the troops forced you to adopt a closer approach to the audience.
>
> That the troops like straight stuff if well done and well put over and not for too long.
>
> That he and Beatrice Lillie had been completely outstarred at one RAF camp by the crooner Sam Costa who was stationed there.[3] They had watched his performance with sickly smiles.
>
> That Noel Coward when they meet lectures him on what he should do but never listens to him. That the English version of café society had been manufactured largely by Coward's glamourisations.
>
> That Coward had terrific understanding of ordinary people because he had been through the mill as for instance Terence Rattigan had not but maybe he, Coward, ought to mix around a bit more.
>
> That when he, Gielguid, appeared as a guest star in the *Hi, Gang!* programme he was at the BBC from lunchtime until the show went on about 6.20 p.m.
>
> That Vic Oliver, Ben Lyon, and Bebe Daniels worked like slaves all the afternoon.
>
> That Oliver goes to his room after dinner every night and works on gags for an hour.
>
> That when they met he, Gielguid, said 'I've always wanted to meet you, I thought perhaps we could share toupees,' which he didn't think had been very popular.[4]

I got to Oxford at 3.45 p.m. and had tea at the Randolph Hotel with Donald Hamilton the architect, the man who suggested roofing Oxford streets so that there wouldn't have to be a black-out. Oxford at the moment is a boom town, the hotels are crowded, the streets are packed. One is immediately struck by the contrast between the students and the Forces. The students look appalling, long hair, stupid clothes.

We are billeted at Brasenose, two to a room and five to a batman. I am not too happy about the latter idea. I am sharing with a Scot. He is off drink because he killed two people in a road accident which cost him £1,800. The rooms are rather blowsy and very bare though they have a certain amount of furniture, not very homey furniture though. After reporting to the Adjutant we were free for the night. I find that the Commandant

---

2   John Gielguid, the illustrious actor, later knighted, who performed abridged versions of Shakespeare and other great dramatists for the troops through ENSA during the war.

3   Beatrice Lillie, usually known as Miss Bea Lillie, actress and comedienne.

4   *Hi, Gang!* was a massively popular, morale-boosting comedy show on the radio. Ben Lyon and Bebe Daniels were a famous American show-biz couple. Vic Oliver was a half-Austrian actor and comic, who is now chiefly known for having married Winston Churchill's daughter Sarah against her father's wishes. Lyon, Daniels and Oliver were the regular *Hi, Gang!* team.

of the School was at school with me or rather vice-versa. We both took organ lessons.[5] This may or may not be a good thing.

The course looks appalling, 9 a.m. to 7 p.m. every day, and night work.

I had dinner by myself at the George; it was crowded and quite pleasant. You see more solitary diners in Oxford than anywhere, and more odd ones. The town might be run by the Café Royal.

My room mate didn't get in until after midnight, he had been locked out and had to climb over a wall. He says he has been court-martialled for striking a brigadier out in France. I hope he doesn't strike me.

I slept on the floor in my valise but by using cushions from the window seat as a mattress it was quite comfortable.

Breakfast was quite reasonably good. The dining hall is dark and timbered with refectory tables and benches. I met another man who was on the preliminary, a nightmare course, a regular from the RVR.[6]

After breakfast the batman told me that it was a very hard course and there were usually one or two in hospital. He pointed out of the window at a figure hobbling across the quad bent over two sticks. 'That gentleman was on the last course,' he said. I could not easily forget this conversation.

At 9 a.m. my old school chum gave the opening address. There could be no less ardent old boy than I but I felt most concerned that he should be a success and indignant at any critical sniggers. Actually he spoke well, pithily and at some length.

We spent the morning drawing equipment. Crash helmets – 'Experience has shown them to be necessary' – waterproof clothing – 'It doesn't fit but we can't help it' – tools, maps and books.

I feel just as if I were back at school. Looking out at the sunshine just as one used to, trying to be comfortable on the benches, praying for the time to pass quickly.

The lock and chain. Padlock must be locked before restarting. All right laugh, bloody funny. But you'll do it.

Map reading test from 5 p.m.–7 p.m. 7 p.m. eh? and every night too.[7]

There was a great wad of papers waiting in our mail pigeon holes including several things to read up by tomorrow. Conversation at dinner was a little sardonic. Found a long review of *What! No Morning Tea?* by Richard King in *The Tatler*.

---

5   The school was King's School, Rochester, which had a high reputation for music. However, Anthony almost certainly took organ lessons in order to get off sports or some other activity which he did not like.

6   Possibly, in fact, the QVR, the Queen Victoria's Rifles, a territorial unit of the London regiment. Anthony may have been misreading his notes. Anthony's later description of this particular soldier certainly suggests he was from the QVR.

7   Anthony is clearly writing the diary during a lecture, because course notes are interspersed.

After dinner I went out with John Irwin who used to be on the *Daily Mirror*. We went to the Randolph. Standing next to each other at the bar were an RAF DSO and DFC and a young man with velvet trousers, rings on his fingers and a red carnation in his buttonhole.[8] Quite a little contrast in war effort.

We spent the evening with people whose whole life seemed to consist of knowing other people. Never was there such a cavalcade of pretentious nonentity names. Every incident considered in the conversation was preceded by 'do you know Hugo Earlyman?' or 'do you know Brian this or Guy that?' All of them taking flats from each other and giving parties at which people threw themselves downstairs or locked themselves in the bathroom or had terrible arguments. There are an enormous circle of these miscellaneous semi-intelligent people. It seems to take an awful lot of mental shams to produce one good mind.

WEDNESDAY

This was the first real day of the course. First a lecture on tactics by the Commandant. This I unfortunately missed because I was engaged in marking up a map which we were supposed to have ready for the second period.

We spent the rest of the morning (we don't get any break) sitting in small groups in the garage listening to lectures on the motorcycle engine. It is a subject which does not excite me. Two hours of it I found rather long, especially in mumbled Scottish dialect. Magneto, dynamo, dear me what a rigmarole.

After lunch we went out for a drive. I couldn't get mine to start, they said I had over-flooded it with petrol.

'Change the plug,' the officer said to me.

'I'm afraid I don't know how to.'

'Good God man, haven't you ever had a car down?'

Really I see no more reason for me to do that than for a newspaper reader to write a news story.

It was a pleasant afternoon. We rode out of Oxford about three miles up on to a long flat open plateau with a dust surface. Here we rode about at will. The Commandant came up to me, 'I didn't realise it was you,' he said. 'How's the world treating you?'

'It's been treating you pretty well,' I said. 'Sir.'

But it makes a long day having to start again after tea.

'Officers will be prepared to discuss the following eight questions tutorially at 1700 hours, Wed 19 March.' We had been given the list for our homework last night; for instance, Question 4:

8　　DSO: Distinguished Service Order; DFC: Distinguished Flying Cross, both highly prestigious RAF decorations.

'"Infantry must in the end confirm all successes in war" – Do you agree with this in view of the success of German armoured formations last year?'

We discussed things like this for two hours, twelve of us and an instructor bunched in a group on the front benches of a large lecture room. The discussion was lively, the arguments progressive but hackneyed to a regular reader of Tom Wintringham.[9]

After lunch there was another tutorial discussion but I was too tired to pay attention. After tea we went across to the Indian Institute. Here in a large basement room with an Indian temperature was a landscape model thirty feet long. The countryside it represented was supposed to be the ground over which an infantry division were advancing in support of an armoured division. We were then treated to a display in which the Commandant and his assistants played the part of the Infantry Divisional Commander and his staff officers. They each had a cardboard label round their necks to identify their roles.

I felt rather fed up in the evening so when someone asked me to go for a drink I went. We went to Whites. You go up an alleyway between two shops. The main features of the place are its gramophone which constantly plays good jazz records. The walls are very highly coloured. There are two bars, one small with a high bar counter the whole length of it, and a lounge bar. My companion was a young regular in the RVR, very charming but very orthodox. His one complaint is that he can't get back to his peacetime battalion. Like many regulars he was drafted to a territorial battalion. 'The trouble is I can't stand the London accent.' he said worried. He said the weakness of regular soldiers was that the Army routine bred a great obstinacy.

SATURDAY

Discussions all the morning. I caught the 12 p.m. to town. We had to change at Didcot. There were five ATS in the refreshment room.

'D'you see they've got the new ATS hats out?'

'Yes, aren't they lovely?'

'I'll have to change my parting, I've done mine the boy's side.'

'Oh so will I.'

Just like listening to the young gentlemen at Oxford.

MONDAY

I caught the 5.30 a.m. from Paddington. I got a compartment to myself so I slept.

I got to Oxford in good time for breakfast.

---

9   Thomas Wintringham, journalist and fighter in the Spanish Civil War, where he became friends with Ernest Hemingway who based one of his characters upon him. In the Second World War, he helped to train the Local Defence Volunteers, later the Home Guard.

The first lesson after breakfast was another play. This time a series of scenes showing how and how not to be a liaison officer. First there was the funny man doing everything wrong, not having his identity card, not having his map marked properly, not saluting the Brigade Major on arrival, leaving the most important information until last, not marshalling his facts properly and all the rest of it. Then a rather nauseating character came on and did everything right.

The rest of the morning was spent in a syndicate discussion. We were split in syndicates of six. Each group has to prepare a plan of advance for an infantry division. The plans will then be called for and commented on in public, each man being responsible for one aspect of the problem e.g. whether the advance should be on a two brigade front or one.

There was a macabre little notice up on the board at lunchtime.

INSTRUCTIONAL TRIAL

Forty-five minutes will be spent on each hazard.

Number 1 hazard … steep descent with greasy surface.

Number 2 hazard … rocky ledged climb.

Number 3 hazard … mud.

Number 4 hazard … steep ascent of slimy stony surface.

Number 5 hazard … water.

We lined up our bikes in the road outside the garage after lunch.

There was the usual appalling symphony of engines revving up. As I sat there, my feet straddled on the ground, waiting to be led off on this devil's chase, it occurred to me that really it would be difficult to devise any more deplorable way of spending the afternoon. Mentally I quivered with apprehension. Premonitions of various degrees of disaster crowded through my mind with the vivid urgency of a life insurance man.

I was pleased to find that I kept up rather better than before. Certainly I am getting much more confidence. We drove about twelve miles out of Oxford. The first episode for me was riding across a ploughed field, which I managed in slow time. Then a ride down a forty foot precipice. There was, however, a slightly less dangerous way which some of the more pedestrian spirits including myself took. Then up an extraordinary morass made of mud and small crazy-paving stones. I was very pleased to get up without falling off.

After these experiences you feel madly confident riding on a level road again.

WEDNESDAY

Today was dominated by my old school chum, the Commandant.

First there was the notice on the board:

The Commandant has been appalled by an unmannerly and unjustifiable attack on the mess waiters with regard to the quantity of food available at dinner on March 25. Officers are referred to standing orders, their sense of decency, and the fact that they have failed to elect a mess committee when required to do so.

From 9–10.30 we had a meet to discuss the advance of a division in which each of us was responsible for answering one question. The Commandant called a name out of the hat and the man had to stand and deliver. I was lucky.

The Commandant then gave a most impressively well-documented lecture on the organisation of the German Army. He described how he had watched the muddle of the German move into Vienna which was before they had had much practice.[10] He thought the reason the Germans had seemed shy about gas was the possible reaction on their horse transport on which they rely far more than people imagine.

He outlined the German policy of hammer blows at the weakest point but questioned whether it would work here. He also wondered whether the Germans would devise a successful alternative and whether they weren't too committed and wedded to their strategy to change it.

'Like the old gentleman who lives above this room. He came to a sherry party we gave in our ante-room and when we wanted to take his coat out of the room, he said, "No, this is the room you leave coats in." We said it was no longer a cloak-room, it was our ante-room, and he said, "This is the room where you leave hats and coats. I have been here sixty-seven years and I know."'

The afternoon was spent in the garage, first listening to another lecture from the Scots mechanic. It was about the carburettor, more I did not learn.

Others seemed to be having the time of their lives, but though I have tried in a mild way I find it almost impossible to be anything but indifferent to the internal combustion engine. From 3–4 p.m. we were ordered to maintenance our bikes, oiling, greasing, blowing up tyres, etc. Someone said I handled the oil can as if I couldn't believe it existed.

From 5–7 p.m. there was another inquest on the divisional advance, continued from this morning.

THURSDAY

Today I travelled 136 miles on a motor cycle. Starting at 8.30 a.m. we rode fifty miles and had a scheme in which we each played the part of liaison officers given a new problem every two hours or so.

---

10   The commandant is referring to the Anschluss in March 1938, when the Germans annexed Austria.

The Commandant and the man who was in *The Mirror* met head-on round a corner and were both removed to hospital. The Commandant, so we are told, landed on his jaw. Irwin snapped his leg. The Commandant is expected out of hospital in ten days. Irwin ought to be able to stand again in six months.

'A Night at the Staff College'

The Staff College was very pleasant, set in a park district and most comfortable inside. There were eight of us. We were received by a Lieutenant-Colonel aged about forty.

'What time were you told to get here?' he said.

'Two o'clock, sir.'

'I've been waiting here since twelve,' he said.

He took us to wash in a very large, white and well-appointed wash-room. Then along a stone-floored corridor to the ante-room. It was large and comfortable, with an outlook downhill to a lake. The Colonel ordered us a glass of beer and then took us into lunch. The Mess room was also enormous and pillared. For lunch we had two pork sausages, boiled potatoes, cabbage, greengages, rice pudding, and coffee in the lounge; also very good brown bread and cheese.

After lunch we were told where to go by the Colonel who had received us. We were acting as liaison officers in a telephone battle, with the Staff College students playing the parts of the various staff officers in a division. The time was supposed to be autumn, 1942; a BEF had landed in Europe and advanced for ten days without much resistance.[11] At this point they had come up against a stiffening German opposition. We were to be attached in pairs to the various divisional headquarters. He took us round. They were large rooms, empty at the moment except for tables. The Staff College pupils were out for the afternoon reconnoitring the actual ground, then they would come back and work all night planning and organising the attack.

We were free in the afternoon. De Stacpoole and I went for a walk in the grounds; I bought a couple of books; but we couldn't go far because we were hatless and de Stacpoole, being a regular, felt unnatural without one.[12]

We came back and had tea, sitting next to one of the students. He said that the college was run by a number of officers, nearly all lieutenant-colonels. They worked from 9 a.m. to 7 p.m. and there was a lot of spare-time work.

---

11   BEF – British Expeditionary Force. Advancing without much resistance seems very wishful thinking in view of what actually happened in Normandy in June 1944.

12   De Stacpoole was another motor liaison officer with whom Anthony had spent some time in training.

After tea we went across to Divisional Headquarters. This gradually filled up with captains and majors. A lieutenant-colonel who was umpiring our room came and introduced himself.

Another colonel asked if I would be so kind as to get a couple of chairs. The battle had begun.

A major came running across the room. 'Are you a liaison officer?' he said.

'Yes, sir,' I said eagerly.

'Would you get me a couple of chairs?'

When I got back another man told me to go to 5th Infantry Brigade and ask for their strength return. 5th Infantry Brigade were in the next room but one down the corridor. I walked along and got the message. I asked if they had any news or other messages for me to take back. They said no. The atmosphere was now about as hectic as possible, voices all over the room, everyone phoning.

'Will you render your casualty return ... Brigade three is cut off ... Where the hell are you? ... Speak up, man ... Where's Jackson?' etc., etc. At this point there were a series of small explosions outside the window. Headquarters was being shelled. Everyone put his tin hat on.

A Canadian major told me that General Awful, the Divisional Commander, was fifteen minutes overdue at 5th Infantry Brigade. I was to go and look for him. I went along the passage to 5th Infantry Brigade, who said he hadn't arrived. A colonel pulled me aside.

'You're someone else, you don't know the General's missing,' he said, 'Come in here to 6th Infantry Brigade; their maps have been destroyed by bombing and you don't know where you are.'

The Brigade Major of 6th Infantry Brigade told me to get some more maps. I went back to Division, and after twenty minutes interval, to allow for my motor-cycle journey, I asked the GSO3 for maps.[13]

'Aha, maps, but of course,' he said, and wrote '100 maps' on a piece of paper. I went back to the Brigade who wanted the maps, and on the umpire's instructions said there were none available. I went back to 5th Brigade and asked for any further news of the General. They had just sent out a party to look for him. They told me to wait. There was a great noise outside, and an enormous man entered dressed as a French peasant in a tam-o'-shanter and a blue smock. I should have said before that we were all wearing gas masks. The peasant talked French at great speed and tried to steal papers off the table. He said he had blown up a bridge at Goring. As they were taking his fingerprints in green ink, the General's body was brought in on a stretcher. I thought it would be Ralph Lynn.[14] It was now 7.15 p.m. I went to dinner at 8 p.m. I sat next to a tall, red-haired lieutenant-colonel.

---

13 GSO3 – General Staff Officer Grade III.

14 Ralph Lynn was an actor who often played in the Aldwych Theatre Farces, which were beloved by Anthony and his brother Geoffrey. Lynn specialised in playing a monocled upperclass twit.

He said: 'They say we're all crackers at the end of our time here. Very hard work, you know, trying to keep two or three jumps ahead of the class, normally manage to keep half a jump.'

For dinner we had soup, fish and chips, and cheese.

There was very little drinking. 'Whisky one-and-six a time; got to do something about it, you know,' said the Colonel, 'And most people drink before meals instead of with them; do myself, I know.'

After dinner I went into the library, very military but a good one; no ban on Secker and Warburg. I was reading in one of the alcoves when I heard a voice up the other end, 'Well, I'll lock the door then, sir,' and a key turned in the lock. I couldn't get anyone to hear for twenty minutes.

Back at the battle there wasn't much doing. My opposite number and I went to bed at 10.40 p.m., sleeping on the floor in one of the lecture rooms. It was very stuffy, and we kept being woken by the French Canadian Captain, who was playing French Fifth Columnist parts, and kept on changing his costume. At 3.45 a.m. someone woke me. 'Are you a motor contact officer? Everything's boiling.' I was wanted. I dressed quickly and reported. The job they wanted me for was to go and wake someone else. Then I had to wait in case the General wanted to go forward to observe the battle. He wanted me to walk down the passage with him if he did.

To be woken at 3.45 for this is bad for morale. I felt as if it would be a luxury to fall down on the floor and sleep. It reminded me of a sergeant who used to say: 'You don't want to think, "Oh —, another night without sleep," you want to say, "Oh, boy, another forty-eight hours and I'll be having a lovely kip."'

So far as I was concerned the exercise rapidly petered out after this. We kept going over to the ante-room for cups of tea and biscuits. The place was crowded all the time. An officer asleep in a chair was being pointed out; he had been there asleep ever since yesterday afternoon, so it was said. I had a bath about 7 a.m., which made me feel better, and breakfast afterwards. Then I sat around reading the papers, and started riding home at 10.30 a.m. with one or two stops to telephone and to admire the Thames.

★★★

After the Motor Contact Officer course ended, Anthony was ordered to report to London, a posting which was the answer to all his dreams – 'Yes, sir, to London. Boy, oh boy!' However, this delightful interlude only lasted a day before he was sent to join the Guards in a large pleasant house in Surrey next to a golf course. This particular interlude did not last long either. Once again, the diary has no dates, but the following entry would probably have been in early to mid-May 1941.

'Wednesday: I Went Down to the Garage ...'

WEDNESDAY

I went down to the garage to draw a motorbike at 9.30 a.m. I hadn't been on one of the beastly things for three weeks; it was too good to last.

We started about 10 a.m. I rode in a group of motorbikes just behind the first truck. These convoys travel at about 12 mph. The last time I rode in one on a motorbike it was all I could do to keep up, but now I have become a rough riding-star it was rather tedious. We were on the road for four hours. At one point I broke away from the column to get a cup of coffee and, oddly enough, found myself at the same place where I broke away from the column on our way to Chichester and was told off by the Major for doing so.[15] However, on this occasion I rejoined the column without comment.

At about 2 p.m. we arrived at a house where Brigade Headquarters was set up in the grounds. I hung around trying to keep up with the situation, which was no great strain, I must say, but no one wanted me except the Brigade Major, who wanted me to move my motorbike; so I withdrew to the RASC truck in the rear and wrote. It was then 2.40 p.m. and high time we had lunch.

'What do you do most of the time?' I asked the RASC officer.

'I don't know really. If we were on active service I'd be about the busiest of the lot, but now it's a rest cure.'

Lunch appeared at 2.45 p.m. We had it in the house in a very pleasant room looking on the garden. Cold meats, tinned peaches and cheese.

'Well, deck-chairs and a sunny corner this afternoon, I think,' said the Irish Guards Colonel who was acting as Brigadier for the exercise.

'And shall I say a late dinner, sir?' asked Lord Rosse.[16]

'Eight o'clock, I think,' said the Colonel.

I dozed on the lawn after lunch until the Brigade Major called me over and sent me to find the MT officer.[17] A cloud then came over the moon. I rode around miles of country lanes without finding him. Eventually I rode up to a small group of transport parked under some trees and was asked for my identification card. I said I hadn't got one and had never had one, which, owing to one thing and another, I hadn't. So being a lieutenant quartermaster, he arrested me and took me to his Battalion HQ. I was identified by the acting Adjutant, but it was one of those stupid stories which everyone laughs at. I have an unholy knack of appearing ludicrous in military conditions. When I got back to Brigade it had been reported and they all seemed to find it funny.

---

15 See 'Defending the Realm', page 43.

16 Lord Rosse was the Brigade Intelligence Officer.

17 MT – Motor Transport.

Halfway through dinner I was called out to ride behind the Brigadier's car to the new and advanced Brigade HQ. This was about eight miles away, temporarily established in a garden. I rode like the wind to salvage my reputation, found the complicated way perfectly and arrived very soon. They had all gone; they had moved. No one had told me, and as I was so late I hadn't been there to hear.

It was now 10.45 p.m. and getting dark. Anyway, I was riding the thing round until 1 a.m. and feeling most unhappy. When I finally arrived at the new Brigade HQ, I didn't know whether to report to the Brigade Major with my completely out-of-date message or whether nothing said soonest mended. I decided to say nothing and went to bed. I was called at 4 a.m. to be Duty Officer; this meant sitting waiting in case anything happened. About six o'clock the Brigade Major sent me out to the Welsh Guards to tell them the situation.

'You ought to be back in an hour,' he said.

I found the Welsh Guards in a rather broken-down, isolated house. The officers were sitting round on the floor.

'Ah, it's our Quisling,' they said.[18]

I found I hadn't the remotest idea of what the situation was to tell them, so I asked them what they wanted to know. They wanted to know when they were going to be moved.

I rode back like a mad thing and told the Brigade Major, who said they would have been told this by this time. I was then approached by the Staff Captain and told to find the conblasted man I couldn't find last night. He was 'somewhere on the road between Herriards Common and the Brentworth House'.

Let me draw a veil over the rest of the day. Exactly the same thing happened. I couldn't find him and when I finally gave up and went back to the Brigade they had moved and no one knew where.

I rode on again up roads crowded with men and trucks. But no one knew where Brigade HQ had moved to. Eventually I saw three ambulances and followed them.

I may mention that by this time I was completely exhausted, and shortly afterwards I was stopped by an umpire who pointed to a man in the ditch with a rifle pointed at me and said I was captured. I was sent back to their HQ under escort. Unfortunately, I had the entire operation orders in my map-case – quite wrongly, of course. But I pointed to some aeroplanes and while my escort gaped I managed to stuff them down my trousers.

I finally got back to the Brigade HQ at tea-time.

After lunch next day I was called in by the Brigade Major and told that I had been transferred back to London with effect from tomorrow.

---

18 Vidkun Quisling, head of the puppet Norwegian government under Nazi rule. Anthony is jokingly being called a traitor. The Welsh Guards were probably the unit to which Anthony was attached though he does not make this clear.

PART TWO

REPORTING FOR *WAR*,
JUNE 1941 – SEPTEMBER 1944

REPORTING FOR *WAR*

At the end of June 1941, Anthony received a wire telling him that he was required for temporary duty at the War Office. The posting was for fourteen days with a view to a probable, permanent staff appointment. The posting was to a new department within the War Office which would soon come to be called ABCA, the Army Bureau of Current Affairs. Anthony would remain based in London, attached to the War Office and ABCA, for the rest of his time with the Army.

At ABCA, he and his new colleague, Stephen Watts, ascertained very quickly that they were in at the start of something huge, an extraordinarily radical movement to educate the troops which was powered by a blend of idealism and pragmatism. The new bulletin on which Anthony and Stephen were working was primarily intended to supply raw material for education officers so that they could get the men motivated by the key issues behind the war. The bulletin would also give the men a good perspective on what was happening in the war as a whole (for example, in the RAF and the Royal Navy), one useful side-effect of this being to stop the grousers who were always convinced that there were cushier billets elsewhere.

Stephen described how he and Anthony gave the bulletin its distinctive identity:

> Cotterell and I decided on the title *WAR*, and I drew its glaring red and white cover. Also, while doodling away those warm summer afternoons, I devised the beehive shaped monogram of the letters ABCA which became our trademark. Cotterell was emphatic that our first publication should be called *WAR* because it afforded the opportunity to answer the telephone with the words 'This is *WAR*', which are susceptible of a variety of dramatic enunciations.[1]

WAR's first issue appeared on 20 September 1941. By now it had been decided that ABCA would have two bulletins, *WAR* being published one week and *Current Affairs* the next. *WAR* dealt with military subjects and was written almost entirely inside the War Office by Anthony and Stephen, although articles by other soldiers were invited

---

1   Stephen Watts, *Moonlight on a Lake in Bond Street*, pp. 107–8.

and soon began to appear. *Current Affairs* was written by outside writers, civilians as well as soldiers; it ventured into social, some would say political, issues.[2] A beautifully designed Map Review was also printed fortnightly, with photographs and features on one side and a map on the reverse showing the current military situation in some theatre of war. The map was designed by Abraham Games, one of the best poster-designers of the century.

As described in the Introduction, Anthony gradually modified the material which *WAR* published until he was essentially acting as a war reporter. He chose his own assignments and the way in which he wrote about them, always having in mind that his material could be used to create books which would get his name before a much wider audience than that for *WAR*. His *WAR* articles are often very short and comparatively terse versions of much longer book chapters or potential book chapters. For this reason, only two WAR articles have been included in Part Two; the other exerts are from his books or unpublished papers where he could be much freer with his material.

By 1943, Anthony was writing vivid accounts for *WAR* of his various reporting assignments, these assignments being chosen by himself and voluntarily entered into despite their dangers. He still gave a great deal of factual information but he had a masterly lightness of touch with the didactic stuff. In the article which follows, published in issue 36 on 23 January 1943, the title he chose was a fairly typical joking reference, being a quote from the popular song *And what did they see?/They saw the sea.*

---

2   Having become a footnote in history, ABCA is almost invariably cited in only two contexts: firstly, in discussing the British Army as a social institution, and secondly in analysing the Conservative defeat and Labour victory in the 1945 election, frequently supposed to be partly due to ABCA which was blamed for radicalising the troops.

'AND WHAT DID THEY SEE?'

WAR issues were often confined to a single subject, with perhaps one or two additional short features for amusement or information. Issue 36, published on 23 January 1943, was dedicated to the Merchant Navy and the convoy system. The only other feature in the issue was a short 'Prisoner's Quiz', in which men were asked if they knew how they should behave when captured, the answers being given on the back page.

The convoy system was a means of protecting merchant shipping by grouping vessels together under armed escort. Convoys were critical to Britain's survival and at this period of the war this was a highly topical subject. The crisis in the Battle of the Atlantic was approaching and finally came in March 1943.[1] The battle was effectively won by 24 May when the German Admiral, Karl Dönitz, diverted his U-boats to easier targets. 'The Germans were now smashing themselves against a convoy escort system of ships and aircraft that for the first time in the war had no loopholes to be exploited.'[2]

Anthony's main intention in this issue was to show how all three services were involved in protecting a routine coastal convoy, 'the point emerging that inter-service co-operation is not confined to high days and spectacularly important convoys'. In the interests of accuracy, he travelled with two coastal convoys, first in a destroyer and then in a merchant ship.

The following extracts, all written by Anthony, give an idea of the typical flavour of a *WAR* issue concentrating upon one single, highly important topic, but making it as interesting as possible.

---

1   Most historians define the crisis of the Battle of the Atlantic as being March 1943, but others, such as Duncan Redford, argue that it occurred in November 1942. See Duncan Redford, 'The March 1943 Crisis in the Battle of the Atlantic: Myth and Reality', *History*, Vol. 92, No. 305 (2007).

2   Eric J. Grove, *The Royal Navy since 1815* (Palgrave Macmillan, London, 2005), p.204.

'Lines of Thought' (Editorial)

Dr Johnson said: 'No man will be a sailor who has contrivance enough to get himself into a jail, for being in a ship is being in jail with a chance of being drowned.' How do your men feel about this? In any group of soldiers there is usually at least one who wishes he had been a sailor. Ask him why. This is also the moment to hear the experiences of anyone who has been at sea: and this is one case where discussion would be reinforced by reference to the most recent news stories, and to the current ABCA Map Review No. 5.

'Once Round the North Sea'

We sailed about 1.30 p.m. There were about a dozen officers and men on the bridge, several more than normal because this particular destroyer is a flotilla leader, and so carries the flotilla staff. She is commanded by a captain instead of a lieutenant-commander, and has a crew of 206 instead of about 130.

Another destroyer came with us. The water was calm and the sun very trying. Going down the Thames estuary they had a practice shoot at a target towed by an airplane. Very noisy. This was stopped on the approach of an incoming convoy, part of which was approaching the wrong side of a particular buoy. We made towards them, and the Captain spoke to them through a microphone.

'You're off your course. There was a ship mined here only a few days ago. Do be careful,' he said. They changed course immediately. 'Hasn't been a ship mined here for weeks,' he said to me. 'But it makes them jump.'

I am writing this down in the Torpedo Officer's cabin, which has been allotted to me. There is a bunk and a desk; the wall behind the desk is being used as a message board for signal forms and eight pictures of a girl.

Bread and jam for tea in the ward room. Some sailors came in and started passing ammunition through a hole in the floor. At about 6.30 p.m. there was another practice shoot.

At 7 p.m. we caught up with the north-bound convoy, for which we were to provide an escort through the North Sea danger patches. There were forty-nine ships of all kinds and sizes steaming uneventfully in parallel straight lines, strung out farther than you could see.

Stew and rice pudding for dinner. Afterwards I went up to the sickbay, where the doctor was playing draughts with his steward. The sick bay is about 14 feet by 7 feet. It has a bunk on which the doctor sleeps, a desk on which the steward sleeps, and a floor on which the Flag-Lieutenant and I slept, the cabins below deck having been battened down for water-tightness.

Wearing the regulation woollen-hooded coat, I went up on to the bridge. The whole ship was now at action stations. During action stations there are fourteen look-outs at a time, operating in half-hour shifts. Every gun and torpedo tube is manned, and the bridge is packed tight. You have to find a place and stay there; there was no room to move about except the Captain who paced up and down behind the glass windscreen. The reason for this overcrowding is that the ship is an old one, built during the last war.

The order was given to put on steel helmets to establish that everyone had got one. At 8.50 p.m. underwater explosions were reported. The stern of the convoy was being bombed. At 9 p.m. it was bombed again. You could see the red tracer and H.E. fired up in reply, but it was too far down the convoy to make much noise.

A wireless started up just behind where I was standing and a toneless, nasal voice reported the Nazi plane to be going away at 5,000 yards. Superimposed on and tending to drown the voice there was a tenor singing 'Maid of the Mountains'.

'Cut out that damned tenor,' snapped the Captain, bent over the receiver.

'Can't, sir; overlapping frequency, sir,' said the Flag-Lieutenant.

The first bombing had happened less than ten minutes after the last of our protecting day fighters had gone home. It was now almost dark, and the outlines of the neighbouring ships were beginning to merge with the darkness.

Then we heard the familiar de-synchronised hum. We put our tin hats on. She came out of a dark cloud at about 1,000 feet and flew across us from right to left. They opened fire with everything. The whole ship was suddenly like a fountain of red tracer and explosions. It was a dark night but you could see her quite clearly as she came across – a Heinkel 111. She machine-gunned us and dropped two bombs which hit the sea just in front of us. We steamed through their swirl. There were definite hits with pom-pom on the Heinkel and a lot of red tracer disappeared in her.

'We got her, by God, I think we got her,' said the Captain, but we hadn't. All the same it was very satisfying.

A few minutes later the head of the convoy opened fire on another aircraft. There was nothing passive about this convoy, the merchant ships by themselves put up a considerable exhibition. Five minutes later there were bombs astern, a minute later there were more bombs on the port quarter and one ship was machine-gunned. A man was wounded.

From then on it was very quiet. There were periodic alarms and at 9.25 p.m. an aircraft flew astern. A 'darkened object' was reported and we turned off from the convoy and steamed towards it, but it wasn't anything. The idea was that it might have been a German E-boat lurking to put its torpedoes into the convoy.[3]

At 11 p.m. cocoa and corned beef sandwiches were served on the bridge, and after that I went to bed.

---

3   German E-boat – a fast, surface attack boat.

For breakfast we had corn flakes, bacon and tomato, toast and marmalade. The sailors had bread and jam and tea. They told me they preferred it this way. The messing was done differently from the Army system. They were given a midday dinner and a certain daily issue of tea, bread and jam; for the other meals they were given a messing allowance and if they had a cooked breakfast they wouldn't be able to have a cooked supper without running up the mess bill. However, if they liked to buy something for breakfast they could get it cooked. Mostly they preferred extra time in bed.

Sleeping quarters in this destroyer were congested. There wasn't room for them all to sleep at once. Some slept in hammocks but most of them on the floor, on tables or on lockers.

An ordinary seaman's day was likely to be something like this: on watch from 12.30–4 p.m.; free until 6 p.m; on watch from 6.30 p.m. to 7.30 p.m; then supper (maybe liver and bacon and chips). Darken ship and guns' crews close up at dusk with all hands on deck until 2 a.m., then some time during the night another three hours on watch. Of course, they aren't at sea all the time. This particular destroyer had been doing about two days a week at sea.

During the morning we left our northbound convoy and turned to join a southbound one. There were forty-nine ships in each convoy.

We got back punctually to the scheduled minute on the morning of the third day.

'Same Way, Different Ship'

That is the naval side. Here is an account of the same trip in a merchant ship. I had to be at the pier at 6.40 a.m. There was a man in bed in the office who when he got dressed turned out to be a naval lieutenant. He said the ship hadn't turned up yet. Beyond the office there was a peace-time seaside concert party hall, still littered with some of the old equipment. It is now used as a conference hall where the Merchant Navy masters are given their sailing orders.

As there have been more than a thousand of these convoys, a certain note of repetition is beginning to creep into the meetings. They are given their route, which is of course constantly varied; the long list of buoyed channels which the convoy will follow; latest information about wrecks and wreck buoys; what time and where practice rounds are to be fired; they are reminded of their evasive action orders and other standing orders.

Each Master is given his position in the convoy and his ship's number, which is indicated by pennants. The ship I was to travel in hadn't arrived in time for the conference, so her sailing orders and I were taken out on a drifter.

She was a collier carrying 4,000 tons of coal, or, if needs be, eighty Army trucks. You go aboard from a pitching drifter up a pitching rope ladder. The Master showed me into his cabin, which had a bunk down one side, a tall cupboard, a settee and a desk, a small iron safe under the desk, and a small glass-fronted bookshelf. In the saloon next door the Mate was having bacon and sausage for breakfast. I joined him and the Master sat and watched.

'Hope we have a better trip than last time,' he said.

'Aye,' said the Mate.

'Terribly rough last time.'

'Aye,' said the Mate.

'Chap fell down the hold. Broke both wrists, internal injuries and lacerated his brain.'

'Conscious all the time,' said the Mate.

'Terrible sight he was.'

'He was that,' said the Mate.

Greatly encouraged, I am writing now in his cabin. It is 10.10 a.m. The Master and Mate are complaining that the start is unnecessarily late. Also about some other Masters who make a great rush to be away first.

This is partly to be home first at the other end and partly because they hate the idea of straggling. Some of these convoys may be fifteen miles long, each ship about 600 feet behind the one in front. In these narrow mine-infested waters round the coast they may have to stretch out with not more than two or three abreast, so as to have room to manoeuvre. Deep-sea convoys can be more compact, with more ships travelling abreast, and because U-boats normally attack from the flank this reduces their target.

This was a slow convoy (5 to 7 knots). A medium convoy travels at 7 to 9, a fast at perhaps 14 knots. Very fast ships travel unescorted, but most merchant shipping was built for economical steaming, not for outdistancing submarines.

PARACHUTIST

*I*n October 1943, Anthony went on a parachuting course, hoping to use this new skill when the much-anticipated invasion of Europe took place. He was fascinated by the airborne forces, and had been so since late 1941, when an article had appeared about British parachutists in the seventh issue of *WAR*, published on 13 December. It was written by Lieutenant-Colonel Flavell, the commanding officer of the 2nd Parachute Battalion. Almost a year later, Anthony wrote a long article for *WAR* which clearly demonstrates why he was so fascinated.

> The everyday atmosphere of the airborne forces, like that of any dangerous trade, is essentially matter of fact.
>
> Of course, things aren't exactly easy. It is a hard life, permeated with a tremendous idealism and sense of purpose. Discipline is rigid, smartness is a must. It is difficult to get in and difficult to stay in. If they think you are unsuitable in any way, out you go. Tomorrow. Just like that.
>
> One thing that the airborne authorities are most anxious to emphasise is that brains are more important that a tough appearance, and that aggressive behaviour in public-houses constitutes no criterion of anything but unsuitability.
>
> Their platform is that toughness is mainly mental and therefore the first requisite for a recruit is plenty of native common sense.[1]

The article ended with an account of the Bruneval raid, a high-profile attack on a radio-location station in France which had taken place nine months earlier in February 1942. The commander of this raid, Major John Frost, would be Anthony's CO at Arnhem bridge in September 1944.

Anthony wrote an extended piece for *WAR* about his parachute training which was published in December 1943.[2] A longer version appeared in *An Apple for the Sergeant*. He also wrote a short story about his experiences entitled 'The Sergeant's High Jump', which was published in a service newspaper called *OFF PARADE* on 15 January 1944.

1   Anthony Cotterell, 'The Airborne Forces', *WAR*, issue 32, 28 November 1942.
2   Anthony Cotterell, 'Parachuting as a Career', *WAR*, issues 59 and 60, 11 and 25 December 1943.

'The Sergeant's High Jump'

'May I ask a question, sir?' he said.

'Certainly.'

'Isn't it true, sir, that the higher percentage of accidents in motorcycling as opposed to parachuting is simply because there are more people learning to ride motorcycles? So that really our chances of being injured while learning to parachute are much greater than in learning to ride a motorcycle?'

'Nothing of the kind. Absolute nonsense,' said the Flight Lieutenant firmly. 'The comparison is made with full allowance for the number of people engaged. It is a simple mathematical fact that you stand less chance of getting hurt in this course than if you were learning to ride a motor-bike.'

The equanimity of the audience, which had been slightly punctured by the Sergeant's question, was mercurially restored.

For the purpose of parachute training we were divided into sections of ten men, each under a sergeant instructor. I noted without feeling that the pessimistic Sergeant was in the same section as myself, and we embarked on five days' ground training.

They train you very thoroughly with every kind of fair-ground machinery. You learn to fall and to land properly in every conceivable position. You slide down chutes, you swing through the air in a harness which unpredictably collapses when the instructor presses a button and thus tests your quickness of reaction. You speed across the roof of a hangar suspended only by your hands from a monorail and attempting to maintain yourself in the correct position. You are dragged across the field at considerable speed while you learn with desperate eagerness how to release yourself from your harness without presenting more than a minimum target area to the enemy.

In all these activities Sergeant Trevelyan displayed the same blend of resolution and pessimism, but with consummate and scientific instinct he spotted where lay the possibility of mishap in each case, and told us, before unwaveringly launching himself.

For instance he was a source of inspiration in aperture training. This is the business of learning to project yourself through the hole in the floor of the aircraft. American paratroops jump through a door at the side; British troops jump through a hole in the floor. It's really perfectly simple. You sit with your legs through the hole. The instructor shouts 'GO!' as intimidatingly as he can. You push off with your hands and disappear through the hole in the position of attention, with your head kept firmly upwards and backwards – landing on mattresses a few feet below. If you don't follow the instructions you are liable to ring a bell if you crack your head on the side as you fall.

Sergeant Trevelyan thought there was more danger of banging his head on the near side of the hole if he kept his head back as instructed than if he kept it a little forward as he jumped. After banging his head good and hard three times he still wasn't wholly convinced.

There came the evening before our first jump. We all felt jumpy but not in the right kind of way. There's something about the idea of throwing yourself out of an aircraft which reduces everyone to a common denominator without much bearing on that individual's record in the face of other kinds of danger. You don't get some people who like it and others who loathe it; everyone is horrified together right from the start.

As I was getting into bed Sergeant Trevelyan asked me to do him a favour. He put a large scroll of paper in front of me. 'Would you witness it?' he said. 'It's my will.' There was an undercurrent in my laughter, and I went to bed thoughtfully.

For your first jump they take you up in a balloon. You clutch the sides of the basket, ignore the instructor's attempts to joke and try to resist the temptation to stare mesmerised at the receding earth. At about 500 feet the basket started rocking in the wind.

'Some sort of freak wind,' explained Sergeant Trevelyan. 'Hope it doesn't catch us when we are landing. Nasty injuries.'

'Complete bleeding optimist as usual, I see,' said the instructor.

The balloon came to a halt at the regulation 700 feet from the ground. There was a momentary pause while we composed ourselves. Sergeant Trevelyan pulled a letter out of the pocket of his jumping jacket and handed it to the instructor.

'I think I may be killed,' he said. 'It's a last letter to my mother.'

'Action stations, Number One,' shouted the instructor.

I swung my legs into the hole.

'GO!' thundered the instructor.

I left the Sergeant and all his depressing effects behind. It was the same with every jump we did. He wrote a new letter nightly or perhaps he brought the old one updated. Nightly he dreamed and daily he asked blood-curdling questions. He was jumping as well as anybody, disappearing through the hole like a ramrod and landing like a feather, but this didn't reassure him at all.

Our fourth jump was on Sunday evening. We dropped in two sticks of five, so having delivered the first five the aircraft had to circle the dropping zone and run up for the second five.[3]

I knew that Trevelyan was jumping fifth. I saw the little streak borne from the belly of the aircraft and watched for the parachute to develop. It never did.

Trevelyan dropped like a stone. At first with deliberation and then dreadfully faster. The Flight Lieutenant just had time to shout: 'Jam your legs together. Jam your legs together!' through his loud amplifier, and then the body hit the ground. The awful thing was that up to that split second of impact you knew that the poor devil had been as well and strong as any of us. And now he was dead; killed right before our eyes. The ambulance shot past me, followed by another car, and people started running towards the body. I suddenly felt too sick to move.

---

3   'Stick' was a collective name for a group of parachutists.

Then the body sat up. Then it stood up.

Then I saw Trevelyan running towards me. The ambulance went past him and Trevelyan waved to it. He was ignored. The ambulance went on, looking for him. Twice again it passed him and took no notice of his signals. The ambulance described another agitated small circle and stopped. Trevelyan came on running, weak but determined.

'Lie down, man!' I shouted at him, afraid he'd fall to pieces. I thought he was a human case of delayed action bombing and would disintegrate on some fixed stimulus, perhaps into powder like the people in *Lost Horizon*.[4]

'Where's the instructor? I've not reported yet,' panted Trevelyan.

I just looked at him. At that moment the Flight Lieutenant came running up, incredulous and shaken by what he had seen.

'Are you the man?' he said.

'He's the one all right,' I said. 'Sergeant Trevelyan, Section J 8.'

'Jumped number five, sir,' said the miracle man, reporting in the approved way. 'The parachute failed to open, sir,' he said, as if mentioning a small technical detail.

'But are you all right?' said the instructor, like a man talking to a ghost.

'I rather expected something of the kind to happen, sir.'

'What do you mean, "expected it to happen"? It's a million to one chance of its happening.'

'Premonition, sir,' said Trevelyan rather loftily.

'How the devil did you land? What was it like?'

'Side right, sir.'

'But are you all right?'

'It made me tingle, sir. Very fast landing, otherwise nothing. Wrenched my toes upwards.'

The doctor came up and looked him over. He hadn't even sprained his ankle.

'You realise that this makes you the luckiest man in the world?' he said.

But Trevelyan didn't seem concerned.

Back in the camp we jumped down from the bus. There was a sharply anguished yelp from Trevelyan.

He had sprained his ankle. The man who had successfully jumped 600 feet from an airplane had failed to jump 3 feet from a bus.

'I knew something like that would happen,' he said. 'It's a fool's game, parachuting.'

---

4   *Lost Horizon* – a highly popular film directed by Frank Capra, which had come out in 1937. It was about Shangri-La, a magical hidden valley in the Himalayas.

WITH THE AIRMEN

*I*n 1943, Anthony embarked on a series of flights with the daylight bombers of the United States Army Air Force, the USAAF, and the day and night bombers of the RAF. He wrote up his experiences in two chapter in *An Apple for the Sergeant*, 'Ships that Pass in the Day' and 'Did I ever tell you about my operation?'. A shorter, terser version of 'Did I ever tell you about my operation?' appeared in *WAR*, issue 62, 22 January 1944. However, the *WAR* article about the USAAF ('Daylight Bombing', issue 54, 2 October 1943) was almost completely factual with none of the entertainment value of 'Ships that Pass in the Day'.

Anthony's flights with the USAAF mainly took place in the summer of 1943; he flew on the B-17s of the 384th Bomb Group which was based at Grafton Underwood. (I am indebted to Fred Preller for working out the crews, commanding officer, and chronology of 'Ships that Pass in the Day', using the aircraft loading sheets and other records of the 384th Bomb Group.[1]) The missions took place between 30 August and 3 September, and it was only on the last flight that bombs were actually dropped. In February 1944, Anthony returned to Grafton Underwood and flew another mission.

Anthony was clearly fascinated by the Americans and how difficult English people found it to behave naturally with them. During 1943 he wrote a number of pieces on the American Army for *An Apple for the Sergeant*, and ended by concluding that there were 'considerable differences of spirit and approach' between the American and the British military.

Americans look on the Army more as a nine-to-six job. Their loyalty is more akin to the pride of a business man employed by a first-rate firm. Whereas the British soldier's loyalty is based on the feeling that we mustn't let the old place down, plus personal attachment to officers.[2]

---

1   Fred Preller is the webmaster of the 384th Bomb Group website: www.384thBombGroup.com (last accessed 30 December 2012).

2   'Quit Horsing Around and Police Up', from *An Apple for the Sergeant*, p.140.

In flying on the USAAF and RAF bombing raids, Anthony was gambling with his life. Ernest Watkins, who worked with Anthony on *WAR* after Stephen Watts moved on, watched Anthony voluntarily take on these assignments with something like horror. In his autobiography he makes it clear that he himself kept clear of dangerous situations during his work for *WAR*, and was appalled when he inadvertently strayed into them. He wrote that Anthony 'had far more courage than I had', but he was also at pains to stress that there was no element of idiotic showing off in what Anthony did:

> There was never any touch of 'Look, Ma, no hands!' or 'You can do this if you try' in anything he wrote. No moralising, nothing exhortatory. He described ordinary men with ordinary fears using their skills and experience to succeed in some dangerous duty. It was their confidence in each other that held them together.[3]

Watkins admired Anthony's courage but very much wished to avoid emulating him. On one occasion, however, he felt that he absolutely had to. He wrote of his attempt to fly operationally with the USAAF: 'I was driven to it by the example of Anthony. The decision to make the attempt brought me no joy of any kind.' When he was barred from the flight at the last moment due to a hitch in regulations, he felt the most intense relief. A sense of guilt always remained, but he knew that he could never have showed Anthony's insouciance.

> While I had been away, Anthony had slipped down one afternoon to the RAF station at Gatwick and taken an evening bombing mission over the same set of targets. He said he got back to London in time for a late supper at the Savoy. I believed him.[4]

What was clearly Anthony's most significant trip with the RAF took place on 20 December 1943, the day after his 27th birthday, when he took part in a major raid on Frankfurt. His account of this operation in a Lancaster of 619 Squadron is one of the very best pieces of contemporary writing about Bomber Command.[5] It was a raid in which 650 aircraft took part, forty-three of which were lost.[6] The winter of 1943–44 saw appalling losses in Bomber Command, and Anthony could quite easily have been killed. With stark realism, some of his crew mates did not expect to survive their tour. They could see with their own eyes how many other crews were disappearing off their station, Woodhall Spa. In addition, the authorities published losses very accurately. After

3   Ernest Watkins, 'It is Dangerous to Lean Out', p. 173.

4   Ibid, pp. 185–6.

5   USAAF bombing flights were always known as missions, RAF bombing flights were always known as operations.

6   Martin Middlebrook and Chris Everitt (eds.), *The Bomber Command War Diaries* (Penguin, London, 1990), p. 460.

they got back, Anthony was given the figure of forty-two aircraft lost on the Frankfurt raid.[7] No one was covering up the appalling loss rate.

But his account is not particularly sombre. He was fascinated by the surreal experience of seeing Occupied Europe from the Lancaster's operational height of around 20,000 feet, whilst the crew occasionally argued whether some flak-infested area was Aachen or Brussels or Antwerp. He found the situation both ridiculous and utterly bizarre, hearing his crew mates talk of the cities of Western Europe in terms of their previous operations – 'They knew them not by their cultural monuments, their political significance or hotels, but simply by their flak and searchlight barrages.'

The editorial to the *WAR* version of 'Did I ever tell you about my operation?' demonstrates what Anthony found most impressive of all in dangerous military situations – the comradeship of highly trained specialists working as a team:

> Perhaps the outstanding military moral is the complete unity of the bomber crew. This unity grows from their technical interdependence and from the nature of their work. A similar spirit is natural to the tank crew, the parachute stick, the mortar team, or in any situation where everyone feels that everyone else knows his job. There could be an interesting and useful discussion on the teamwork situation in your own group.[8]

The extended version of 'Did I ever tell you about my operation?' forms the last chapter of *An Apple for the Sergeant*; the book also includes a photograph of Anthony with the aircrew and ground crew of T-Tommy, warming themselves by the ground crew's brazier just prior to take-off. The flight to Frankfurt marks a cut-off point, for though Anthony may have written some other detailed pieces nothing survives except the material he wrote on D-Day, the Normandy campaign, and the run-up to Arnhem, which are the following chapters of this book.

'Ships that Pass in the Day'

In a horrified kind of way I had always wanted to go on a bombing raid.

Arrangements were made for me to fly with the American Fortresses. First I was sent on a course at a Combat Crew Replacement Centre, where they give refresher training to reinforcements newly arrived in this country, and also prepare non-flyers who have to fly for one reason or another.

---

7   619 Squadron fortunately suffered no losses on the night of the Frankfurt operation. W.R. Chorley, *Royal Air Force Bomber Command Losses of the Second World War, Volume 4: 1943* (Midland Publishing, Hinckley, 2007), p.436.

8   'Lines of Thought', *WAR*, issue 62, 22 January 1944.

There were two others in the class, Colonel Jock Whitney, the American millionaire race-horse owner and tycoon, and a young man who was introduced as General Eaker's aide.

The Colonel was youngish and amiable, though naturally not unaccustomed to having his point of view appreciated. General Eaker's aide was volatile and instantly well-informed about almost anything.

The schedule was rigorous and devoted mostly to the .50 calibre machine-gun, which we were supposed to learn to fire and maintain in case the occasion arose. We worked under a corporal instructor in a gymnasium which had been partitioned into classrooms. For some periods we joined the general class. It was reassuring to find that none of them took notes. I never have much confidence in people who take a lot of notes in lectures. They were all in leather or mackintosh jerkins and were obviously suffering from a sense of anticlimax, having arrived in this country geared for action and being immediately plunged into this end-of-term revision.

'When you hear the term "tail attack" it doesn't mean he's overtaking you. He'll never do that. It means he'll end up at your tail. He's gonna have to follow a curve of pursuit until he ends up dead behind your tail. That's a very common form of attack. With our ships it's usually from above …'

'How many in here can judge a second exactly every time?'

One hand was raised.

'I can do it, but it takes practice,' the instructor went on. 'That's the way to estimate speed.'

We were taught how to behave when forced down into the sea. You all go into the radio compartment and pack down on the floor like sardines, sheltering your head in your arms and keeping your knees slightly bent. There is a terrific forward momentum when the aircraft hits the water, and no matter how smooth the sea may be, the water comes up to your waist. There is a considerable jolt on landing and another when she finally settles, so you don't move until she comes to a standstill.

The engineer and his assistant get out first to see that the life rafts have successfully launched themselves from the wings. You all climb in, carrying the emergency radio, and get away quickly; not because of the suction but because of the unpredictable behaviour of the tail when the aircraft breaks up.

Even if the Air/Sea Rescue people know your position exactly, it may be thirty-six hours before you are picked up.

We went for an altitude flight, partly at 30,000 feet. There was no particular sensation except a sudden feeling of coldness and a progressive tendency to flatulence.

Next day we went for an artificial altitude flight in the oxygen cabin. There were five of us, the Colonel, the Captain and two strangers. We sat locked in a sort of fortified caravan with white walls and a thick glass panel at the end through which the doctor watched us. He addressed us through a loudspeaker. We sat facing each other as if in a tram.

The doctor's amplified voice: 'We'll go up at 4,000 feet a minute and come down slower in case anyone has ear trouble.'

In a very short time a mist formed in the cabin. 'You're getting in a cloud,' said the voice. It was appreciably colder, like an autumn morning, though outside the cabin there was heat-wave weather. There was no sound except the persistent tapping of the pumping machine. One man was rather affectedly reading the *New Yorker*.

Voice: 'Now we're nearing 10,000 feet. Put your masks on.'

A little later: 'Now we're doing 20,000, going on 25,000. Take out pens from your pockets or the ink's liable to leak.' My stomach began to rumble.

Presently, one at a time, we had to take off our oxygen masks, stamp our feet and hands, then write our names as many times as we could before passing out. The rarefied atmosphere feels quite normal without artificial oxygen. That is the danger of it. You don't realise that you are just going to pass out. I managed to write my name once, but I wasn't conscious of the second attempt, which was a meaningless jumble, tailing off as I lost consciousness. The others managed to write their names two or three times. Evidently I am not the Himalayan type.

There was a great sense of stomach comfort as we descended to 20,000 feet, though a slight painfulness in the ears. The idea is to inoculate people against the temptation to feel that they can do without their oxygen if, say, they want to move about the aircraft. I found it a completely convincing demonstration.

There were many more lectures on the .50 calibre gun.

'Whether it be one gun or a lot of guns we always do the paper work, using similar triangles ... lock the gun in that position ... this distance here is 'x' ... gives us the distance from the line of bore to the line of sight ...'

In lectures you are either bored because you understand what the lecturer is saying or because you don't. (Thought recorded at 1.40 p.m., the afternoon's work starting at 1 p.m.)

The Captain was an intelligent follower: 'I don't see that. How can it be a straight line from the back of the barrel to 'x'?'

The Colonel was dogged: 'I missed something there. I'd like to have you go over that again. I didn't quite get it. What I'd like,' he said, 'is a lecture on calibres, the bigger ones and all that.'

'We don't need that,' said the Captain.

'May as well get ourselves a little free education,' said the Whitney millions.

There was a constant stream of new arrivals from America. At night their voices could be heard in different parts of the hut. One man said that General Montgomery had been made a Lord and would get a great palace and a hundred thousand pounds a year.[9] He regarded this as decadent and feudal.

---

9   Referring to Bernard Montgomery, 'Montie'. Montie was knighted for his generalship in North
     Africa. The stuff about the great palace was, of course, nonsense.

'But we get as much as an English full Colonel as Second Lieutenants,' said another man. 'I wanna go home, damn it.'

Next morning we drove down to the miniature range at the far side of the airfield. Our instructor had brought the wrong key, so we sat waiting in the car. It was 8 a.m.

'You got egg all over your mouth,' said the Colonel to the Captain.

'I'll clean it off with some of that soap from your ear,' riposted the Captain.

Presently the keys arrived and we fired the .50 calibre on the range; it makes the most formidable noise.

A week or two later I was sent down to an airfield for the actual excursion. The first opportunity was on the Monday afternoon. They were going to bomb airfields in France.

MONDAY[10]

After briefing, the pilot and I drove round to the aircraft in a jeep. The pilot's name was Sprague; he was ruddy-cheeked and taciturn. The aircraft was parked in a circular bay just off one of the runways, with a group of men working on it. The pilot disappeared to superintend, and I was approached by a young man who said: 'You the navigator? Yelvington's my name. Afraid I'm just a greenhorn. This is my first mission.' I was about to console him that we all have to begin somewhere, when it suddenly occurred to me that my very life might be jeopardised by his greenhornery. Sympathy instantly evaporated. It turned out that he was to act as co-pilot on this mission to give him some experience for operations with his own aircraft.

Presently eight men drove up in a truck, each carrying one or two machine-gun stocks. They sat down on the ground and cleaned them. We were each given a packet of Spearmint and a Mars bar. An hour went by before climbing into the aircraft, which felt its way out on the runway at 4.45 p.m.

I sat in the nose surrounded by guns and ammunition upon a sort of counter normally used by the navigator, who was sitting on a box of ammunition studying his maps with a pair of dividers. The compartment was bullet-nosed, mostly of glass, and filled with belts of ammunition stored in knee-high wooden frames overflowing rather untidily on to the floor. Right up in the nose the bombardier sat on another case of ammunition, making adjustments on an instrumental panel.

I will now switch into the present tense, because most of this was written in the aircraft.

The whole thing is in a state of frenzy and vibration and uncomfort. Not at all in keeping with the spectator's view of the way a bomber seems to drift into the air; it makes me apprehensive about my stomach.

---

10   This was Monday, 30 August 1943.

The ships are crawling towards the take-off like great bats in the sunlight. I am suddenly alarmed that I have left my parachute behind. It is handed to me to keep on my lap. No room elsewhere.

Both young men are very preoccupied. There seem to be no arrangements for being sick. No sign of the paper bag provided by commercial airlines. One of the three enormous machine-guns is banging about uncomfortably near my head, which it hits from time to time. Now we are moving. Just passing the ambulances. I think it would be more tactful to keep them out of sight.

We are flying just to the right and behind the leading ship. In the air the bats look like newts.

'If I use this gun, scram back there, Major,' says the navigator, 'and if I use that one, get over there.'

A pleasant sense of fatalism comes over me. The business of not being bothered by responsibility or having to make decisions. There is nowhere to put anything. Have just put my cigarette butt in my pocket. Seems a pity to dirty the floor. The bombardier has gone aft, so I have a perfect uninterrupted view through the glass nose. A large irregular hole in the glass nose has been patched. Shrapnel, I suppose. Oh dear.

The thing about being an Englishman with Americans is that one feels bound to behave with as near an approach to sang-froid as is possible, though I suppose that would apply if one was with the English. They were rather tactless at the briefing. It hardly seemed the time for the Colonel to complain about faults in the gunnery, even small ones, or to paint nightmare pictures of the vulnerability of loosened formations. Funny to what extent your main concern is how other people will react to your behaviour.

I am not overdressed. Just a summer flying-suit, over-boots and an American jockey-cap. In fact the others are wearing more than I am; and with my low blood-pressure.[11] The navigator is still doing advanced geometry. No one tells me anything. I hope I am pulling my weight. I just noticed fifteen other Fortresses out to the right. Probably been there quite a while. The hell of an observer I make. We are approaching a solid bank of cloud. The land below is disappearing. It is just like suddenly finding yourself in the Arctic. There is another formation of eighteen on our left.

Navigator: 'We are going up now. Put on your oxygen mask. Bombardier, check the Major's oxygen gauge, it don't seem to be working. I can't see it going up and down.'

Sometime later the mission was cancelled owing to weather not being clear enough for precision bombing. We turned back from the English coast.

I was surprised to find myself feeling frustrated instead of reprieved; as if I had made an unsuccessful attempt at seduction. All those hours of flying just to turn around and come back; and incidentally that was quicker said than done. We had to fly several hundred miles and then go through all the business of circling round waiting our turn to land. Then, when you landed, instead of feeling heroic, you felt plain ludicrous.

11   A typical Anthony joke against his own lack of military physique.

We got back at 8 p.m. I ate in the Combat Crew Mess-hall, which was much more rough and ready than the Ground Officers' Mess. The idea of separate messes is to cater for the flyers' eccentric hours. Sometimes they have to eat very early, sometimes very late. By American standards 8 p.m. is outlandishly late for dinner. I went to the movie show. They were showing *Desert Victory*, which was very well received.[12] It was a big hut with backless benches and a far from perfect projector.

Next day, Tuesday, there was another mission.

TUESDAY

Briefing was at 1 p.m. Much the same as yesterday. The main excitement is when you come into the room and see for the first time where you are going. The route is marked with coloured strings and pins on a giant map. Close-up pictures of the target are shown. Details of the route are given. 'Cloudy', the weather-man, forecasts the clouds and conditions over the target, and the Colonel summarises the situation and points a few morals, e.g.: 'Anything that heads towards you and looks like taking pictures with a flash-light – let him have it.'

The ship was just queuing up to take off when a message came for me to get out. The tyre of the leading ship had a puncture, so it couldn't take off, and the Colonel, who was leading the group, was transferring to this aircraft, leaving no room for me.[13] I clambered out. There was a high wind on the runway produced by the madly revolving airscrews of the ships queued up for take-off. It was difficult to stand up, especially when loaded with parachute, oxygen-mask, life-belt and odd clothing. I found myself and kit standing Chaplin-like beside the queue of bombers waiting to take off. Just then Major Beckett, the good-looking deputy Group Commander, drove up through the wind in a jeep and okayed the idea of my getting on the next ship but two. I got in just as it was moving off and sat with the waist-gunners while the ship threw itself along the take-off and up into the air. Then made my way forward and found myself enclosed in the bomb-bay, stuck between two iron frameworks loaded with bombs. The doors were shut on either side and I had a general sense of taking part in an Abbott and Costello chase.

But the new nose was roomier. It was more open. The ammunition had been used to furnish the place with more care. I seemed to have interrupted something. The navigator was reading the *News Chronicle*, and the bombardier a Penguin book. I was given a box of ammunition to sit on; unfortunately, it had no lid and was not fully loaded, so I was suspended.

---

12   *Desert Victory* (1943) – British Ministry of Information film about the North African campaign.

13   After being bumped, Anthony flew with the William M. Price, III, crew in B-17F 42-30043, named *RUTHLESS*. The colonel who bumped him was Colonel Budd J. Peaslee, Group Commanding Officer. Thus Anthony appears on two different aircraft loading sheets.

Through my headphones I can hear the arrangements of getting the formations fixed. I can see more aircraft than yesterday, because this ship is further back in the formation. There are nine Forts immediately ahead, four out of the left-hand window and eighteen out of the right. Presently will come the problem of whether or not to spit out one's chewing-gum before donning the oxygen mask.

It is now 4.45 p.m. and am wearing mask; nothing has happened; nothing to do but watch the little red ball which bobs up and down between the gauge to show that the oxygen is working all right.

Sample conversation on the inter-phone.

'Ball gunner to navigator. Ball gunner to navigator. Over.'

'Carry on, ball gunner.'

'What's that ship out on the right?'

'Must be part of another formation.'

'Thanks. I just wanted to know.'

Pilot: 'We are coming right in on the English Channel now.'

The navigator and pilot keep saying numbers.

Just over Beachy Head. The ship is bumping about a little. The bombardier is having trouble with his 'chute; he cannot get it on. They are testing the guns, which make pleasantly little noise against the noise of the plane. We are now over Dieppe. The navigator and bombardier have suddenly busied up. The compartment suddenly seems much too small and my presence quite unwarrantable. I am kneeling, which is very appropriate and most uncomfortable. Crouched sitting on my right heel I cannot see a thing, being diffident of getting in the way. I am trying to take a look, but whenever I get to the window there is nothing in sight. The folly of all this becomes more apparent minute by minute. I wish I had brought my flak under-pants. I cannot move forward without getting in the way, and I cannot move back because I am nearly at the end of my oxygen tube tether. Parts of my body feel very hot, parts very cold. Presently I find a way of half lying, which still further restricts the view but reduces intense muscular fatigue. The weather is wonderfully sunny. We have just passed a crippled fighter being escorted home by four others. The navigator and bombardier look like the Wright brothers leaning forward in this apparently frail glass case, sprawling among the maps and ammunition.

We skirted Paris. I could just make out the Eiffel Tower. It was exciting to see it.

The formation out to our left was going through a heavy flak barrage; little bursts of dark brown smoke all in around them. One of their aircraft fell away, having been hit. Presently there were some little bursts in our formation. I tried not to care. The maddening thing was that the pilot didn't seem to make any effort to go any faster or dodge about. We just mooned drearily forward.

Dotted all over the sky were groups of aircraft, bombers, fighters, American, British, and some German. They all plunged purposefully along about their different business.

It was like a sort of market day or a lot of people hurrying to work. I didn't get any particular sense of massed power; even the aircraft just ahead looked quite small and innocuous, though their guns were roaming across the sky. It seemed absurd to think of all the work and organisation which had gone to bring each one of those groups to fly there that sunny afternoon.

I gave up trying to see out of the window, and after a while I became attuned to the circumstances with a sense of satisfaction which I felt must be punctured by something.

And no wonder I was beginning to feel serene. I found that we were back over England, having got to the target but again being unable to drop bombs because of thick clouds. I there and then determined that, come what may, I would be present at the dropping of at least one bomb on enemy-occupied territory. I felt that someone was trying to make a fool of me. The crew felt the same, though they were consoled to some degree by the fact that the excursion counted as one of their operational tours.

WEDNESDAY

The weather was too bad for anything but training.

THURSDAY

Here we are again sitting in the nose of another aircraft, but with the same navigator and bombardier that I started with the first time. These ships vary quite a bit in design. The ammunition boxes are built differently. There is a minimum of room in this ship. The engines have just started; we are a bit late owing to something wrong with the bomb-bay doors. I remembered to bring along an air-cushion. Today we are supposed to go to an airfield by Saint Nazaire. As we start I bump my head sharply against a gun.

I seem to have been doing this for months. There is no sensation of excitement, although there has been during the day. I am not awfully comfortable, and have to crouch down to avoid being hit on the back of the head by this gun, and sit with my feet out of alignment. My two companions don't talk much. I write industriously in the hope that they will be deluded into thinking that I am making a significant record of this matter. The weather is not good at all, being cloudy. Another group of Forts has just passed by the window.

The navigator is using a pair of dividers on a map of the Brest area. The rear gunner has just come crawling up through the hatchway to borrow a blanket, having very injudiciously forgotten to bring the connecting plug for his heated suit. It is really wonderful up here. The sky is a 'Lost Horizon' blue.[14] It doesn't seem likely one could come to any harm. I find I have not eaten my Mars bar from the previous time. I eat it. Too quickly. I am sure it is a mistake not to prolong one's pleasures.

---

14   Anthony is referring to the highly popular 1937 film, *Lost Horizon*.

I am trying to remember what to do in the way of first aid if one of these men gets wounded.

4.10 p.m. Have just put on my oxygen mask. You get used to it very quickly, though you notice it when you move around, and you can only move in a very restricted range. To show my new confidence I have just put a stick of chewing-gum into my mouth, lifting my mask to do so.

Later. I have just found myself thinking how sad it would be if I were killed. Sudden picture of my family opening the little bag with my things in it sent back by the Americans. I wonder what they would do with the American cigarettes and the orange I picked up off the floor during this morning's lecture by an RAF sergeant. Would they eat the orange, or keep it as a souvenir?

I have just a faint feeling someone is squeezing my intestines. I suppose it is the elements of the bends that afflict people in high altitudes. I find myself wishing we could be shot down in a comfortable way, and have a comfortably exciting escape, but this mood is quite different from the ideas I had over France on Tuesday when we were passing through flak; the folly of it all was then uppermost.

These young men are very reassuring to be with. There is no resolute determination; on the other hand, no frivolity; just deadpan. There are ships in front and on either side, but one doesn't seem to derive any support from being with so many. Each ship seems strictly on its own for the purpose of self-preservation. The bombardier has just put on his winter coat. There is some kind of draught somewhere, and 25,000 feet is no height for a draught. I have just asked where we are, and we are approaching the English coast. Shortly afterwards we pass by the Channel Islands. They look very small from our height.

Slight doubt by the pilot as to whether we are being led back to England. We have been turning to the right or Atlantic for some minutes.

Sure enough, we are going home again. Talk about sickening. Immediately the incentive evaporates you feel tired, bored and cold.

FRIDAY

I was called at 2.15 a.m. by a blood brother of Humphrey Bogart. Briefing was at 2.30 a.m. We were going to the same target as Tuesday. Breakfast was quite something – an orange, cornflakes, bacon and two eggs.

Out in the darkness some of the ships had lights on their noses, which made them look more like insects than ever. There was about an hour and a half before take-off. You have a tremendous feeling of worthwhileness; the new day is not going to be wasted as far as you are concerned.

The dawn did not break, it flowered into an anticlimax of coloured mists.

I am riding behind the pilots. They are conducting a testing dialogue. 'Oil pressure coming up 4,' says one. 'Oil pressure coming up 4,' says the other. Both pilots suddenly rub their faces with burnt cork. I ask and learn that this is to reduce the sun glare, which is very intense at high altitudes. The testing process continues as we queue up to go off. He throttles up each of the four engines in turn, announces, 'No. 1 checked. OK,' etc.

We are airborne at 6 a.m. The co-pilot calls out the speeds as we race along the runway. '50, 60, 70': at 130 we rise.

The top turret gun is just behind me. The gunner: 'See them cracks in the windscreen? That's concussion from firing. That's about the sixth set of windows we had in.'

The pilot suddenly reaches up over my right shoulder and fires a Verey light. Down below the ground is shrouded in mist like a Mongolian ghost world. The turret gunner and I lean over the pilots' shoulders. Two faces decapitated by the high backs of their seats. Both monotonously chewing gum. Things happen, time passes, slower when you are standing up. There are some thirty dials; the only one I understand is a clock which is two hours twenty-five minutes slow. These Americans refer to light mist as fog.

I am standing with my feet apart, each on a narrow ledge, with a hatch below me. The turret gunner points out the door through which we entered. 'Learn how to use that door. Pull the red handle, the door falls from you, get out head first; feet first you are liable to hit your head on the door with wind resistance.' My stomach is playing me up a little. Standing makes you more conscious physically, so I sit down and read a chapter of Eric Ambler's *Cause for Alarm*.[15]

This 'plane is called the *Black Ghost*.[16] The pilot has just fired another signal. Each time the turret reloads the pistol.

Turret gunner: 'That's a funny sector we're going. First time we lost five ships, then we went three times over and hardly saw a thing. Then we had fighters and flak everywhere. Now today I don't know what we are going to have.'

The ground is hazy, but the aircraft are sharply defined in the sunlight, as if each one had an individual coating. I can see six ships, four out ahead, one alongside, one behind. The propellers from this angle seem to lollop over lazily and irregularly. We are approaching a snow-like cloudbank. It is like crawling up a shore. Air speed is 150. The ships each rise and fall all the time, but it is not noticeable inside. The group ahead are just flying up a valley between two banks of cloud; there almost seems to be a danger of crashing against the clouds.

I don't know whether it is a tribute to Eric Ambler or cowardly escapism, but I keep wanting to read that book instead of concentrating on the situation. We are approaching the French coast. 'Chutes on. Also wearing flak helmets. The other day mine was too small, but now I have one that is too big. The guns have been tested and the pilots have suddenly become more watchful. If I lean back at all the turret catches me in the back,

---

15   *Cause for Alarm* – a 1938 spy thriller set in Fascist Italy.

16   Anthony flew with the Ralph R. Pulcipher crew in B-17F 42-5843, which is confirmed in 384th Bomb Group records as *BLACK GHOST*.

and, when revolving, starts to drag me round, so I have to hang on in a sort of fly-like position to the back of the pilot's seat.

Well, here is France. How the hell I can get out of all this paraphernalia if necessary I don't know. I suppose he will be firing the Verey light again. I feel nervy at the prospect of this mild explosion. One or two other things may explode, come to think of it. We are going over Dieppe. I can see a lot of our fighters, I am glad to say. I wish they would cuddle up a little closer. I am holding my flak helmet above my eyes like a man holding on to his hat in a high wind. I must look a BF standing here trying to write notes, hoping something will happen, and hoping it won't.[17] Now, what's that phrase a variation of?

It is 8.30 a.m. and I am suddenly conscious of cold toes. So is the pilot apparently, he keeps on stamping his feet. We have started turning. If we don't drop bombs this time I shall resign. I write 'Are we going home?' on a piece of paper and hand it to the co-pilot, who writes 'If we don't find this target we will get another.'

Up above you can see fighter trails. There seems to be a dogfight going on. This approach is interminable. The thing just seems to go steadily forward with no sense of straining to get there and away. Just as I write that, flak starts up everywhere. It is much fiercer than the other day. Little black, pointed, flat toadstools dispersing into fantastic tree shapes. It jumps up all round like Jack-in-the-Boxes. The formation ahead of us is passing through a barrage. You can't hear anything except the normal roar of the 'plane. The guns have just started working for some reason. Their stuttering makes the ship shudder, but it is nothing like the alarming noise they make when you fire them on the ground. You cannot hear much except the noise of the 'plane; if you listen you seem to hear explosions like punctures, but it might be imaginary noises in the ear. The shadow of the turret guns keeps passing back and forth across the cockpit. I look out for fighters. We are now west of Paris. Apparently we have been cruising round Paris for quite a time. I can see the Eiffel Tower. Now we are in another flak barrage. They seem to fire a great number of rounds. My face is painful, as the mask is too tight; my feet are cold; I don't think we are going to drop the bloody bombs. I try to scratch my nose, but of course scratch the mask. I am getting pretty tired and fed up.

There are some enemy fighters out to the right. Three or four little specks. They don't seem capable of doing anybody any harm. I know it is silly, but you cannot seem to work up any strong feelings.

Then the guns started; I could see tracer sprouting from the nose, and I caught sight of an enemy fighter out in front. There seemed to be tracer pouring into it, but it didn't seem discouraged, it seemed to hang there rather uncertainly, and then little stabs of flame appeared as it fired at us. Then it dived off past the right window. Two others did the same thing. Somehow they were not particularly frightening, not so frightening as the flak, because you are conscious of their being much smaller than you, and driven by

17   'BF' – bloody fool.

someone in the same condition of being in a strange element, whereas the flak comes up directed at you by a lot of people with nothing else to do. You feel something in common with a man who is also in a contraption thousands of feet above the earth, but the men on the safe ground below are very definitely on the other side of the counter. At this point I rather naively inquired what had happened to the 'plane on our left. Apparently it had been shot down, but I had not noticed it. A few seconds later I saw a Fortress diving down on its own. You knew that inside it there were ten men faced with the immediate prospect of death, but this idea was oddly unimpressive; not nearly so fascinatingly horrible as, say, the sight of a man being marched off to jail.

Presently we turned and the formations broke up into a line, one 'plane behind the other, for the bombing run. They couldn't bomb in formation without bombing the aircraft flying below.

As each bomb drops a red light flashes on the panel in front of the pilot. Afterwards the formations rally as quickly as possible and make for home. Apart from a little flak and the pilot's heel becoming frostbitten we didn't have any more trouble.

We got back just after 11.30 a.m.

A few months later I went down to fly another mission from the same station.[18] Yelvington, the 'greenhorn' of the first occasion, had now flown some twenty missions and was one of the most experienced pilots. The whole place had developed tremendously; they were now able to send twice as many aircraft as before. Everything had multiplied, improved, accelerated and matured.

Owing to the unfavourable weather we were restricted to targets in Northern France, which the crews now regarded as a dreary little milk run, though when I first visited a Fortress field, little more than a year before, a mission of the same depth was considered quite an adequate height of daring.

Later in the same week I flew on an RAF daylight operation over Northern France in a Mitchell medium bomber, which is much smaller and frailer than a Fortress, and even lacks the reassuring quality of the name Fortress. Everything is smaller and vibrates more. On a medium bomber airfield there is none of the sense of drama associated with heavy bombers. The preparations and briefing are much more spontaneous and informal. The operations are shorter and I started on mine with the inescapable feeling that it was some kind of sporting event. A feeling possibly enhanced by a letter from the AOC read out at the briefing, which had entreated the crews not to bomb any but military targets so that in years to come they would be able to look back and congratulate themselves on a good fight cleanly fought in accordance with principles of international law.[19] I found that the pleasure of taking part in such attractively clean and well-regulated fun almost disap-

---

18   The date was 28 February 1944. Anthony flew with the Joseph L. Bedsole Crew in B-17G 42-97477, named *PORKY'S PIG*.

19   AOC – Air Officer Commanding.

peared on arrival at the French coast. In the Fortress my confidence grew, in the Mitchell it evaporated. And though six Fortresses had been lost and hardly a shot was fired against us in the Mitchells, I was much more anxious to get home in the Mitchell than I was in the Fortress. Perhaps it was something to do with my digestion.

'Did I Ever Tell You About My Operation?'

I was given permission to fly on an RAF raid. On the way from the railway station to the bomber station we came across a mysterious white something drawn across the road. It was a parachute. Only a few minutes before my companion had remarked that it was a ghost-train sort of night, and with the wind and rain driving across the Lincolnshire fens it was alarmingly like an illustration from a spy thriller. There didn't seem to be anybody on the end of the parachute, which had got entangled in the hedge. Just as we were getting thoroughly soaked the parachutist appeared wearing a flying helmet and a civilian overcoat. He was an American airman, one of the crew of a US Navy Liberator which had been forced to bale out through lack of petrol. The Flight-Lieutenant asked him what time he had baled out, how many others had baled out, and what kind of aircraft they had baled out of. The airman, whose name was Clark, said that he was the tail gunner; he had baled out at about 5,000 feet; and there had been ten others in the aircraft; one of them had been injudicious enough to open his parachute before jumping: he had jumped with an armful of canopy and a ripe prospect of disaster. 'She was a good ship. Pity to have to throw her away,' said Clark. He didn't have much to say except when the conversation drifted away from his recent experience, when he switched it firmly back, and told us how he had kept from pulling the cord as long as possible, had been dragged a long way when he landed and had lost his boots. We stopped the car at the next phone box to ring up and institute a search party for the others. Certainly it solved the problem of what to talk about on arrival at the bomber station Mess. This was very comfortably situated in a requisitioned hotel.[20] We got there about 10 p.m. and were given bacon and eggs. The sleeping quarters were admirably luxurious. There was a bathroom attached to each bedroom.

The next day, Sunday, was my birthday.[21] I was called at 8.15 and found that my roommate was a tough little man who told me that he was starting his second tour of operations today as rear gunner to the new Wing Commander. He didn't expect to survive this second tour, which, he thought, on looking out of the window at the relatively clear sky, might very possibly start tonight. He told me that Sunday was just like any other day. The lateness in rising was habitual; there was a bus at 9 a.m. to take the crews from the Mess to

---

20   The Petwood Hotel, Woodhall Spa, which was the Officers' Mess.

21   Anthony's birthday was on 19 December. In 1943 he was twenty-seven years old.

the aerodrome.[22] My conductor, the Flight-Lieutenant, appeared as I was finishing breakfast and afterwards asked me to sign a form which instituted the following legal position:

'No compensation will be paid by the Air Council or by any officer or airman, RAF,
in respect of any such loss or injury. I agree to so bind myself, my heirs, executors and
administrators as to indemnify the Air Council and any officer or airman, RAF, and any
person in the service of the Crown, against any claim which may be made by any third
party against them or any of them arising out of any act or default on my part, during or
in connection with the said flight.'

We then drove round to the airfield. I was taken in to meet the Wing Commander,
a tall, thin young man just returned from the Middle East, and about to start his first
operational tour with Bomber Command. I was subsequently introduced to the Group
Captain. I went back and spent the rest of the morning in the Adjutant's office except
for a brief excursion to the Flying Control room, where they control the traffic of aircraft landing or taking off from the airfield. After lunch I was taken into the Squadron
Leader's office and introduced to the pilots.

The Squadron Leader was a very young DFC with the attractive air of decision
induced by being a young Squadron Leader with the DFC.[23] He sat behind a table;
it was a very small room, with a coke-stove in one corner, one easy chair, and along
one of the walls a chart showing the aircraft state and photographs of the crews. There
were half a dozen pilots in the room. I was introduced to the one who had been
selected as my escort. He looked even younger than the others. His name was Knights.[24]
He took me to draw a parachute and then with the rest of the crew we were taken out
in a crew bus to the aircraft *T for Tommy*. The rest of the crew were similarly young. The
aircraft was a Lancaster. It didn't look sensationally large despite its sensationally large
bomb load. The pilot Knights showed me round it and indicated where I would stand
for the operation, while the rest of the crew cleaned it. Apparently a pilot had to pay
a half-crown fine if the Squadron Leader found any uncleaned portion of the aircraft.
We weren't there for long, as we had to be back at 4 p.m. for a post-mortem discussion
on the last Berlin raid, which had taken place a few days before.[25] It was held in the

---

22   The aerodrome was Woodhall Spa.

23   DFC – Distinguished Flying Cross.

24   The Knights crew for the Frankfurt operation was as follows: R.E. Knights (pilot), K. Twells (flight
     engineer), J.H. Bryant (bomb aimer), J.R. Bell (navigator), H. Rowan (Roman? wireless operator),
     A.W. Hobbs (mid-upper gunner), P.W. Dorham (rear gunner). 619 Squadron Operations Record Book,
     National Archives, AIR27/2131.

25   This was the disastrous raid of 16/17 December, when multiple Bomber Command accidents occurred
     on return to England due to fog. (See my book *Fire By Night, The Dramatic Story of One Pathfinder Crew
     and Black Thursday, 16/17 December 1943*.) 619 Squadron did not suffer any crashes due to bad weather but
     had one spectacular crash-landing at the base due to fighter damage incurred earlier. The pilot Tomlin and
     his flight engineer received immediate decorations. This was the Tomlin crew praised by the group cap-
     tain at the meeting which Anthony attended. The Squadron also had one crew shot down. W.R. Chorley,
     Royal Air Force Bomber Command Losses of the Second World War, Volume 4: 1943, p.429.

briefing-room, which was about the size of a small Church Hall, with a table and forms for each crew. The Group Captain conducted the meeting. Apparently it was the first of the kind held on this station. He explained that after each operation the report and photographs brought back by each crew were individually considered. He hoped that if the post-mortems were held in the presence of all concerned, very useful lessons might be learned. It might help to counteract the tendency to think you knew a thing when you weren't really sure. But criticism was to be constructive, not destructive. 'When I ask why were you twenty miles off track, I don't mean why the hell were you twenty miles off track, I just mean why were you twenty miles off track.' The various special-ist officers, Intelligence, Radio, Ordnance, etc, and the two Squadron Leaders and the Wing Commander sat on each side of him. The Group Captain sat alone at a small table raised on a shallow platform. He had a pile of dossiers before him, one relating to each crew. He took these in turn.

'Tomlin came back with two engines U/S and a third likely to go.[26] Very good per-formance. Now the point is this – he asked for radio priority and he couldn't get it because another aircraft already had priority. Now, was it really necessary for the other aircraft to have priority, and why was it necessary?'

The navigator of the crew concerned stood up and said that they had become uncer-tain of their whereabouts because he, the navigator, had been attending to another member of the crew who was unconscious through oxygen failure. The Group Captain went into the question of why there had been an oxygen failure. He prescribed a revised and tightened-up arrangement for inspecting each man's oxygen mask before taking off.

One crew had complained that the door of the aircraft had blown open. The room became divided into two schools: those who maintained the official view that it was mechanically impossible for the door to blow open, and those with experience of doors inclined to blowing open.

T for Tommy, Knights' aircraft, was the last to be considered. There was laughter in the post-mortem when the Group Captain read out that Knights had bombed on the reciprocal, i.e. had turned and made a second run-up, flying in the opposite direction to the main stream of bombers. It was considered very funny. 'I don't know what to say to you,' said the Group Captain. 'Don't know quite what to say. Yes, I think you were justi-fied. After all, you achieved your primary object. Dropped the bombs on the target. Yes, I think you were justified. Very creditable.'

The rest of the day was our own.

The crews don't know whether or not there will be an operation on any given day until about 10 a.m. Next morning the pilots were hanging round the Squadron Leader's office in the same way as yesterday. Nothing definite had come in by 10 o'clock, when we went out to the aircraft, though the weather was considered ominously suitable.

---

26 See previous footnote.

Accumulators were being charged out in the aircraft, the radio was being tested. A girl's voice said, 'I hear you strong and clear,' 'I hear you strong and clear.'

Discipline was loose but definite. Or rather there didn't have to be any. The sense of interdependence between various members of the crew was complete. They all looked to the pilot for guidance. Each one was conscious of his own important part in the crew. Apart from the pilot the outstanding character was the tail gunner, who was referred to as 'the old man' or 'Dad' because of his pessimistic and hypochondriac tendencies. Apparently Dad was inclined to be an alarmist, to see fighters in a clear sky. But this increased the general confidence in him as a tail gunner. They were convinced that no fighter could possibly catch Dad napping.

'Look at this, that's ominous,' said Knights. A 4,000lb bomb was being towed up to the aircraft on a ground-level buggy. The engines were given a ground run. There was a sense of pleasurable excitement as they started up one by one. The compartment warmed up very quickly. A new zest was detectable as it became evident that there was going to be an operation tonight. The sense of adventure was infectious. You felt that you were taking life by the throat and shaking it.

After a cup of tea at the YMCA mobile van we drove back to the Mess for lunch at noon. My room-mate was changing. He put a small German dictionary in his pocket. 'Come in handy in the Stalag,' he said.

There was an atmosphere of quietly mounting excitement at lunch. People's minds were obviously slightly ahead of the current meal. Certainly mine was. Someone asked me to pass the parsnips, and I said 'Yes, thanks, I will,' and helped myself to some instead.

Pilots were to be briefed at 1 p.m. We sat around on wicker chairs and forms in a small room just off the main briefing-room. The windows looked out over the airfield, but the aircraft were too dispersed to be visible. This room was the Intelligence Library. It was covered with training pamphlets and intelligence reports. We were still waiting at 1.35 p.m. The pilots were discussing possible destinations.

'I hope those sons of bitches aren't sitting there waiting for us,' said one pilot, and Knights said, 'They're sitting in their cockpits having cups of tea brought to them, just sitting there waiting for you.'[27]

It was decided that it wasn't likely to be Berlin, because the petrol load wasn't large enough. They discussed the characteristics of the new Wing Commander in briefing.

'I used to like the way Abercrombie briefed,' said one. 'Made you feel you'd won the war before you got up in the air.'

'I never enthused,' said his neighbour.

Eventually the target map was brought in and unveiled. Cords marked the route to and from the target. It was Frankfurt, in south-west Germany. 'I hate that name,' said Knights. 'Biggest concentration of searchlights you ever saw.'

27　Meaning the German fighter defence, which was deadly accurate.

Roll-call was then taken. The Group Captain came in and sat up on a table.

'Met, will you give your story?' said the Wing Commander. The Meteorological Officer started his technical monologue illustrated by a large and complicated cloud diagram. It didn't mean much to me. 'No front definitely affecting your route … bases should be OK to land all night …' and so on.

The Intelligence Officer described Frankfurt. Population about 570,000, a very important town; a commercial and financial centre, with very vital railway ramifications, also of considerable importance as an industrial centre. The docks had been badly damaged some weeks before.

The pilots had each been issued with a map of the target area set in a map-case, on the back of which there was a space marked off under various headings for them to make notes. The Wing Commander said that there would be several hundred aircraft on the raid (he gave the exact figure). The attack would be in five waves. He read out which aircraft would be in the various waves.

He went on to give particulars of the petrol load, the bomb load, and the overall or all-up weight of the aircraft. One of these aircraft weighs as much as a small convoy of motor lorries.

'You'll set course over base at 1750 hours. Must be comfortable at your height shortly before crossing the enemy coast. Remain at maximum height all the way to the target. You can climb up afterwards.'

There was to be a spoof attack on Mannheim, to divert the enemy defences; this would go in earlier. There would be coffee and sandwiches in the crew-room at 3 p.m., transport at 3.35 p.m. They were to be at the aircraft by 4 p.m. First take-off at 5 p.m. Zero hour would be 7.35 p.m. Zero hour for the last wave would be between fourteen and seventeen minutes later.

We moved into the neighbouring room for the main briefing. Here the crews were sitting, each of them on their separate tables. Ours was in the middle of the room. Knights started telling them what had gone on in the pilots' briefing. When all the pilots had finished telling their crews the Group Captain stood upon the platform at the end of the room and read out one of the Prime Minister's messages of congratulation to Sir Arthur Harris.[28] The Group Captain said he was sure they would all be glad to hear that Sir Arthur had sent a message expressing their appreciation of the Prime Minister's thoughtfulness. 'And I'm sure you will join me in congratulating our late Wing Commander – Wing Commander Abercrombie – on his very well-deserved bar to the DFC. I wired him congratulations from us all.'

He went on to say that Frankfurt had often been scheduled as a target but bad weather had often interfered. Tonight was perfect. 'The Met merchant won't dare to show his face if anything goes wrong.'

28   Sir Arthur Travers Harris, Air Officer Commanding in Chief of Bomber Command.

'Now let's have fourteen first-class aiming-point photographs for the Wing Commander's first trip. Have a good trip – fourteen aiming-points, remember, and fourteen back.'

We went to dress ourselves. I put on the whole rigmarole: flying suit, fleece-lined boots, sweater, parachute harness, and Mae West. My conducting officer had come over from Group Headquarters especially to see me off. We were taken out to the aircraft in a crew-bus and he came in his little car.

'Feeling all right?' he said.

'I think so,' I said.

'Well, you've got a first-class crew here – at least, I think they are,' he said. 'I'll just have a word with them. How many trips have you done?' he said to Knights.

'Twenty-three,' said Knights.[29]

'Ah, that's fine. Well, take very good care of him. Take very good care of him indeed. Weave in and out all the way there and back.'

'Sure,' said Knights.

'Well, I think I'll be pushing off now. I think I told you I'm going on leave tomorrow, I've a good bit to clear up. Well, have a good trip, Major. Hope you come through all right.'

After he had driven off a corporal of the ground crew came up. 'I've often thought I'd like to go on one of these trips just to see what it was like,' he said. 'But of course what I'd really like would be to be on aircrew myself.

'Oh yes, of course I was all packed up and ready to go back in the 1938 crisis. I talked it out with Dad – I was working for him at the time. "I'm going, Dad, I feel I must," I said to him. "If that's how you feel, son, I won't stand in your way," he said. "I wouldn't speak to you if you felt any other way." But then, you see, I got married and that made things different. I had another talk with Dad in 1939, told him I was volunteering for aircrew. "You can't do that. Things are different now, you can't possibly leave Gladys," he said. Then I saw he was right. I hadn't realised what a big difference it made being married. I was still keen to join up even if I couldn't go in aircrew, but Dad said I'd better not do anything hasty. You see, I was reserved for quite a time. Then I couldn't keep from wanting to get into it, so I volunteered. Been in it more than two years now.'

'Been posted about much?' I asked.

'No, I haven't much. Matter of fact, I live near here. Doesn't pay you to move about too much, you know. They don't get a chance to see what you can do. You do much better by staying in one place. That's how I got to be corporal. Still, I often wish I was on aircrew,' he said. 'If it wasn't for Gladys it would be a very different story. But it's different when you're married.'

---

29   The first tour of a Main Force crew was thirty operations, so Knights had seven left to do. Happily, the Knights crew appear to have survived the war as they are not listed in Commonwealth War Graves Commission records.

'It is, too,' I said.

'Well, I'd better be looking at my other aircraft. Hope you get back all right, sir. May see you later, then. I shall be here when you get back.'

We stood around warming ourselves at the ground crew's fire which was burning outside their little shack.[30] It was pretty cold. My excitement was constant but not urgent. But the sense of drama was satisfying. Things were very quiet. No sensation of being surrounded by an air armada waiting to take off. Just a small party in a corner of a big windy field.

It was about twenty to five when Knights said, 'Well, better be getting in.' They started engines at 4.50 p.m. The pilot and the engineer started going through their checking and testing drill. I stood just behind them in the gangway, which leads past the pilot's chair from the nose where the bomb-aimer was reclining to the navigator's position just behind me. The navigator was a rubicund country boy in appearance. He sat at a table which grew out from the wall of the aircraft and worked at his maps. I had a very good view out of the long right-hand window. I could see out of the left-hand side, but only a limited range of vision, owing to the high back of the pilot's seat and the black-out curtain which partitioned off the navigator's compartment. Outside I could see the ground crew shivering with their hands in their pockets.

'Is the door shut, Bill?' asked the pilot over the intercom. On hearing that it was he began to start the engines, one by one from right to left, until the four of them were roaring. Almost immediately the cabin began to get noticeably warmer. The feeling of dull tiredness into which my excitement had faded cleared and was replaced by the sense of high, nay lunatic, adventure. The aircraft edged out on to the taxi track. Other aircraft were lumbering in the same direction. Presently we wheeled into the runway past the little group of blue figures standing to watch the take-off and wave goodbye.

The sense of adventure was further enhanced by the gathering darkness into which the aircraft ahead was just disappearing, followed at about a thirty-second interval by our own. The pilot and the engineer were meanwhile carrying on their technical dialogue. 'Undercarriage,' said the pilot.

'Undercarriage up,' said the engineer.

'OK.'

We flew over a river. 'Let me know when I'm right over the 'drome,' said the pilot.

'OK,' said the navigator. 'OK, that'll do.'

'OK, navigator.'

There was a band of olive green, orange and scarlet across the general greyness of the sky: it was like marzipan. Turning round, I could look down the length of the aircraft; it looked much bigger in the air than on the ground. There was a slightly sinister red glow from each of the four engines.

30 See the photographic section of this book.

The navigator asked the pilot to give him the air speed and height. '170, 11, 200,' intoned Knights. We started passing large formations of aircraft flying in the opposite direction and distinguishable by their navigation lights. Sometimes they flashed past seeming to be dangerously near. All this time we were climbing. At ten to six I noted that the stars were looking down.

'OK. Turn right now,' said the navigator, and we started wheeling round.

'What's the weather like?' asked the engineer.

'Pretty mucky,' said Knights; 'Good job we're case-hardened, Ernie.'

I noticed that Knights always looked behind before turning. In the Squadron Leader's office there was a list of instructions for pilots headed 'Experientia Docet' in which one of the rules was: 'Always look behind before taking off. Also before doing a turn in the air. The machine you are flying isn't the only one in existence. Neither are you the only fool. Make a habit of this, but not the habit that makes you screw your head round without seeing anything.'

There were other rules. 'A good pilot when travelling by train or car should sub-consciously be seeing the passing country in the light of forced landing-ground.' 'Always regard the other man as a fool. Then if he turns out to be one, you won't be surprised.' 'Do everything in the air smoothly – one might almost say with rhythm. Treat the machine as you would a lady.' The one which I hoped Pilot Officer Knights had taken most to heart was: 'A steady, consistent pilot is of far more use than a bril-liant, erratic one.'

'Is that the coast?' the rear-gunner's voice suddenly asked over the intercom. I looked down and just made out the division between land and water.

'Yep, Norfolk,' said Knights.

'Are we going in or coming out?' asked the rear-gunner.

'Going out over the North Sea.'

'There's a convoy off Great Yarmouth,' announced the navigator.

At 6.25 someone asked if we could have the heat lowered. I couldn't identify the intercom voice, but he said he was getting fairly sweaty.

The rear gunner excitedly announced the approach of an aircraft, then said, 'OK. Lancaster.'

'Keep a good look round, Dad,' said the pilot.

Distant flashes and searchlight cones began to be visible. The aircraft broke into an odd swaying motion. As we drew nearer the Continent the whole horizon was punctu-ated by signs of strife. These activities were forbiddingly widespread.

'Coast coming up,' said Knights presently.

'You're heading straight for flak,' said the bomb-aimer.

'That's right, run right into it,' said the engineer sarcastically.

Knights was suddenly concerned that his windscreen was icing up. The engineer bent up forward and rubbed the rag round it.

'Two searchlights on the starboard bow,' said the tail gunner.

'OK,' said Knights.

The aircraft started weaving slightly. There was no need to tell me that there were two searchlights on the starboard bow. They were creeping with sinister purposefulness round the sky, every now and then executing a dart as if to demonstrate their reserve of mobility. They seemed to stroke the sky all around us, playing cat and mouse. It seemed unlastably good luck that they didn't find us. There would be no trouble about the morale of searchlight detachments if the men could be taken for a ride in a bomber and experience the attention and respect induced by the weapons they wield. I looked at my watch, which I could read quite plainly in the reflected light of the searchlights. It was 6.45 p.m. We seemed to be passing through a belt of searchlights, which, in the way of searchlights, switched on and off without apparent logic. There seemed to be no telling where they would spring up next. There was a lot of gunfire, but nothing came near us. Our relative position to most of the clusters of searchlights took a long time to change, which meant, I suppose, that they were much further away than I imagined. Quite suddenly, after flying in this atmosphere of action and enemy protest for some time, we were in the clear again. We were in fact clear of the coast, or in the fighters' parlour, according to how you felt. Incidentally, there isn't much you can feel.

'I think everybody's early, Bob. There's no searchlights at the back now,' said the tail gunner after a little while. The tail gunner seemed to be easily the best-informed commentator on the social scene. He seemed to know the most and talked the most.[31] Perhaps his isolation stimulated his appetite for sociability. Presently he said, 'There's one going down in flames. Right behind us.'

I looked back and couldn't see anything until the engineer pointed it out. I could distinguish a faint, shapeless glow of flames.

It served to emphasize that admission to these quarters was not free. The gate was shut behind. The house was haunted. Europe was all around us and we were all alone. Looking down on the ground, you could see odd, inexplicable, unaggressive-looking lights from time to time. They had no apparent operational significance, and may even have been blackout infringements of the grosser kind. But they served to emphasize our sense of being cut off. I need hardly say, because it has been said so often already, that this gives one a tremendous sense of comradeship with the other members of the crew. Your companionship with each other knows no inhibitions of temperament or prejudice. Friendship is perfect and complete. The idea of carrying an irritation or a resentment against one of them into the air seems quite out of the question.

'Fighter flares in front,' said Knights. 'Keep a good lookout, Dad.'

---

31 Anthony adds a footnote about the rear gunner, whom he calls the tail gunner, here: 'He said his main job was keeping warm and seeing the fighter first. Fighters usually approach from astern and below, unless they get an aircraft silhouetted against a cloud, when they approach from above.'

I began keeping a good lookout immediately. I saw a row of orange flares hanging pendant in the sky. They seemed to be quite a distance away but I distrusted them none the less. Having already underestimated the distance of some searchlights, there seemed no reason why I shouldn't be overestimating the distance of these flares. Back in the rear turret, Dad seemed to be having a whale of a time. He kept asking Knights to switch the aircraft in different directions so that he could get a better view of points where he thought he saw a fighter. (Incidentally, though he had nearly finished his operational tour and been on many severe raids, he had never yet been opened fire on by a fighter.)

The Ruhr, 'Happy Valley', was now pointed out to me. I looked and saw nothing but distant cones of searchlights. 'I think that's Cologne,' said the engineer, pointing at nothing in particular. It wasn't really a very satisfactory view of the Ruhr. But I felt glad to have seen it. It felt very grand to be able to look out of the window and say to oneself, 'Oh yes, of course, the Ruhr.'

'That's Mannheim. Looks as if they're going in early,' said Knights.

We could see it quite plainly ahead of us to the right, though it must have been about a hundred miles away. We could see the clusters of searchlights, the flares, the fires and the flashes. Mannheim is about fifty miles from Frankfurt, and it was about this time that we began to come in sight of our target. There were the same flashes and searchlights but much more clearly defined. It was quite unlike what I expected. Everything was so neatly beautiful.

'Hello, Bob, Junkers 88 coming up, starboard,' said Dad in a suddenly urgent voice. Knights threw the aircraft over to allow the gunners to get a better view.

'No, OK, sorry, it's a Lanc,' said Dad. I looked up and saw that it was indeed a Lanc. Coming towards us in what seemed like a sideways motion. One second a vague shape, it alarmingly materialised and defined its outline. There just seemed no possibility of avoiding collision. It was all over in a second, but it seemed quite a time. It passed just to the rear and slightly high. I looked up and saw its underbelly skim over us. 'Jesus, did you see that?' said Knights.

'I thought we'd had it that time,' said the engineer. The aircraft was still rocking from the impact with the other aircraft's slipstream. We were now coming up to Frankfurt proper. We could see what looked like hundreds of thousands of electric light bulbs carpeting the ground. It took me some little time to realise that these were incendiaries. They looked so regular and artificial, so naively pretty, that one couldn't associate them with any work of destruction. There was a large, long area of them shaped like the lobes of a gigantic liver. The sky was suddenly filled with the regular grey puffs of a flak barrage. These barrages seemed to me extraordinarily consistent in their strength. They don't just throw up a few hundred rounds and stop. They continue with what seems unlimited regularity. With the flares dropped by the Pathfinders, the flares dropped by the enemy fighters, the waving searchlights, the bead-like pattern of incendiary fires on the ground, and the flashes of gunfire, there was a sense of supreme experience and excitement.[32] Knights was working to keep us out of the clutches of some peculiarly inquisitive searchlights, and away to the right another aircraft had failed to keep out of the way. We could see it wriggling in the cone of searchlights, which were doing their best to hold it there while the guns concentrated on it. The cruel thing is that one's only sensation is one of relief that the searchlights are temporarily diverted elsewhere. One feels no urge to go to the assistance of the unfortunate aircraft that is cornered. Of course, obviously it would be senseless to do so, but it seems extraordinary that one doesn't feel any urge to do so. I noticed the same indifference to the troubles of others when flying with the Americans. There is complete unity within the individual aircraft, but for some reason that is where it ends. Nor is it simply the expression of my own individual idiosyncrasy. It was obviously a general state of mind.

All this time the pilot and the navigator were keeping up a running dialogue on how the time was going for the approach to the target. Apparently we were a minute or two early, so we had to lose that amount of time. It was pretty impressive, if the word isn't too banal, to hear the young men talking about losing a minute or two while passing through this fireworks display. I hadn't much idea of what was going on. I didn't know whether we were running up to the target or still cruising around, and I didn't want to disturb the crew in any way. It hardly seemed in my best interest to do so. I was anxious that they should give their best, and concentrate closely on the work in hand. But presently I realised that we were running up.

'Get weaving, Skipper, the night's too long,' said someone.

'I can't see that river,' said Knights.

'Bomb-doors open,' said whoever's business it was to open them.

'How're we doing?' said someone.

'Fine,' said someone else.

Apparently the first time over the target conditions weren't satisfactory. They couldn't see the Pathfinder flares which they were supposed to bomb, so we flew across the town, then circled round and approached the target area from another direction. Coming back on to the target it was like bright daylight. It is very difficult to describe. Nothing that I have ever read on the subject of bombing gave me anything like the impression which I actually had on the spot. I expected something of the atmosphere of a fire-blitz on the ground. I hadn't allowed for the sense of detachment produced by being so high. You knew that down there was a town of half a million people undergoing the most horrible ordeal. By staring round the engineer's shoulder I could see the bomb-aimer preparing to press the button which would release another 4,000 lbs contribution to this ordeal. But it seemed quite unreal. The incendiaries were dropped first and then the 4,000-lb cookie. Just beforehand there was an appreciable tenseness of the crew. The pilot, of course, had to keep the aircraft flying as level as possible for the bombing run.

---

32   The Pathfinders were the elite target-marking force of Bomber Command.

He turned and half rose from his seat as if he were willing the aircraft to a supreme effort. I tried to write down the dialogue between pilot and bomb-aimer, but it was too fast for my hobbling shorthand. I wrote it down, but now I can't transcribe it. I did not feel any appreciable lightness of the aircraft when 'Bombs away' was announced. All I knew was that the dialogue of 'Steady', 'Hold her steady', 'OK, Bob', 'OK, bomb-aimer' and the sing-song intonation of numbers just before the dropping, subsided. Knights asked the bomb-aimer if he thought they had obtained a satisfactory picture; the bomb-aimer thought he had. They were all professionally satisfied with the delivery of the bomb. There was a sense of achievement. The engineer pointed out the burning streets of Frankfurt. I could just make them out from an orange streak in the carpet of fairy-like lights produced by the incendiaries. I tried to think of the spectacle in terms of what was going on below, but it was just impossible to worry about. Mostly, I suppose, because we had plenty to worry about above.

The amount of fun and fury and fighter-flares was extraordinary. The sky was simply full of trouble. Yet oddly enough it was difficult to think of us in this particular aircraft as actively threatened by sudden death. I don't mean that, speaking for myself, I wasn't afraid. Certainly I was in a state of great alarm. But I didn't really expect that we in this aircraft would buy it.

There seemed to be plenty to buy. The tail gunner reported that he counted forty-nine fighter-flares. Just afterwards he reported a fight going on behind us to starboard. I looked back and saw the flares and stabs of flame. This and the one we saw just after crossing the coast were the only two aircraft we saw going down, though we later learned that forty-two aircraft had been lost that night.

'Is there a small defended area on the starboard?' Knights asked the navigator. Two or three of the crew got into an argument as to whether it was Aachen or Brussels. 'That's Antwerp a bit further up,' said one of them. It was ridiculous, to hear the young men talk of the cities of Western Europe in terms of where they were last Friday – no, I'm a liar, that was Thursday – knowing their way so matter-of-factly round the Continent in these bizarre circumstances.[33] They knew them not by their cultural monuments, their political significance or their hotels, but simply by their flak and searchlights barrages. They all looked alike to me, but I was told that after only two or three trips you remember the way awfully well. There was quite a lot of flak going up over Brussels. We crossed the coast in the neighborhood of Rotterdam, and just before doing so were nearly caught by searchlights. 'Hello, they're having a go,' said Knights, as the light seemed to lift the fuselage. The aircraft started weaving as, amid incongruously facetious encouragement by the crew, Knights went about the routine of evasion. When you consider how large the coast of Europe is it seems extraordinary how difficult it is to cross it without coming up against resistance of one kind or another. 'Keep a good lookout,

---

33   Anthony writes Tuesday but probably misread his notes – it was actually Thursday, 16 December.

Dad. See we're not being followed,' said Knights. 'OK,' said Dad. It seemed a long way back over the North Sea. I was getting very tired of standing. The engineer let me sit on his seat for a spell, but then he had to have it back to go on with his business. Coffee was now served from thermos flasks. I opened the paper bag of rations with which we had been issued. There was an orange, a packet of chocolate, some boiled sweets, and two packets of chewing-gum. I ate the chocolate, but with difficulty, as it was frozen hard. I then ate the orange, which was also frozen. In fact the emotional experience of eating that orange was quite lost. It was painfully cold in the mouth. We were now down to 10,000 or 11,000 feet and had taken off our oxygen masks. It wasn't long, but it seemed long, before we were skirting the English Coast. There were searchlights here too, but what a difference in their attitude! These were kindly lights pointing the way to security, not fingers of fate contriving our doom. It was now something past 10 p.m., and we were due to land at 11 p.m. That last hour seemed interminable. I found it odd that I felt no particular sense of achievement, as I had anticipated. All I felt was awfully tired.

The landing-grounds were illuminated by circles of tiny lights. And over each aerodrome there was a guiding cone of searchlights. The odd thing was that, at this height, they seemed so very close together. It was as if all the landing-grounds were in adjoining fields, instead of being many miles apart. I got to the point where I didn't think we were ever to land, but eventually we did.

We were driven back to be interrogated, and then home to the Mess for bacon and egg.[34]

I got to bed sometime after 2 a.m.

This crew had been on operations for some time, and expected to finish their term in a month or so. The operations weren't at all monotonous, said Knights, but they were all of a kind. After the first few trips you learned your way round. Some crews regarded the business as getting progressively easier with each raid, but this crew made a point of regarding each raid as the first. They thought that was the surest way of getting through.

FOOTNOTE

The American Fortress crews with which I flew on daylight operations said that they would be scared stiff to fly at night in the RAF fashion, while the RAF crew said that they would be scared stiff to operate by day.

There seems to be a moral lurking somewhere here.

34 'Interrogated', the slightly unfortunate term for the debriefings which took place of all Bomber Command crews once they returned from operations. The Knights' crew summary of the raid says, amongst other things, that their photograph of the aiming point was a failure due to 'fire-tracks and cloud'. 619 Squadron Operations Record Book, The National Archives AIR 27/2131.

RAMC

Anthony's book *RAMC*, published in late 1943 or early 1944, is about the Army medical system for treating casualties. It is a straightforward factual piece of reporting but includes several vivid anecdotes and pen portraits. Its subjects range from front-line first aid and the system of casualty clearing stations to the type of hospital and convalescent depot found back at home. Much of the information relates to the BEF campaign in France up to June 1940 and to the North African campaign up to May 1943. The book missed the invasion of mainland Europe, which began in September 1943 in Italy.

As the book jacket prominently tells us, the book was an 'authoritative account prepared with the assistance of the Army Medical Department of the War Office and the Royal Army Medical Corps'. So convincing was Anthony's writing on medical matters, utilising his knowledge of anatomy and his medical studies at Guy's, that readers who did not know who he was would assume that the book had been written by a medical officer.[1]

Whilst the book was in draft, it was read by Robert Graves, the famous author, the father of Jenny Nicholson who was Anthony's girlfriend. In June 1943, Anthony wrote to Graves thanking him for his suggestions on how to improve the book. The handwritten letter was sent from the *WAR* office at 47 Eaton Square in Belgravia, London. In it, Anthony explained the reasons behind his apparent carelessness where book writing was concerned, for which it seems he had been criticised by both Jenny and Graves:

> The trouble is that I have been educated to take great care and trouble over newspaper articles, to make each one as good as possible of its kind; and to regard books as mass production work in which broad effects compensated for relatively careless writing. This inverted snobbery was reinforced by sub-editing books for serialisation purposes.[2]

---

1   The assumption that Anthony was a medical officer has also been made by the modern historian, Mark Harrison, in his book *Medicine and Victory: British Military Medicine in the Second World War* (Oxford University Press, Oxford, 2004).

2   Anthony Cotterell to Robert Graves, letter, 7 June 1943, the Poetry Collection, University at Buffalo, the State University of New York.

RAMC is certainly very different from much of the work included in this book, although there is nothing slapdash or careless about it so perhaps Anthony had taken his lessons to heart. Its main difference lies in the fact that Anthony wrote it as a serious, authoritative piece of work which completely excludes himself from the picture, even though he is the interviewer of the numerous medical officers and patients who appear in the book.

★★★

Malingerers

Malingerers can often be caught out quite simply.

If a man claims to be deaf he should be taken quite seriously. The doctor goes through the tests and talks to him in an unnaturally loud voice as if he were deaf. Then afterwards, when he is sitting writing some notes and the man is relaxed, the doctor looks up and says, 'Turn to the left will you,' or something of the kind, and the man is usually taken in.

On the other hand there was a lance-corporal sent to a base hospital because of deafness said to have been caused by a bursting shell. When the specialist examined him there was every indication that he had been deaf long before the shell burst.

The fact was that five years before he had tried to enlist in a regiment in which the men of his family had often served and had been rejected because of the deafness which he had had since childhood. He took up lip-reading, studied it for three years, and tried again. This time he was successful. He found no difficulty in training and was promoted to lance-corporal. But when he got to France and went on night patrol, lip-reading wasn't much use.

'French Farce'

Up to the end of April 1940, one in eight of all BEF cases evacuated home from France was suffering from stomach trouble. The surgeons were not exactly being overtaxed.

At Metz there was a Casualty Clearing Station dealing with casualties from British units in front of the Maginot Line. From March to early May this sector had more fighting than anywhere else, and there was a fairly constant supply of patients. Mostly they had been wounded on patrols or by odd bombs or shells. They were regarded almost in the light of civilian casualties, or as men who had been accidentally injured on manoeuvres. It was just bad luck rather than a logical attempt by the enemy to destroy them.

The RAMC were housed in a French military hospital about twenty miles behind the line. The place was well-equipped and conditions ideal. The wounded took from four to twelve hours to reach them, and the operations were pleasantly successful.

The unit consisted of five officers, six sisters and forty-three other ranks, including Major R.S. Handley, the surgeon, on whose recollections this account is based.

The spring weather, the Moselle river and its wines, and the excellent cooking of a French widow woman made life pleasant enough. Halcyon was the word for it.

Until the Germans attacked the Metz sector on May 12th and 13th. The attack was expensive and unsuccessful. But the Casualty Clearing Station was worked to its limits for three days. In this time they took in ninety wounded and did fifty operations. Major Handley found that he averaged rather more than one operation an hour and sixteen hours on end was as much as he could manage.

Endurance was not the only difficulty. The gas was turned off during air raids, so often sterilisation was a problem. Their things could only be scrubbed between cases.

During the rush they used sulphanilamide powder for the first time. This treatment was then in its early stages and they were astonished by the excellent results. What later became a commonplace was then a revelation.

A French doctor was called in to give a blood transfusion. He arrived with the donor and a very neat little pumping machine for giving direct transfusion. The patient and the donor were duly connected and the French doctor started turning the handle of the pump. It was very simple, he kept saying. Indeed it was so simple that the patient received several times the normal volume of blood in a minute (he had 250 c.c.) Having so far been comatose, he sat up and 'called the Almighty and his mother to witness that he could not breathe'.

But in the end it was a successful transfusion. The patient was married two months later in England.

When the Maginot Line was outflanked the Casualty Clearing Station was moved to Le Mans and Major Handley was posted to Rouen. He arrived there on the evening of June 5th 1940, and was operating an hour later. He was attached to a general hospital which had just been opened and was getting some 1,200 casualties a day. There were four surgical teams working continuously in eight hour shifts, two on and two off. By the time they had eaten and left their tents to shelter from the more vicious raids, there wasn't much time to sleep in their eight hours off.

After five days the Germans arrived on the further side of the Seine, and the hospital had to pack what it could and go. Major Handley was operating on a stomach when the Seine bridges were blown up. He finished the operation wearing an unsterilised tin hat and left two hours later at dawn.

Fusilier William Close

When Wavell chased the Italians to Benghazi, Fusilier William Close went along.[3] He was then chased by the Germans back to Tobruk.

He had been in Tobruk about six months and one evening he was stripping one of the guns in a dugout up on the perimeter. The perimeter of Tobruk was twenty-two miles long – a flat, rocky plateau. In the daytime you could see the Germans shaking their blankets and it was a military crime to stand up. Food had to be brought in at night. The machine-gunners, Close amongst them, were split up in sections of five. One man on guard all day, two at night. Guns had to be cleaned every two or three hours because of the sand.

The sun was setting this night in August 1941. About 5.30 p.m. they saw a mortar flash. It was impossible to locate because the mortars were being fired on bogies and then being pulled back into the cliff. They seemed to be trying to find the British machine-gun positions and just about one second later they succeeded. It was like an express train – you could hear the wind – Close was thrown forward prone on to the gun. He half thought he was dead. He was sure that he was blinded. But, in fact, the corrugated iron roof and four layers of sandbags had saved him. He could not see a thing. There was blood running in his eyes and he could feel it dripping on his chest. The first thing he heard was the Section Leader threatening to shoot the first unmentionable to raise his head.

The enemy mortaring was still going on. About fifteen or sixteen shells swept the whole area, the nearest only 25 yards away. He sat down till he heard the Corporal shout, 'This way, Bill'. Then he crawled along the slit trench into the next gun-pit. Two other men had been in the same pit with him. One was injured in the arm, the other blasted in the face. The Platoon Sergeant had meanwhile come running up. He put splints on the boy with the broken arm, but there was nothing he could do for Close. They waited there ninety minutes for the stretcher-bearers who could not come up until it was completely dark. Close could feel the shrapnel sticking out of his face. Half his face seemed blown away. He wanted to feel it but they would not let him. They tried to cheer him up with jokes but he was not listening.

He was carried 600 yards on a stretcher by four Australians to a South African dressing station called the Fig Tree. Here an Australian padre asked him if he wanted to cable home that he was all right. It didn't seem quite the moment to cable home that he was all right, but he did. The Padre gave him ten cigarettes and sent for his mate to whom Close wanted to give all his personal property. His wounds were starting to throb now. He kept wanting to scratch his eyes, but they strapped his arms down and gave him a

---

3   Wavell – General Sir Archibald Wavell, who was relieved of his North African command by Winston Churchill in June 1941.

shot of morphia. The morphia wore off. The ambulance jolted too much but in about twenty minutes' time at the next dressing station they gave him a cup of tea with no milk or sugar and another shot of morphia. They also asked if he was all right. This, he thought, was too much. 'It's the rich food's my trouble,' he said.

At Tobruk Hospital he was operated on immediately. They took the shrapnel out of his face and cleaned his eyes. He woke up next afternoon bandaged all over. He was still blind. He didn't believe them when they said he would see again.

At midnight the same day he was taken out in a barge to a destroyer and not many hours later he was in Alexandria, where they operated on his eyes. About a month later they put him in a dark room and gradually removed the bandages. He could just make out the multi-coloured revolving wheel with which they were trying to coax his eyes back to work. They washed his eyes four times a day and every day tested them differently. The film of blindness gradually thinned until at last magically he could see again.

The Medical Board graded him 'B', so that he would be given a job at the base depot and not sent back to the desert. He went to see the Medical Officer and persuaded him to grade him 'A.1.'. He wanted to be back with his old company. Three weeks later he was taken back to Tobruk by destroyer and almost as soon as he got back Tobruk was relieved. They got back to Cairo for Christmas.

The first day of May 1942, he was dispatch-riding for the Platoon Commander, right in the rear of the platoon. The armoured division was pushing ahead trying to harass the enemy enough to relieve Rommel's pressure on Tobruk. It was very tough riding on the desert tracks. Easy to fall, and fall he did. The bike skidded on soft sand and he was pinned underneath. This time he had bought it. Both legs were fractured. The pain was much worse than his previous gunshot wound. He wanted to scream the place down.

They took him back to Sidi Barrani. The rest of the company went on. He hasn't seen them since. Many of them are dead or prisoners. He had been with 'Y' Company nine years and to him it was almost like losing all the members of your family. He is back in this country now. When interviewed he still couldn't walk without crutches but they said he would be able to. They wanted to discharge him from the Army but he didn't want to go. So after much pleading they were sending him back to Newcastle, now Category 'C'.

D-DAY

*A*nthony's typescript diary of the preparations for D-Day, named here 'Prelude to D-Day', runs from 20 May until 5 June 1944. It ends at ten o'clock in the evening with him on the boat going to France. After 6 June, D-Day itself, he wrote a detailed account based on the notes he took during the assault and at the beach-head. This account was published one month later in *WAR* under the decidedly unserious title 'A Day at the Seaside'.[1]

In the fortnight running up to D-Day, Anthony was living in a marshalling camp with a group of RAMC officers. These medical officers were his ticket to the opening stages of the invasion, the only way he could get round Montgomery's ban on non-operational personnel being amongst the first waves of assault troops. He had carefully cultivated his medical contacts for months, having got to know many of them through research for his book *RAMC*. Anthony had great charm, and he had evidently charmed the RAMC who were actively colluding with him in dodging Montgomery's ban.

Taking a belt and braces approach, Anthony had also applied to drop by parachute with 6th Airborne Division. When official permission for this was refused, he was offered by way of compensation an attachment (which he does not identify in the diary) which meant he could legitimately arrive in France – but some hours after the invasion had started. He turned this down, preferring his connivance with the medical officers. The MOs were going in very early in the assault to establish Field Dressing Stations. However, before the ship got to France, Anthony managed to change his arrival time on the beach-head from two and a half hours after the first assault to a mere forty-five minutes. As there is no further mention of his medical officers, he seems to have parted company with them before the actual trip to the shore.

It had always been his plan to attach himself to a military unit once he was in France. Looking around the marshalling camp prior to the invasion, he found exactly what he was looking for in the 8th Armoured Brigade, a prestigious tank brigade who had fought its way to victory in North Africa. Its emblem of a red fox's mask, stamped on a yellow background, had been much in evidence all along the North African coast to

---

Tunis in the pursuit of Rommel's forces. Part of the diary concerns Anthony's arrangements with the Brigade for sharing with them the fortunes of war in France.

A Brief Note on the Text

'Prelude to D-Day' is based on Anthony's typed diary with some very minor insertions or substitutions from the parallel texts: 'Sitting on the Fence', 'Is This the Way to the Second Front?' and 'On a Steamer Going Over'. These changes have not been footnoted in order to preserve readability. For D-Day itself, there is no corresponding diary material amongst his papers, but given the unusual informality and liveliness of the account in *WAR* (usually Anthony edited his *WAR* articles to make them rather more formal and impersonal), it fits in perfectly with the diary. 'A Day at the Seaside: Going on Shore' remains a totally unique slant on what happened on that momentous day, 6 June 1944.

'Prelude to D-Day'

SATURDAY, 20 MAY 1944

1.40 p.m. to Southampton (same line as to Dorchester).[2] Stood all the way. Met by two doctors, taken to sub-area (2) HQ, thence to Mess.

The Brigade Major answering the phone: 'SOPT here', 'Veterinary surgeon here', etc.[3] The phone never stopped ringing, each call a catalogue of unforeseen complications connected with the difficulties of phasing in.

At the HQ they were tearing up and packing. There was an exhilarating pre-holiday atmosphere. Really men's reactions are too much.

Administratively it was a wonderful opportunity to get all sorts of things for nothing, to tear up embarrassing correspondence, to abandon courts of inquiry, to indent for things and, miraculously, get them. All the things which had never been available were now suddenly available for the asking. And through all these transactions ran a stimulating sense of impunity, summarised in the current tag: 'They can't touch you now.' It didn't matter much what you did, they wouldn't leave you behind.

After tea we stopped at the ordnance depot to see how they were getting on with filling a lot of cans with water, this being part of the process of bituminising. If water is left in, it rusts and discolours. This has no injurious effect, in fact, medically, it is liable to be improved – but men won't drink it except in the dark. They didn't seem to be getting

---

2   Anthony knew this railway line very well from his first few months in the Army, his initial training camp having been at Dorchester.

3   SOPT – possibly one of the following: Senior Officer Physical Training or Staff Officer Physical Training or the School of Physical Training. Then again it may be Anthony misreading his notes.

on very fast. There was a hydrant nearby which would have speeded things up considerably, but it hadn't been requisitioned so they weren't allowed to use it.

Major Bowman took me out to the camp where I was to stay. We drove at a steady 40 mph until we came to a jeep parked in the road. In trying to avoid this and the oncoming traffic we then drove steadily into a telegraph pole. I had the sense to brace my right arm but not my left, so that I was flung forward on to my left arm and bent the rail to a remarkable extent. Considering the speed of impact we were very lucky. Apparently no more damage to the car than a smashed wing. Bowman and the driver felt a considerable anxiety to have it repaired before the next evening when the Commander, whose car it was, was due to return. After pulling the mudguard straight we continued. Inside the car there was no damage except the rail bent by my arm and a pencil mysteriously shattered.

The camp was five miles out of Winchester, a mixture of huts and square American tents.[4]

Pleasant atmosphere of irresponsibility due to having everything packed up.

After dinner, drinking. Slept well.

SUNDAY, 21 MAY

Up at 7.45 a.m. Mistakenly early. Slightly put off breakfast by the whisky. Not a very good breakfast anyway. Very cold morning. Went down to Medical Office where a bit of hanging about was going on. Then discovered Lawson from the Fusiliers who told me that he and some others from the battalion were working as static staff on the camp.[5] He and Kelly took me off on a jeep ride to recce wiring on a neighbouring camp. Lawson was to be in charge of a wiring party. The wire is to keep the troops from getting out of the camp.

I hope it won't keep them from getting into Europe. Of course the effect is purely psychological, nearly all the men in these camps having been trained for years to cope with barbed wire.

We were taken round by a very subalternish subaltern, who pooh-poohed the official estimate that eighty rolls were needed for this camp. The actual requirements were much nearer 800. So just for one thing there wasn't the slightest hope of getting it done in time.

---

4   'Is This the Way to the Second Front?' adds the following information: 'The marshalling camp was
    hidden away in the grounds of a big English country house. Here, camouflaged under the trees, were
    several thousand troops […] For good dramatic measure there was also an aircraft factory hidden in the
    grounds, and the big house was used as offices by an armaments firm.
        An exciting situation.
        But however anxious you may be to liberate Europe or to get in there and fight, you can't remain
    tense with purpose indefinitely. After waiting for a week or two something sags. The tense becomes past.'

5   Anthony's base unit was the Royal Fusiliers. He was on attachment to the War Office, and thence to
    ABCA. Had he got into serious trouble at any stage, he would have been sent back to the Royal Fusil-
    iers in disgrace. He knew Lawson from the posting at Malvern, see Part One, 'Defending the Realm'.
    'Static staff' – i.e. they were semi-permanent whilst the other units were passing through.

I had lunch with Lawson and Kelly in their Mess. The food and conditions were a great improvement. When I returned I asked if anything had happened. Needless to say nothing had.

After lunch I met the blood transfusion captain with whom I am travelling under the guise of a field surgical unit, and we hitch-hiked into Winchester.[6] People in general seemed to be showing remarkably little initiative in getting out of the place.

Winchester was not very promising until we found the Royal Hotel where, after initial hesitation and some calculations of capacity by the chef, it was decided that we could have dinner, also a bath. The key positions were all held by grey-haired ladies. The housekeeper was told to conduct us to bathrooms. She gave us a towel and tried to select the right key for the soap cupboard. 'Lock and key, of course,' she whispered, 'Everything's under lock and key.'

She runs the place like fifty years ago. She thinks it is fifty years ago. Locking up the soap, I ask you, who wants soap?

My companion was telling me how REME use contraceptives to waterproof accumulators.[7]

Pleasant bath.

Madman head waiter who took unlimited time to decide which table we were to have. Afterwards we got up to go and asked for our bill at the door. 'Please go back to the table, sir, and he'll bring your bill. He gets so worried, so many people.' The old fool put his hand to his head and joined in asking us to go back so that he could work out where we were.

Dorothy Parker did a story about a woman who was meeting a negro singer and made a tremendous business of declaring how anti-colour bar she was when she wasn't. Same story could be done about English soldiers' opinion of Americans.

We walked home. Hitch-hiking wasn't very successful, and my companion wanted to get into training. He rather sneered at my theory that half-prepared was no better than unprepared (for it seems to me that endurance under stress bears no relation to endurance under training). Unfortunately we went the long way round so that we had to walk about seven miles.[8]

While warm in bed I wasn't quite so comfortable. I wonder what causes those aches in the hip region.

---

6   'Under the guise of a field surgical unit' – this refers to Anthony's subterfuge in getting to France at
      an early stage of D-Day in contravention of Montgomery's orders. The blood transfusion captain was
      almost certainly Captain Parfitt.

7   REME – the Royal Electrical and Mechanical Engineers.

8   Anthony remained completely averse to physical exercise except when absolutely necessary. As he
      wrote in 1943, 'Looked at one way, my whole military life has been motivated by this strange, strong,
      inner urge to sit down.' An Apple for the Sergeant, p.137.

MONDAY, 22 MAY

Up just in time to be in to breakfast by 0830 hours. Bacon and fried bread and marmalade.

Afterwards PT. A little too soon afterwards, perhaps, because it made me feel appalling. However, there was no reason not to have a nice lie-down, and I did so.

Overheard in the latrine.

'Haven't even got anything to bloody read.'

'Read? What for?'

'I like a nice bloody read.'

Up to now I have thought very little about the prospects of the next few weeks. I have heard no one discuss it seriously. One man asked whether there was any scientific possibility of the Germans having electrified all the water.

I have been given some rather snazzy formation signs, a red anchor on a pale blue background.[9]

Statements by a batman: 'If it has to come, the sooner it comes the sooner we get finished with the job. Fellow on the train said "I'll give you the tip, don't try any travelling after Monday. They're taking all the trains off." I reckon it's bound to start any day. Look at all these lorries gone away loaded up with six or seven ton. You can't keep them long like that. Harm the wheels.'

There was a route march available but I didn't feel up to it.

Sooner or sooner still, any diary I keep comes to an illness. I think we are coming to one now. I seem to have caught the same curse (caused, he says, by primitive sanitation and infected water) as one of the doctors in the tent. Identical symptoms – like incipient seasickness – so I took advantage of my present irresponsibility to lie down from 4 p.m. to 7 p.m. when I had been invited to dinner with the Fusiliers. Before that I lay in the sun correcting proofs.[10]

Kelly: 'Just been having a most interesting conversation with an American in the next room. Never saw such a chap for reading the most extraordinary books. Psychology, science, history, every damn thing. He says it's to get a general picture. "But don't you get worried when you can't remember it all?" I said. "I get awfully worried when I've been reading a book halfway and realise I don't know what it's about." He said he only gets a very general picture. "I'm going to wash now." He pointed to two books by his bed. "There's Tolstoy's *War and Peace*, Pepys' Diary and (lying on a chest) *Macaulay's Essays*. See if you can get through them before I get back."'

---

9   These were D-Day beach group formation signs.

10 Anthony would have been correcting proofs either for *WAR* or for his forthcoming book *An Apple for the Sergeant*.

Chicken for dinner. Well, well.

Someone looked in the post-box and said: 'Well, damn that, there's two letters I posted last night. No one's touched them.'

Lawson: 'That's what I like about this place, everyone's completely honest.'

After dinner they were censoring letters, complaining of the length, particularly as the writers frequently apologised for brevity, or announced their intention to continue writing long daily letters. 'Christ! he only saw the girl on Friday,' said Lawson, holding up a particularly voluminous one.

'Marvellous how they find time to do it. How long do you think it would take to write eight pages like that?' asked the Colonel with the naive curiosity of colonels.

Recurring remark in letters: 'I'm sorry I upset your mother.'

The sad thing about having a day off is the acceleration of flying time towards the end. One minute there is a pleasant vista of empty hours in which to read or idle, and then all of a sudden it is nearly time to go to bed.

An air raid during the night.

TUESDAY, 23 MAY

The batman: 'See this concert last night? Very good. Monte Rey was there. Least some say it was Don Carlos. I say it was Monte Rey. I saw a picture of him and I say it was Monte Rey.'

Went to see the Armoured Brigade where the Staff Captain almost immediately invited me to join them in France.[11] I accepted. Interviewed a number of their RAMC orderlies and went to a lecture by Clay to the beach group medicals.[12] He first complained that there would be a shortage of sweets on the other side. This, he said, could be offset by buying £10 worth here, which would mean about one pound of sweets a head. Did they want them bought out of unit funds or would they like to leave the unit funds at their present level (about £30) and buy as individuals. Needless to say the vote to deplete unit funds was almost unanimous.

The ensuing lecture was about behaviour on landing. The news emerged that we were landing in a built-up area. Somehow it is difficult to imagine anything but fishing villages or lonely cliffs.

The lecture was rather above my head, being bound up in domestic organisation: where Sergeant so-and-so was to go with his four men; the possibility of finding a bombed building to provide a suitable billet for the cooks; the varying times and tides at which transport would arrive; the way whole blood was to be brought across from England every day in a service of motor launches.

---

11   8th Armoured Brigade, with whom Anthony would travel in Normandy.

12   This was the medical beach group with whom Anthony had arranged to cross to France.

I had lunch in the Armoured Brigade Mess with the Staff Captain, who continued to suggest that I should join them.

I wonder if the doctors are poisoning the water as part of the scheme.

I must practise surrendering to myself in the mirror to see if I've got it right.

I spent the afternoon interviewing seven men from one of the armoured regiments. Then I saw the Staff Captain, who took me to see the Brigade Major – very young, bemedalled and welcoming. Said that he would fix me in.

I caught the train from Winchester to London. Slight sense of guilt about going off when others can't. The excursion is legitimate, but nothing in the Army seems legitimate when it is pleasant.

Got to London 10.30. After being informed that the Savoy Grill kitchens had closed also at 10.30 p.m., I walked down to the Corner House where, in the queue, I got talking to a RAC trooper who complained about the war putting back his career.[13] 'I'm a bank clerk,' he said. 'Some people think of that as a dead end sort of job, but I think that's wrong. It's all in how you look at it. If you go into it saying "I'm going to be a bank clerk," a bank clerk you'll stay. Just that and no more.'

I quite agreed with him.

'But if you go in saying "I'm going to be a bank manager," that's pretty different.'

He paused to allow this audacious observation to sink in on me. As I didn't protest at the heights of his ambition he continued:

'I know several gentlemen who are bank managers, and have a very nice time. Belong to yacht clubs and that sort of thing. Of course, being a bank manager puts you in the way of all sorts of plums, secretaryships, you know. You have to be careful though. The banks have strict rules.'

WEDNESDAY. 24 MAY

'I thought you'd gone,' people said. 'What, back already?' etc. The usual dissatisfaction of returning immediately after brave farewells.[14]

London very sunny. The prospect of going away keens up the senses.

Letter on my desk reporting final failure of airborne application. Few hours later arrangement was reported by which I arrive overland a few hours afterwards. Not nearly so satisfactory as where I am now.[15]

---

13   The Savoy was one of Anthony's favourite haunts in London; it was the place where all the journalists gathered. RAC – Royal Armoured Corps.

14   Anthony had gone to the *WAR* office, where he worked with Ernest Watkins, probably to deliver copy for *WAR*.

15   'Where I am now', meaning with his medical officers who were going to land in France early on D-Day.

Caught the 7.50 p.m. at Waterloo and walked back into camp with a padre. One never gets over the pathetic, new-boy feeling of returning after leave, even a few hours. The people who stayed behind seem at such an advantage. Captain Parfitt was in the tent. He immediately showed me the official way of turning a gas cape into a sleeping-bag.

The two Majors, Clay and Dill-Russell, arrived late in the tent, and rather unusually cheerful.

THURSDAY, 25 MAY

One thing I like about this camp is you get a lot of sleep. The batmen come in about 7 a.m. with tea and hot water, but there is no earthly need to get up until 8.15 a.m. Breakfast is served up to 8.30 a.m. and thereafter for periods varying with the rank and personality of the latecomer. I got up a little early this morning, around 8.10 a.m.

'Well,' I said, 'Another day.'

'Wasted,' said Parfitt, 'Add that one word and you've got a more accurate picture.'

After breakfast there was PT. But not for me. I went for a walk in the woods where I am sitting writing. A negro has just gone by reading a book while driving a jeep. I wonder how long that will last.

'Why, there you are. You're back,' said Clay to me.

'Bloody fool he must be,' said Dill-Russell.

'I'm worried about those lorries,' said Clay.

'What lorries?'

'I'd rather have them at D+6 and complete them half-loaded.'[16]

'There's nothing you can do, old boy. Nothing you could have done. You've done your best.'

'I could have found out for myself instead of taking someone's word.'

'All you have to do is tell 'em they can't touch them.'

'Oh, yes they can.'

I walked back just in time for the 10.30 a.m. elevenses in the Fusiliers' Mess. Sultana cake and a large mug of coffee. I read the *Royal Fusiliers Chronicle* which seemed creditably spritely. Well, the morning was getting on now, and I retired to our tent where I worked until lunch at half past twelve.

Steak pie and a salad for lunch. Some found this an intolerably unorthodox combination. Cold steak pie and salad, yes; hot, no. It was pointed out that by waiting a little they could have cold steak pie and salad, but that wasn't good enough.

Afterwards I accompanied Clay and the staff of the Field Dressing Station on a route march which lasted until tea-time and left me with one sore foot. This I attributed to the unequal frictions due to walking in the gutter, and had a hot shower.

16   D+6 – D-Day + 6 days. Probably actually D–6.

I went to the movie show. There are two houses.[17] The queue was about 60 yards long. I went to see 'For Whom the Bell Tolls' but it turned out to be another film called *Flesh and Fantasy*.[18]

The cinema was a marquee and the programme was compeered by the projectionist.

'I'm sorry to say there will be no smoking,' he said. 'This first short film hasn't got a title. It's called "Freddie's Band" – "Fred Headley's Band".'

The film started immediately, without any credits, titles or other foolery. It was one of those dreadful pictures of a blaring dance band, photographed from eccentric angles, and thoroughly foolish. Quite a bit of the convincing power of a film is lost when it isn't shown in orthodox cinema surroundings. You don't accept the story to the same degree; it seems amateurish and it feels natural to barrack. You become aware of the way the actors execute a tantalising, unnatural pause before their first kiss, particularly when half the audience is shouting, 'Go on, get stuck in,' and further obscenities. There was an ironical jeer from the Africa Star holders when Barbara Stanwyck said she had stayed at Shepheards, Cairo, and recalled the orange blossoms in Palestine.[19]

Parfitt was already in bed.

'Another ration of oblivion,' he said. 'You know when I was first put on this thing my first feeling was annoyance at having my life revised.[20] Then I got the willies. And now I am thinking I don't have any feelings at all.'

---

17 In 'Sitting on the Fence', Anthony refers to being Turkish-bathed in the camp cinemas which were in tents which got very hot in the sunshine and were always overcrowded. As he later discovered, there were actually three of them – the Windmill, the State and the Minsky, so dubbed by the Americans who had previously occupied the camp.

18 *Flesh and Fantasy* (1943) – a film with three separate stories, all with a supernatural element.

19 The Africa Star – the campaign medal for those who had been in the North African campaign. Shepheards was a very swanky and famous hotel in Cairo.

20 'When I was first put on this thing' – Parfitt is referring to his uniform.

FRIDAY, 26 MAY

Briefing.[21]
After which Dill-Russell was suddenly very cheerful.

It was a good drying day for washing. Gave in money for changing into francs.

Work until 2.30 p.m. Inadequate dinner supplemented with soggy NAAFI cake.

In the Mess, briefing and confinement produced a more than usually crowded and excited atmosphere.[22] Names were listed for the D-Day+365 Reunion Dinner, provisionally at the Adlon in Berlin, alternatively at the Railway Hotel, Dunkirk. There was a delightful atmosphere of burnt boats and happy-go-luckiness, though there was nothing to drink but stout. Pontoon played. Boots on the stone floor. Gramophone records give way to *Songs from the Shows*, then *While You Work*.[23] Puddle on the floor where someone upset the beer. Cigarette ends all over the floor don't seem unpleasant because so much in keeping with the benches, the rusty stove, the biscuit tins on the elementary bar, the gym-shoed mess waiters, the not very good light.

SATURDAY, 27 MAY

Mice in the tent all night.

Really delightful to wake up having had enough sleep at 7 a.m. and not have to get up. Holiday atmosphere.

10.30 a.m. tea in the NAAFI.

Some of the young officers are sex-consciousationists. Amplify.

---

21   The doctors with whom Anthony was travelling had their own operation order, 'nine pages long with five appendices, crammed with extraordinary information'. Anthony gives details of these orders in 'Sitting on the Fence':

'A reserve of pyjamas was being landed. Each heavy anti-aircraft gun of one particular regiment would land with ten stretchers strapped to it. [...] A hospital carrier would arrive on D+1, and thereafter daily.

From D-Day there would be a daily delivery of whole blood – approximately 100 pints – brought across the Channel by Naval Despatch Launch.

Each Field Dressing Station would land with enough hospital supplies for 200 patients for fourteen days; also 2,000 tins of self-heating cocoa, 2,000 cigarettes, 2,000 tins of self-heating malted milk, and twelve packs of playing cards.

Beach dressing stations, each of two doctors and twenty-five other ranks, would land ninety minutes after H-Hour and set up on the beach fringe. The main medical area would be a few thousand yards inland. (These arrangements were in addition to the assault units' own medical resources.) The medical job of the beach group was to establish a full-dress evacuation system as quickly as possible, and also to do emergency surgery and transfusion.'

22   'Confinement' – no one was allowed out of camp once briefing had started except for very privileged people with special passes. Some of the ordinary soldiers were very disgruntled: in 'Sitting on the Fence' Anthony notes: '"No leave, no Second Front," wrote the wash-house wall commentators.' It was different for officers, as can be seen from Anthony's description.

23   *Songs from the Shows, While You Work* – popular BBC radio programmes.

1 Platoon photograph at the end of the initial training course. Anthony is fifth from the right, back row, half hidden behind his fellow soldiers. (*An Apple for the Sergeant*)

2 Anthony as a new conscript, 1940. (Geoffrey Cotterell)

3 Anthony (right) at the time of his training as a signaller, with fellow conscripts Baker and Daly. (Geoffrey Cotterell)

4 The Cotterell family at Ham Frith, used as a publicity shot for an article that Anthony was writing. His brother Geoffrey is on the left, with a Royal Artillery badge on his shoulder. (Geoffrey Cotterell)

5 Anthony in the *WAR* office with Captain Lionel Birch, probably 1942. (Geoffrey Cotterell)

6 Cover of *WAR* for the Normandy campaign issue, 19 August 1944. (Author)

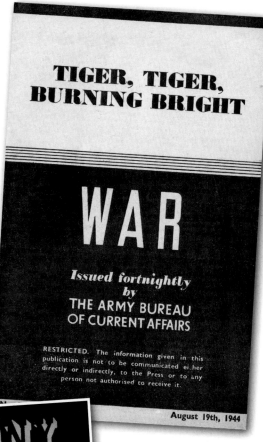

7 Cover of *An Apple for the Sergeant*. (Author)

8 Anthony training as a Motor Contact Officer. (*An Apple for the Sergeant*)

9 Anthony training as a parachutist. (*An Apple for the Sergeant*)

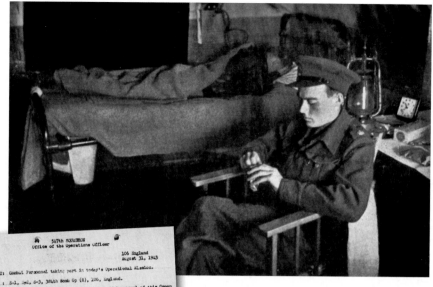

10 Anthony at Grafton Underwood in the summer of 1943, when he was attached to 348th Bomb Group, USAAF. (*An Apple for the Sergeant*)

11 Loading sheets for 348th Bomb Group.

12 Anthony with the Knights Crew and their ground crew at RAF Woodhall Spa, prior to take-off on 20 December 1943. (*An Apple for the Sergeant*)

13 Anthony with the Knights Crew. (Geoffrey Cotterell)

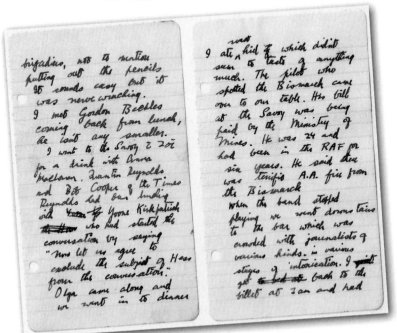

14 Sheets from Anthony's handwritten diary
(29 May 1941 entry, which mentions the sinking of
the *Bismarck*). He used this diary as the basis for his
books and articles. (Author)

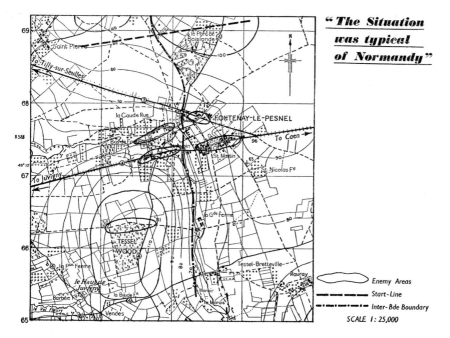

15 Map of the Fontenay-le-Pesnel battle, printed in *WAR*, 19 August 1944. (Author)

16 British Sherman tanks being unloaded in Normandy in 1944.

17 1ST Parachute Brigade HQ in May 1944.
From left to right, back row: Captain W.A. Taylor,
Lieutenant S.G. Cairns, Lieutenant Pat Barnett, Captain
R.E. Morton, Captain C.R. Miller, 2nd Lieutenant
J. Szegda; front row: Captain Bill Marquand, Major
John Fitch, Brigadier Gerald Lathbury, Major Cecil
Byng-Maddick and Captain Bernard Briggs.

18 Manuscript of 'Jumping to a Conclusion', written at
1 Parachute Brigade HQ prior to the Arnhem operation in
September 1944. (Author)

19 The man on the right
is thought to be Anthony,
talking with the journalists
and members of the Army
Film & Photographic Unit
who were on the verge of
leaving for Arnhem to cover
the MARKET GARDEN
operation, September 1944.
The man on the left is the
famous Canadian journalist
Stanley Maxted. (With thanks
to Andrew Reeds)

11 a.m. tea in static Mess. Read the papers. Peculiarly difficult to take any interest in the Italian front.[24]

Went to get a mess tin.

Sat in the sun listening to the amplified radio.

The music echoing in the trees, the men marching about, washing their clothes, and cutting each other's hair in the sun. The patches of bright sunlight in the ground shadow made by the trees. The coolness of the tent. All very stimulating.

The idea that a high proportion of the men will be killed or maimed doesn't really seem likely. Any more than a non-sufferer can really sympathise with a hay-fever case.[25] You accept it as an intellectual proposition that the victim is seriously in trouble. But you can't really feel for him.

Lunch with the Staff Captain of the Armoured Brigade. Decided that I should join them on the evening of D-Day. Worked after lunch and then set out to the tank park to find the Brigade Major with whom I had tea. Decided that I should travel in one of the reserve tanks, the tank crew being normally five, but the reserve ones carrying only four, leaving a spare seat.[26]

Washed my feet with hot water secured from the cookhouse and read *The Soldier's Guide to France*, which had just been issued.[27]

Received my 1100 francs in exchange for £5.10.0., and drew my chocolate and cigarette ration. Stood in a queue for twenty minutes but no overheard mention of Second Front.

Superior dinner in static Mess.

Went to *Hellzapoppin*.[28] Tent too hot so came out.

---

24 The mainland of Italy had been invaded by the Allies in September 1943, but this campaign was now increasingly looking like a side-show.

25 A reference to Anthony's brother Geoffrey, who suffered from debilitating hay-fever.

26 The particular tank unit which Anthony was joining was the Sherwood Rangers Yeomanry.

27 *The Soldiers Guide to France* was a pocket-sized handbook, containing advice and instructions, together with some French phrases. It was issued to all troops. Anthony quotes some of its advice in 'Sitting on the Fence', and adds the following: 'There was a considerable drive to learn the words and phrases which formed the second half of the book. Those who had been misled into a holiday mood by the French pay parade were brought sharply back to earth by such ominous phrases as "Poovon noo dormer dong votrer grong?" (Can we sleep in your barn?)'

28 *Hellzapoppin* – jazz movie, 1941.

SUNDAY, 28 MAY

Arrmoured briefing.

Brigadier effectively quiet.[29]

My plan is simple. To put Dublin Toffee issue in bags vomit.[30]

Hot shower in the hot afternoon. Worked until supper time. Bags vomit good for shoes and paper waterproofing.

Major Clay: 'Now, Major, some local colour. The famous Clay socks. The armband I wore at Dunkirk, the boots I wore at Madagascar.'[31]

The point now arises whether I need my hair cream.

Major Clay's duel with a rat and his sweets.[32]

'Chap in the washhouse thought me mad, I washed my hands with three pieces of soap running. Rats been at them.'

He said anent nationalisation: 'Do a ward round of twenty patients quite satisfactorily from a clinical standpoint in an hour. Six private patients may take a morning and wear you out.'

Amazing how little you want, isn't it, when you come to start packing.

Conversation between a corporal and a sergeant: Corporal had never been farther away from Liverpool than Gloucester, except once to London to see the Station Art Exhibition. 'One chap from our office went down somewhere near Monte Carlo. One chap went to America. Great fuss. We made an agreement not to ask him any questions when he got back.'

---

29   This brigadier was the Brigadier of 8th Armoured Brigade, Bernard Cracroft. In 'Sitting on the Fence' Anthony gives more details of this briefing: 'I spent the following morning at the briefing of the senior officers of an armoured brigade by its brigadier. Operationally, it was unpunishably far ahead. Mostly it was a maze of timetables and arrangements for mutual support.

      The brigadier was a tall, youngish man with red hair and a subdued voice which was extremely effective in urging the audience to hit the enemy hard with every weapon at every opportunity. There was no prefabricated belligerence in his voice, no overt appeal to animal emotions. He made cool, calm blood-thirstiness sound like a sensitive idea.'

30   Bags vomit – in 'Sitting on the Fence' Anthony elaborates: 'During the day the troops changed old socks, shirts and drawers woollen for new ones, and were issued with their "bags vomit". Each man had two of these brown, waxed-paper, shopping bags, with instructions not to throw one away until it had been fully used. But right now one of the two bags contained 12 ounces of mixed sweets bought with unit funds to maintain the men's energy in the early food-scarcity days.'

31   Clay is mockingly giving Anthony some copy for his article, by pointing out his own articles of dress.

32   Rats were everywhere in the camp. In 'Sitting on the Fence' Anthony notes that the camp staff were trying to secure 400 extra rat-traps, one trap having caught six in a single afternoon.

MONDAY, 29 MAY

Fitted my equipment.

Drew a mess tin and a pair of PT shoes.

Was shown over the Sherman tank in which I shall presumably be riding.

Attended the Fusiliers' cake and coffee party held in the open air.

Back in the tent. Parfitt said, 'Now I must cut my mirror in two.'

'Cut your mirror in two?'

'Too big. You can cut it with a flint. Make one out of a stone.'

He went outside and threw a stone on the ground until he had cracked it. Then he pulled to pieces his rather elaborately made mirror, sawed the glass in two and stuck them together back to back.

'Every man a substantial pension,' said Major Clay.

'It was Christmas Day in the workhouse, the happiest day in the year,' said Major Dill-Russell.

'It's tragic that a man like you, of culture and some education, should be reduced to this. They give pensions for shattered limbs, but nothing for your ruined mind,' said Major Clay.

'Every man an egg for breakfast,' said Major Dill-Russell.

Simple humour. I wondered whether the rats had reconnaissance rats out to report that we all had a bag of sweets.

'They're briefing now,' said Major Clay.

'The rat commander,' said Major Dill-Russell.

With the other bit of his mirror Captain Parfitt made one for me.

Parfitt sweating in the tent:

Colossal problems that beset the mind. Where shall I put my towel. What shall I pack in my mess tin? How many socks shall I put in the dry wrapper? How shall I carry my jerkin? These are matters of great moment.

I've thought of a scheme. Why fool around with front studs. Just sew on a button the length of one and there you are.

'Parfitt,' I said, 'if you have a button just coming off, is it better to pull it right off and start again, or reinforce the surviving strands?'

'When you're just about to invade enemy country pull it off. Unless you can guarantee that all the threads bear an equal strain,' said the sage.

Later. Rum ration issued.

Clay: 'Have you got your seasickness tablets?'

Dill-Russell: 'Don't want any of those.'

Clay: 'You'll upset the whole arrangements.'

Before the rum ration I had been to a briefing of the Armoured Brigade Signals Squadron. They saw the model of their bit of Europe for the first time. Questions constantly asked for but not many asked. Three men asked them all. Is it a feint we're in or the real thing? Plus questions about the use of bogus names in which they were being briefed, they having a specialised interest in people losing their way and asking them for it.

Water shortage in the camp, the wells having become contaminated.

Dinner in the static camp.

Saw a Deanna Durbin film; pretty awful.

The Mess empty-ish. They were packing up.

I glanced at *The Field* which had an article 'Public School Cricketers of 1941'.

At 3 p.m. I was taken to meet the tank crew whom I am supposed to meet. They land on a neighbouring beach.[33] I find myself wondering whether it is really probable that I shall be able to meet them. However, we arranged to look out for each other. I might wear a red carnation.

TUESDAY, 30 MAY

The day clouded by prospect of packing and arranging.

Had to meet the Brigadier in charge of the Armoured Brigade at 9 a.m.[34] Walked down from his tent to his office. He wasn't exactly a tower of technical strength on the subject of feature writing, but he was very cordially keen on the idea of his men who had had to keep very quiet about their secret equipment.[35] He gave me a chit saying that I was free to ride on any vehicle.

I went down to see the tank to see if they could take my bed roll. The tank had gone so I shall have to carry it. On the other hand, I shall have it with me.

Packed up.

Spent the rest of the morning trying to phone London.

Some people were up at 5 a.m. to move two miles down the road to another camp.

The craft load in which I am didn't move until after lunch. We were stopped five times for checking in about two miles.

Arrived in a dust-bowl lined with trees and found no tent, so waited around military fashion, drew blankets, new camp beds (or newly packed beds) and waited until a mixed force of one negro and three Scotsmen put up a tent for us.

Tea was dreadful.

---

33   The D-Day plan for the 8th Armoured Brigade was that they were to support the 50th (Northumberland) Division in the assault on Arromanches, part of the Gold Beach landing. The landing beaches, from west to east, were: Utah, Omaha, Gold, Juno, Sword. 50th (Northumberland) Division was landing on two sectors of Gold Beach, 'Jig' and 'King'. It seems that Anthony was to land at 'King' and his tank crew were possibly detailed to come ashore on 'Jig'.

34   Brigadier Bernard Cracroft.

35   Sherman tanks used Duplex Drive, DD, which Anthony, and no doubt countless others, called Donald Duck. This allowed the tanks to swim through the sea. The secret of this was so well kept that the Germans had no inkling of the tanks' versatility.

Conference in Mess tent; on the table floating butter, sweating cheese.

Conference Craft Serial Orders.

Colonel: 'Nucleus Band. What the devil's that?'

'It's correct, sir.'

'What the devil is it?'

'We don't know what it is, but it's correct, sir.'

'Just one of those things?'

Turned out to be naval.

'Major Scott-Joynt will sort us out on B.3 deck.' 'When we march out of here we march out in reverse order to what I read out here.'

Very hot in the tent.

Move out on Thursday C-Day.

Pass the starting point at 10.40 1st June. We'd have another conference at 5.20 to tie up movement for next day. Have to march about two miles but have to see about that. I've got 800 maps to myself.

Water sterilising tablets mixed with seasickness, with result that on the scheme one unit went to sleep.

The cooks after the awful supper (same mince and potatoes as at tea). 'It's no good, tell them, there's no more. Make no bones.'

In the movie a vibrant American voice: 'Move over. Four men on every bench. Give the other fellow a break.'

WEDNESDAY, 31 MAY

Up sharp at 8.30 with the pleasant feeling of having slept enough. Decided to stay in bed. Montgomery kindly had a tin of tea sent in. Reinforced by this I got up and found a surprisingly good breakfast, good bacon, marmalade, butter, etc.

Sat talking with O'Keefe, Parfitt's partner, and walked back to the tent. Someone was playing the flute. Parfitt was applying the principle of leverage to bringing more light into the tent while recommending us to paint a coloured, identifying blob on our baggage and pointing out that the reason for American-style shirts being open all down the front was to avoid the stress round the shoulders when putting it on.

Parfitt was at Guy's, I find.[36]

'I find I got just absorbed in dentistry. One long experiment. Same with medicine. I'd like to wash my battle-dress but it wouldn't dry in time. Takes two days. Ah, now, my special shaving equipment.'

---

36 Anthony was also at Guy's Hospital, training in medicine and dentistry briefly before becoming a journalist. Parfitt had apparently taken the same course.

He puts a stick of shaving soap in a bottle, fills the bottle with water, then puts the bottle in hot water and you have a solution of soap.

'If there's anyone lazier than me I've got to meet him,' said Parfitt 'and if I do meet him he'll no longer be the laziest chap because I shall take a lesson from him.'

He attached his sawn-off mirror to a mess tin by a piece of wire, and poured in hot water secured from the cookhouse.

O'Keefe wanted to frame a picture. Parfitt recommended the use of anti-gas eye-shields cut up and pasted together with adhesive tape.

O'Keefe told about a Guy's student who raffled his watch, taking £3 in shilling tickets, then approached the winner and bought back his watch for £1.

'I'll go mad, I can't stand it,' shouted a voice from the next tent.

Parfitt wondered if there would be time to wash and dry his underclothes by lunch-time.

'It won't dry,' said O'Keefe. 'Dampness in the air.'

'Light a fire,' said Parfitt.

I said his clean clothes would then have a rich layer of charcoal.

'Oh no they wouldn't,' said Parfitt. 'I learned the way to light a fire at school. You take little twigs, match-size, and a piece of paper about the size of an envelope. Start very small and build it gradually. That way no smoke.'

When Parfitt had boiled some water, I shaved and washed.

One of my boots has rubbed my foot into a blister. I took it to be cobbled. Outside the cobbler's tent I came across a man leading a fox on a chain. The fox was huntedly agitated but another younger fox chained up a little way along was quite tame, though very restless.[37]

'I hear that safe-breakers cut their nails right down to the quick, because that part of the finger is more sensitive,' said Parfitt.

The public address system announced *Prelude to War*, a special showing at 1430 hours.

'I'm not going to see that. Enough war and khaki in this camp.'

Notice: 'Any discussion of military affairs in this camp is a court-martial.'

After lunch we discussed whether O'Keefe should call his daughter Pamela or Lois. It started raining and Parfitt only just rescued his washing.

It was torpid all afternoon.

From time to time the flute moaned.

'I once bought a flute and tried to play it,' said Parfitt. 'But I shan't do it again.'

I had a very thorough wash, tea, conference, then went to MI room to have a blister dressed.

Long queues for cinemas.

---

37   The foxes were regimental mascots for the 8th Armoured Division, whose symbol was a red fox mask on a yellow background.

On way back saw a bedraggled-looking deserter being brought into the barbed wire guardroom enclosure. Waiting outside the Camp Commandant's office were two men standing between escorts, waiting for judgment. What a tangle their emotions might be in. Being had up on an over-hot afternoon while waiting to go on the Second Front and over the public address system a velvety, appealing lady sang 'I couldn't sleep a wink last night'.

Parfitt went out and conducted an experiment with heath fires. He dropped a cigarette end, covered it with bracken and blew gently until he had quite a fire going. Then he let it die down and by blowing gently started it again. The inactivity was setting his old brain going, he said. It reminded him of a fortnight he spent with nothing to do in Port Sudan. He spent his time drawing everything he could see, including his view of his spectacles.

THURSDAY, 1 JUNE

Gave in blankets, packed kits, formed up, embussed. Then waited. And waited. Finally started at 10.25.

Examined a sailor's odd uniform. One man said he had had seven new kits in two years. Medical officer ticked off a man for having his first field dressing in the wrong place.[38] Discussed possibility of mail being in the ship.[39]

Passed several troops of commandoes. Someone suggested the collective term 'a risk of commandoes'.

Man having his hair cut by the road behind a wire enclosure. 'Have it all off, mate.'[40]

Whistled at girls: one lady so staid she looked back as if she had forgotten how to respond.

Sang a song: *Have you ever had your bollocks in a rat trap?*

Very circuitous route into Southampton, no doubt to deceive the enemy. Possibly embark backwards and they will think we're coming off.

Route lined with security patrols and notices. 'It is forbidden to loiter or talk with troops.'

It is dangerous to feed the troops with buns.[41]

---

38 Everyone carried a field dressing for use in emergencies.

39 This turned out to be a false hope, as Anthony notes in 'Sitting on the Fence'.

40 In 'Sitting on the Fence' Anthony observed 'One man had his head shaved bald in anticipation of unhygienic conditions in the field. "What's it matter now, we aren't on show," he defended himself, and presently others followed suit.'

41 A parody of warning notices in zoos.
    Anthony added in 'On a Steamer Going Over', 'No one took much notice of us. No flowers, no cheers, not even a hand waved by anyone over the age of seven. However, we did not resent the lack of emotion which would have found strangely little echo in ourselves. We did not wave or sing ourselves, perhaps because we were too heavily loaded.'

After debussing, an agonisingly long walk with my valise on my unfortunate shoulder.[42] Ending in a quayside shed where we marched in in a straggling crocodile, marched all round the shed and came back to a spot just a few feet from where we had entered.

Tea was now served, which I thought was a civilised arrangement.

In due course, at 12.25, we embarked on the LSI which was alongside.[43] Having embarked we searched in vain for somewhere to go, and ended up watching the long queue of loaded-down troops coming up the gang plank and disappearing into the ship's insides.[44]

Eventually lunch. That was certainly different. Served with white table cloths and a leather chair to sit on. Excellent food.

Afterwards more hanging about. In a stationary ship one develops a senseless ambition for the thing to move.

Loudspeaker voice in fairly constant action, e.g.:

'The arrangements for mail are as before. The mail bag will be found inside the flotilla office. Mail will be handed in unsealed, uncensored, unstamped. That's all.'

It also announced that my cabin was M7 which turned out to have six austere bunks, with blue blankets on metal frames. None of the other bunks were tenanted.

Meanwhile the junior captains were in agonies as to whether or not they would get cabins or have to join subalterns and the other ranks in the crowded decks.

At 3.50 p.m. the voice said: 'Attention. Anyone not leaving with the ship should get ashore at once.'

I went up on deck.

A little Green Howards captain: 'We're in a hell of a jam. Our company barber's mucked off.' He said they had had four absentees in his company.

It was a grey afternoon. I couldn't get over the idea it was Saturday.[45] After the usual time-taking complications the ship was tugged away from the dock.

'I always find it exciting when the journey starts even though it isn't for a holiday,' said a major to me.

---

42 Anthony noted the amount that they were carrying in addition to their ordinary kit in 'Sitting on the Fence': 'We had been issued with rations for the first two days overseas. Each man had two 24-hour rations, a Tommy Cooker with two re-fills, a tin of corned beef, a packet of biscuits and of chewing gum; two packets of chocolate and a waterproofed tin of twenty cigarettes, a water-sterilising outfit and an emergency ration. It made an awful lot more to carry.'

43 LSI – Landing Ship Infantry.

44 In 'On a Steamer Going Over', Anthony gives the following details of the ship: 'Including the crew there were nearly a thousand men on board. Sleeping berths were crowded, but by traditional troop-ship standards, not too bad at all. Food was served on the cafeteria system, each man queuing with a tray, and eating at metal tables for four. [...] This was a ten-thousand-ton Victory ship, designed for cargo, but adapted as a landing ship infantry halfway through her building.'

45 It wasn't. This was Thursday, 1 June. Perhaps Anthony meant it felt like Saturday.

'We've had it, chum,' said a second lieutenant to a captain.

'We're fucking off then,' said voices of all ranks.

A good many troops crowded to the sides for the final cast-off.[46] But the camp games continued and no one gave up his place in the canteen queues.

From 4.20 p.m. to 5 p.m. the canteen was open to officers. Astonishing scenes ensued. You said 'chocolate' and they gave you four three-penny bars. There were oodles of everything: tinned peanuts, cheese biscuits, cookies, pepsi-cola, liquorice-all-sorts, bootlaces. I asked if it was advisable to stock up well before the hoarders arrived, but apparently the stocks are built to last the trip.

A colonel, who knew that I would be writing about the events, came up on the dockside and said in the slightly laborious way of someone talking for quotation: 'I've been round everyone. All got their tails up. Right up. It's really inspiring to listen to them.'[47]

No doubt he had gone round and had really felt emotionally stirred, but he couldn't describe it – few can – without sounding phoney.

I watched two marines fishing off the blunt end and listened to the 6 o'clock news over the public address system. Then found that a meal was in progress, I don't know who planned the meal. There was cottage pie and tinned beans, followed by an inch-thick slice of pork some five inches long with salad; cream cakes, bread and jam, and tea.

Parfitt was out on deck deciphering morse signals passing through the armada. We were now stationary in a formation of ships which stretched away out of sight. I asked Parfitt how long he thought we would stay here.

'Five days at least. They've made out duty officers for seven,' said the crank. 'If you find yourself with nothing to do try to find a way of trisecting an angle.'

'I'll do that, first thing I do,' I said politely.

'Probably the last. It's impossible,' said Parfitt.

At 7.45 p.m. I went to draw books for our detachment of seven men. They were being handed out by the Padre from a hatch-way. I was given five books, all more than twenty years old. But they shouldn't have survived that long.

Cocoa was served from 8–8.20 p.m. down in the cafeteria, where the troops sit and recreate.[48] The cocoa was sugarless. The room was noisy. One man beat on a metal chair without any rhythm from when we entered and was still beating when we had drunk our cocoa and left.

The official name 'cafeteria' is a good one. Metal tables with swinging stool seats attached to each of the four legs. Everything very white and metallic with service counter in the middle or, should I say, athwartships.

---

46 In fact, the ship only made a short journey out into Southampton Water, where it remained until 5 June.

47 Anthony was by now famous as a war reporter in Army circles.

48 A pun on the use of the word 'recreation' for troops having time off.

At 9.15 a meeting was held in the cafeteria to hear the ship's Standing Orders read out by Tiny. 'Already some things have been stolen. Any more of this nonsense and there'll be trouble for someone. Thieving we will not have.'

Later on Tiny was measuring the width of one of the hand-carts, being worried that it was too wide for the assault craft exit. The assault craft were suspended from a system of davits. Rather gingerly Tiny stepped on to one and started measuring the exit.

Thereupon a marine officer appeared and switched on the winch which with a great noise started lowering the assault craft towards the water.

Tiny was considerably disconcerted. Practical joking isn't normally the shortest cut to my regard, but the marine captain took me and an RASC captain with a very strung-up voice to his cabin and gave us beer in silver metal tumblers.

Whenever there was a knock at the door we had to hide the bottles and glasses, as drink was strictly forbidden.

The marine was in charge of the flotilla of assault craft attached to the ship. He told us about a marine who with a dupe accomplice had dived over the side, swum to a moored dinghy, rowed to the shore, burgled a store of a lot of miscellaneous military clothing, rowed back to the ship, then replaced the dinghy. He had then held a free issue of clothing, towels, socks, badges, etc. to all in sight. At least it was presumed that he had given the stuff away because no one would give him away. He was under open arrest where he would stay until after what is euphemistically known as the Exercise before facing trial.

FRIDAY, 2 JUNE

I was woken at 6.45 by a voice telling the military fatigue party to report to the cafeteria at once. I got up shortly after 8 when the officers' breakfast was announced. And what a breakfast! To the music of Tommy Dorsey I had tomato juice and grape nuts, leading up to a plate which groaned under a large fillet of haddock, four slices of bacon and fried potatoes. Some rolls, butter and marmalade, some cups of tea, and I was ready to face the deck.

While lying awake last night I heard a running train, a diving plane, a fairground in the distance, a thousand lavatories flushing simultaneously, ten cranes at work, and the hum of a power station. Yet the ship was anchored and in calm water. Why are all these noises necessary?

I am reading *The Skies of Europe* by Frederic Prokosch. Most impressive and, as far as my money is concerned, you have to be impressive to get away with as much earthy observation as Mr Prokosch favours. 'She had grown heavier. I watched her turn in at the gate; and then I saw that she was pregnant.' No doubt about it, Mr Prokosch bravely faces up to the important position of sex. Little blue veins stand out in many of his characters' necks at one time or another. Turn over the page and Mr Prokosch observes that the pregnant lady's pregnancy 'had recently become more obvious, her eyes and even her voice had taken on a dreamy, inward-gazing quality; her skin had a soft, thick, milky look.'

Usually when I meet the girlfriends of men who write like that I find myself wondering how they think it all up from such unprepossessing material.

But this is absurd. I wish I could write Mr Prokosch.

A voice has just said: 'There is a notice up by the gasoline locker which says NO SMOKING. That notice was not put there to decorate the ship. There is to be no smoking in the vicinity of the gasoline locker.'

The absurd and immorally attractive feature of this outing is the bandbox spickness of everything. The assault craft slung from the side of the ship look brand new. One's instincts have been so long trained to economy that it seems a great shame for the assault craft to be used only once or twice. Couldn't we fix up some other landings after Burma?[49]

It isn't only the assault craft. The soldiers are loaded down with new equipment and most of them are wearing new battledress. The canteen is loaded down with supplies. The food is plentiful. The paintwork is new. Everyone looks splendidly healthy, as who wouldn't when the day is punctuated with bottles of sparkling satisfying Pepsi-Cola, the five cent drink in the big bottle.

After lunch sat in the sun on the boat deck. O'Keefe searched the shore with glasses. 'Can't even see a Land Girl,' he said.

It was voluptuously hot. We lay on the boat deck reading Whodunits, sucking boiled sweets called Jaffa Oranges, and discussing the arrangement by which each officer could buy a bottle of whisky from the NAAFI. Occasionally ask how the armada was doing and look up to see if there had been any noticeable changes in the far-stretching formations. There never seemed to be any noticeable to a landlubber.

In the cabin there was some discussion about the whereabouts of neighbouring formations on the maps with real names which had now been issued.

At breakfast a boyishly intense little subaltern raised the Vansittartist flag but no one was interested enough to agree or to differ.[50] There is wonderfully little interest in why, where or when the thing is starting, no doubt largely because of the excellent food and weather.

---

49 'Burma' may have been the code-name (or Anthony's substitute for a code-name) for one of the landing areas on his stretch of beach. However, far more likely it was a mishearing by the person to whom Anthony dictated this text of one of the real code-names for the relevant villages – 'Alberta'. 'Derna' and 'Regina', the likeliest, of course, being Derna,

50 'Vansittartist' – Robert Gilbert Vansittart was an ex-diplomat who sat in the House of Lords and who had become famous – some would say infamous – for his much-argued proposition that the German race was innately evil. In 1940 he gave seven radio broadcasts which were so popular and controversial that they were turned into a pamphlet, *Black Record: Germans Past and Present*. It sold 400,000 copies within the first eight months of publication.

   Anthony was very well aware of his work. The last known words that Anthony spoke after he had been seriously wounded by the Germans on 23 September 1944 were a joke about Vansittart – 'If you get back home before me, tell Vansittart he has another disciple in me'.

I washed my handkerchiefs this morning. Being very evasionist about any practical work I am always very surprised when it turns out all right. I was delighted that they looked rather cleaner than when I started. I hung them in a row along the bunk and dried them with the electric fan. Encouraged, I did my shirt in the afternoon.

This slight technical prowess led me to reflect once again how readily we pay tribute to technical prowess when only too often the work isn't really very difficult or well done. Sailors and doctors are just two classes who get away with murder in this respect. We listen to them pop-eared and open-eyed.

Bitter infantryman reading *Life*.[51] 'Care to hear what Churchill said in 1939 after visiting France. "The war is going well." Cor don't they bluff us, eh?'

Proximity accentuates reactions to people from one extreme to another. The blood-less, thin-lipped, formal-minded little runt revelling in his military routines becomes a pleasantly naive little man anxious to help. The careerist lieutenant, humourlessly deter-mined to correct everybody's faults and playing his military part with exaggerated care, loses his power to annoy as one's adjustment to a new environment robs his corrections of their importance.

I spent some time watching inter-ship signals, brushing up on my morse.[52]

'This is the Entertainments Officer. We are just embarking on our first venture in entertainment, except for the good old wireless.'

An inter-battalion quiz:–

1. 'Name three non-English international tennis players. Here's Corporal McCarthy to give you the answer.'
   Dead silence. Corporal McCarthy does not know the answer.
2. 'Private Thomas, name three non-English international golfers.'
   Dead silence. Private Thomas does not know.
3. 'Lance-Corporal Allen: what is an eagle in golf?'
   Dead silence. Lance-Corporal Allen didn't quite get it.
4. 'Private Blakeley: where does the third man field in a cricket team?'
   Blakeley: 'No idea.'
   Entertainments Officer: 'Nobody seems to know anything.'

The sixth man, Lance-Sergeant Roberts, knew Abraham Lincoln's remarks about the government of the people. But Lance-Corporal Robson didn't know who said 'Friends, Romans, Countrymen'.

How long is a piece of string? Correct answer: Twice half its length.

Two points also awarded for saying that you can't walk more than halfway into a wood.

---

51 *Life*, a pictorial magazine.

52 Anthony had learnt morse after his initial Army training course in 1940, on the grounds that work with the signallers was 'easier on the feet'.

On the boat deck under two boat keels a group of half a dozen men were studying maps of the area.

The marines' parade on the boat deck.

'Are you a marine, Slocombe?'

'Hope so, sir.'

'Then pipe down and fall in. Pay attention to what you're doing.'

Long talk with O'Keefe about gynaecology as a career; from the doctor's point of view one disadvantage, he said, is the amount of night work.

Someone else's kit in the cabin, but he didn't appear until some time after midnight. Very large and red-faced.

I think he is a self-propelled gunner. He suggested that we had the porthole open. I didn't even realise it could be. It looked so irretrievably closed that I hadn't tried to open it even in the daytime. Though had I been a little more alert I should have deduced the possibility from all the other port-holes being open. Ah there I go, self-reproaching again.

SATURDAY, 3 JUNE

Continued my great laundry programme by doing my pyjamas and towel.

The AMLO (Assistant Military Landing Officer – a colonel) looked in and said last night's newcomer had no right to be there.

With the help of Captains Parfitt and O'Keefe, I, or rather they, tried converting my sleeping roll into an assault pack folded lengthwise and bent round my shoulders. The experiment was by no means unsuccessful.

They were experimenting with unloading an LCA under the supervision of Captain Knights who asked some of us to come for a spin.[53] We were lowered to the water and started the engines. But the propellers got embroiled with some rope, of which there was plenty available. So we banged about for twenty-five minutes before being hoisted back. A second attempt with another LCA was more successful.

After dinner I went to a briefing of A Company 5th East Yorkshire down in No. 4 Hold, a ponderous cavern, wire-netted into partitions, cluttered with paint, planks, lifebelts, etc.

They were being given the larger picture, also a final rub-up on the Company's role. Landing at H+5.[54] Then advancing at a rate of 100 yards in one and a half minutes. 'Main trouble will be getting there. Once we get there they've had it. So you know what it means. Everyone follow his immediate leader and keep following.'

---

53 LCA – Landing Craft Assault.

54 H+5 – five minutes past zero hour for the landings.

My pyjamas turned out all right but the towel looks as if someone's batman hasn't been using Persil.[55]

Walking out after tea, Parfitt and I discovered an addition to the landing craft slung from the ship. It contained a carrier and a jeep. Never a dull moment.

Brains Trust: Which famous actor-playwright is now serving a sentence in prison?[56]

Every time I move I wonder how I carry so much.

Look at it (the armada). No hope of finding us in all that lot.

What is the difference between French knickers and cami-knickers? Not had much experience.

SUNDAY, 4 JUNE

At 10.55 the Chaplain: 'A short service will take place on the after-deck in five minutes time. I feel that on a day like this we should all attend. Owing to it being late it won't be possible to hold a communion service afterwards, but the short service – it won't last more than fifteen minutes – will take place in five minutes time.'

About 150 people turned up. The Chaplain had an unusually attractive personality, but his sermon made me laugh a bit on the quiet. He said he had been thinking a lot about what to say to us and in the end had decided that all he could say was 'Have Faith in God'. He then asked whether we were prepared spiritually, materially and in our training for what lay ahead. He thought that we were spiritually prepared because we were fighting for the good things, we were on God's side, while the Nazis were not on God's side. We were prepared materially. Excellent material and – so far as we knew – plenty of it. As for our training, he knew that the naval training was excellent and he had no doubt that so was the Army's.

An agitated voice: 'The Corporal who has two sacks of hymn books belonging to the Padre, deliver them to the boat alongside the port quarter now.'

The weather has been windy and cloudy. The possibility of postponement looms.

The Colonel of the Green Howards was brought into my cabin after lunch. He had come in to see his company on this ship and tell them about the thickened anti-tank defences which now beset their path. The weather was too rough for the LCA to take him back. I lent him a book and presently he went to sleep.

On the floor of the lavatory there was the front cover of *Picture Post* for October 21st 1939. There were two ecstatically laughing soldiers with the caption: 'The New War Song: Run, Adolf, Run, Adolf, Run, Run, Run.' On the reverse side of the page there was a lady urging readers to say goodbye to dull, uninteresting hair. Another lady in bed

---

55 A pun on a contemporary advert for soap powder, 'Someone's mother isn't using Persil yet'.

56 Brains Trust – popular title for quiz shows, after the BBC radio programme of the same name which began in 1941 for the forces.

saying, 'Good morning! I've slept like a top on a "two-light" mattress', and the story of another lady who realised what all men know – that attractiveness is an air of freshness.

The nightly Brains Trust:

'Sergeant Dixon, if someone gave you an aphrodisiac would it be a non-malarial mosquito or a sexual stimulant?'

Sergeant thought it would be a non-malarial mosquito.

'If someone gave you an enema would you bury it in the garden or use it to clear your stomach?'

In the near future I won't need one.

During the afternoon I worked up in the Signals office.

The Colonel went away and a lieutenant-commander, RNVR, arrived instead.[57] He is a kingpin of the naval beach organisation and was equipped only for the austerities of battle. He also had a bottle of Brylcream, which seemed superfluous in a life reduced to a one-blanket basis.

I returned to the signals office at 9 p.m. until 10.30 p.m.

The Lieutenant-Commander slept with no bedclothes and dressed only in a pair of shorts. He told me that he has always slept like this, war and peace. Well, now I have seen everything.

MONDAY, 5 JUNE

They tell me that this was to have been D-Day morning. But it wasn't. After breakfast I had my blister dressed. The ship was very busy, mostly with loading marking poles, extremity signals and transit signs for marking the beaches. Signs of personal excitement, my own and other people's.

I arranged with the Royal Marines Captain to switch my position from the ferry service (H+150) to an LCM carrying a brigadier's jeep and carrier (H+45).[58] This should give what is known as a completer picture and will also save humping my unique assault type valise from LSI to LCT to LCA to shore.[59]

The Royal Marines Captain was a very Noel Cowardish character, one of the school who pretend that everything is completely out of control. He was talking about his farewell speech to LCA crews. He said he could never deliver it without bursting into tears.

---

57   RNVR – Royal Navy Volunteer Reserve.

58   LCM – Landing Craft Mechanised; H+150 – two and a half hours after the first landings, H+45 – three-quarters of an hour after the first landings. Anthony was determined to go in as near as possible to the first wave of assault troops.

59   LSI – Landing Ship Infantry; LCT – Landing Craft Tank; LCA – Landing Craft Assault.

The weather was the main preoccupation. It didn't look too good. Then at 1.20 p.m.:

'Attention. All troops, all services will pre-load all kit except small kit into LCAs between 4 and 6.

'Canteen will close to all military personnel and Naval Commandoes at 8 tonight.

'The purser will change all English money into French at 7.30.

'Library books will be handed in at 8 tonight.'

About 3.30 p.m. the Principal Beach Master, a pale-faced, bemedalled young Lieutenant-Commander, arrived in a lifeboat, together with an Engineer Commander.

Apparently the small stuff has started already, and this is inextricably D minus 1.

At 3.45 p.m. there was a bit of a rumble. 'Those are the engines, I believe,' said the Lieutenant-Commander. He was packing up. 'I always wear gloves. I find you can get a better grip on everything with gloves on,' he said.

While sitting in the canteen two messages were broadcast, one to the Navy, one to the Marines, wishing them good luck in their respective jobs and enlarging slightly on the eve of great events theme.[60] People listened dutifully, but were not, on the face of it, particularly injected with any extra resolve. 'Same old bullshit,' they said, though not in any particular spirit of complaint. Tolerant smiles were more the note.

'Attention. This is the Roman Catholic chaplain speaking. I will be saying the Mass at 6.30 this evening.'

These messages helped to underline the nearness. Singing started down in the troop decks. Very feeble jokes began to seem funny.

At 6.25 the amplified voice said in urgent tones:

'Attention. Men who wish to take their anti-seasickness tablets should take the first one NOW.'

We sailed about 7 p.m.

Rather late in the day I loaded my kit into the landing craft, and came up into the wireless cabin to finish typing this story. It is now 10 p.m. The ship's motion is just enough to be felt. It is a grey, commonplace sort of night, and the English coast is a receding blur. Most people have gone to bed. We are being called at 4 a.m. tomorrow, and the first flight of assault craft is due away shortly after 5 a.m.

---

60 Possibly referring to General Eisenhower's broadcast message, which began: 'Soldiers, Sailors and Airmen of the Allied Expeditionary Force! You are about to embark upon a great crusade, toward which we have striven these many months. The eyes of the world are upon you.'

'A Day at the Seaside: Going on Shore'

Breakfast was at 4.25 a.m.

'Attention. The second seasickness pill should be taken now,' said the ship's amplifier as the liver and bacon was served.

We were passing up a mine-swept channel marked by red lights, about eight miles off the French coast. There had been a good deal of flares and flak in the distance but right now there was nothing. As I came out on deck a solitary fighter flew across the ship.

Over the amplifier the Senior Naval Officer's voice said, 'Telephone operators and winchmen will be required in about five minutes' time.'

I went to put on my Christmas-tree-like equipment, and transferred as much stuff as possible from my trouser pockets to my battledress blouse. In the agitated lightheadedness of the moment I decided that the battledress blouse pockets wouldn't take it all and transferred a good deal back again.

I had been told that with any luck we should step ashore in water not more than ankle deep.

The amplifiers said: 'LCA crews, man your craft. Telephone operators to your stations. Winchmen close up. Serial numbers stand by to embark.'

The first flight of the assault troops formed up by the two rows of rectangular and frail, blue and white assault craft. They were a company from the 50th Division.[61] I joined the miscellaneous party in which I was travelling.[62] We didn't belong to the first flight, but we were being lowered in the same batch of LCAs. The crew began wishing us good luck and made very depressing comments about the choppiness of the Channel. The officers and NCOs of the troops going into the craft were telling their men not to worry, there were miles of time to do everything.

At 5.28 a.m. by my now rubber-cased watch, the amplifier began to order craftloads. 'To your stations now.'

We clambered over the rope-laden side of the ship into our landing craft. It had a Bren carrier and a jeep occupying nearly all the deck space. Gunfire started up. The guns of the nearest cruiser looked as if they were firing big brown puffs of smoke, which lolloped vanishingly through the air.

'Go on, shell the bastards,' men said.

'There's no reply yet. From the shore,' one man said.

---

61   50th (Northumberland) Division.

62   Anthony gives details of his party in 'On a Steamer Going Over'. 'Our ship […] carried a beach company commander, half his company HQ, seven sappers under an officer, and three military policemen, together with a party of Royal Navy beach commandos. All these were to go in at H+45 with the reserve battalion and reconnoitre the beaches, particularly TME exits through which succeeding waves would pass inland. Various oddments would go in with them, e.g. the brigade commander's jeep and carrier, not to mention (from another ship) the brigade commander.'

'There's a hell of a swell on, Sergeant.'

'Not so bad as it was,' said the Royal Marine Sergeant in charge of our craft.

'Do you know which way we're going, Sergeant?'

'Any way you like, son.'

Three naval officers and a Royal Marine major came aboard. Their luggage included two wildly incongruous-looking weekend cases.

'Coxswains report their troops onboard,' said the amplifier.

'I wouldn't miss this for worlds, would you?' said someone who probably hadn't been studying the state of the weather.

At 6.28 a.m. the amplifier said 'Lower away 1, 2, 5, 6, 9 and 10.' They hit the water with a splashing plop.

A double line of Landing Craft Tanks dawdled past some 200 yards away, and they split into a Y-formation. Of course, there were ships all round us. Apparently they were now spaced more widely apart than they had been earlier in the journey, so there didn't seem so many.

Our number came up on the amplifier. 'Get inside lads, get inside,' said the Marine Sergeant.

They cast off the craft from the side of the ship. We were now suspended over the water from a single derrick by a cable split into four, one strand to each corner, in umbrella fashion. We bumped about while we waited for two Marines who had been sent to fetch something. Then we were lowered about ten feet and a Royal Corps of Signals sergeant appeared, breathless and urgent, shouting to be put on board. He stood there with one leg over the ship's side, undecided whether or not to jump, until someone pointed out a rope down which he slid, just as they were finally lowering us into the water.

We weren't being lowered into any mill-pond. Goodness, it was rough, and it went on being rough all the way to the shore.

'All the way to the shore' – what a simple phrase that is. What a wealth of colourful and seasick events it fails to picture. Before landing at H hour + 45 minutes we were to go to the Headquarters ship and exchange the naval officers for the Brigadier and staff of the assaulting brigade. We certainly went to the Headquarters ship. In fact, we started going through her, and tore a gash in her side.

By sucking boiled sweets I just managed to avoid seasickness. Others had no boiled sweets or found boiled sweets no antidote. We had all been issued with vomit bags, but in the event men leaned over the pitching side.

The unfortunate coxswain, the Sergeant in the Royal Marines, seriously injured himself in trying to move single-handed the cable which had supported the landing craft when slung from the ship and which was now entangled in the carrier and would thus prevent its swift rush for the beach. The poor devil writhed about in the carrier and we had to half lift him out. He refused to rest, much as we tried to make him do so. He was obviously in great pain.

The barrage had now started all round us. There were ships and landing craft kicking up the devil's own row. A line of assault craft corkscrewed slowly past us, and I thanked my stars I wasn't expected to assault anybody. There was none of the infectiously emboldening qualities of smooth speed. They were being pitched and tossed and soaked, all very slowly.

So were we. The faces of the Brigadier and his staff when we came junketing alongside to take them off were what is known as a study. The journey down the little rope ladder was not an inviting one. It took some time to exchange our passengers. We now started on the last run-in to the shore. It was a grey, miserable day and it looked a grey, miserable shore, clouded over with smoke and with only occasional signs of firing. A few shells fell casually in our neighbourhood but the splash and noise they made were entirely lost in the noise and splash made by our own side.

We could see the spikes of the beach obstacles above the surface of the water. It was now getting on for high tide.

A little way out the coxswain ordered the kedge to be dropped and from then on the sea, which up to now had mysteriously refrained from swamping us, began to take its chances. Our feet disappeared below sea level, and great dollops of surf came washing over the sides, soaking people from head to foot. Some 40 yards out, the craft stopped, the front door was lowered, and we were invited to make for the shore. The jeep plunged into the water, the water came over the floor, and after a few yards it stuck there.[63]

I loaded my kit onto the carrier. Unfortunately I hesitated just too long to load myself on to it. It made a sudden belly dive into the sea and started unsteadily for the shore. Three men stood hesitating, as well they might. It seemed the moment for encouragement by example and I followed the carrier down the ramp.

The water was quite warm and waist-high. We waded towards a narrow strip of shingle into which men and vehicles were beginning to pour. Running parallel to the beach was a track, behind which clouds of smoke were being generated. Through gaps in the smoke you could see English-looking green fields and a narrow road running up hill and inland, to a ridge some 600 yards behind.

To the right of the road on the ridge an ugly-looking house stood against the skyline. There was machine-gun fire away to the left and in the centre. But the main effect on the beach was of some macabre circus coming to town. I followed the carrier in. The officer in charge of it took one look at the exit from the beach, which was now developing into a traffic jam, and ordered the driver to take a short cut.

But it wasn't that kind of beach. The carrier went a few yards, and stuck in making a turn to avoid a wounded man lying on the beach with a blanket round him. The track came off, and there the carrier was stuck in the traffic line.

63   This was the brigadier's jeep.

The minefield between the beach and the parallel tracks was already being cleared. In one cleared corner sat about a dozen German prisoners whose attitude was remarkably serene. They sat or lounged there like men whose day's work was done, greeting new arrivals with the wry sympathy of people committed to some boring social function. They weren't under any great constraint. Everyone was too busy trying to get along the beach themselves to waste time with prisoners.

British wounded were lying on the fringe of the beach in twos and threes. Beach dressing stations were just being established. There were two sergeants lying together. I asked one what he thought of it. He had been hit in the landing craft and again on coming ashore. He said it hadn't been as tough as he thought it would be. Apparently he was easy to please. They were shivering with cold, though the driver of the broken-down carrier had given them his blankets. I fed them each a little rum.

A few yards up the beach a man was lying dead. An equal distance the other way a man was dying. His clothes were in ribbons, his helmet was gone. So were his legs. He was terribly disfigured, but still lingeringly alive. His mouth twitched and his arm moved a little. A doctor came and looked at him, but there was nothing he could do except cover him with more blankets. The poor devil stayed alive a few minutes more, and died.

Casualties had been sharp but light, considering what they might have been. The main trouble had been an 88 millimetre gun, which had had a disastrous field of fire right up the beach. This particular sector was about 1,000 yards long.

At first the beach looked haphazard. The whole horizon was dotted with LCTs beached at curious angles, either to avoid the underwater obstacles (long poles to which mines were attached), or because they had failed to avoid them. I helped dig slit trenches, which a tank then obliterated. I did some stretcher-bearing with a padre. I rescued a case of tins of self-heating soup which had fallen from a tank as it came ashore and shared some out with people who were wet through.

By noon the sun was out, the smoke screens were disappearing, the beach was remarkably quiet.

Two CMPs walked along carrying marking flags.[64] They put up a big banner a few yards away. It pointed to the exit for tracked vehicles in 18 inch letters. There were also separate exits from the beach for wheeled vehicles and for marching parties.

There were some pretty wet landings both for vehicles and men. Many of the vehicles got stuck. Some of the men were drowned. When the tide went down there were more vehicles stuck in the sand in one particular bit of our beach.

Parties of men were drying themselves. A man dressed in a blanket, gym shoes and a tin hat walked along the water's edge looking for his kit. A man came in the opposite direction carrying a primus stove. Two young officers walked along deep in conference, one of them carrying a large penguin doll. About 20 yards out from the shore a man

---

64 CMPs – from the Corps of Military Police.

stood marooned on the bonnet of his truck. The fringe of the beach was littered with packs, petrol cans, tins of food, greatcoats and discarded boots which already looked like old boots.

A man came up to the driver of the carrier on which my kit had landed.

'The Brigadier's gone forward. Taken Hope with him.'

'In the jeep?'

'No, no jeep, damn all he's got. He's walking.'

'Oh, well, soon be Christmas,' said the driver and crawled back under the carrier to continue his repair work.

Tanks began coming in in great numbers. The tracked vehicle exit which had had some pretensions to a surface was now reduced to a condition of morass. But thanks to professional attention it was still usable.

I came on a man scraping sand out of the engine of a jeep. I asked how it got there.

'I don't know, sir. It was upside down when I found it.'

The afternoon was made hideous by the Sappers exploding underwater obstacles. They went up with a detonating crack and a cloud of smoke, and came down with a shower of pebbles and shrapnel. At 3.45 p.m. three-ton lorries started driving up the sands guided by men who stood at the water's edge signalling with yellow flags. It was much easier for vehicles to land there now the tide was out.

I met a colonel from Combined Operations HQ who was writing a report on the landing and we walked the length of the beach. There were thirteen LCTs beached by the under-water obstacles with varying large holes blown in their sides. Many of them were floated successfully on the second tide. We met the Colonel commanding the Beach Group. He said that he was fighting an infantry battle on the side, having killed five Germans himself.

He went on to say that there were still a lot of snipers and one substantial party, a platoon or more, of Germans about with anti-tank guns and mortars. They had already destroyed an armoured car. A company was being sent against them. Walking up the road we came across part of the company, crouching by the roadside, keyed for action.

We walked on up the one-way road to the village. An information room had been set up in an amusement arcade called the *Salles des Fêtes*. A batch of prisoners were sitting by the village war memorial. The corner was crowded with miscellaneous troops.

There was a good deal of bomb damage, but also a number of houses and people left standing. A small boy stood on one of the garden gates playing with toy binoculars. A larger boy came along carrying a souvenir shell case. We passed a deserted and damaged tank whose wireless was still going, echoing oddly along the country road.

The shops and the two little cafes were shut. We looked in one shop, which had suffered a little from blast, and were surprised to note the extent of its stocks of proprietary goods, like matches and toothpaste. The stocks weren't big, but by wartime standards you could not call them inadequate.

At the next corner we were warned by a military policeman to keep to the left, as remaining enemy elements were about to be shelled. We emerged on to the beach again from this semicircular tour. At this end there was a fairly solid sea wall. Incorporated in the wall was a well-built concrete strong-point, based on the 88 millimetre gun which had given so much trouble in the morning.

The Colonel prevented some sailors from being blown up on booby traps while looking for souvenirs. One of them was drinking Vichy Water, happy in the delusion that it was champagne. The Military Police had established themselves in the pillbox and were talking to a little Sapper who had been resting. He said that after the assault, and after seeing a lot of his pals killed by grenades thrown from the pillbox whilst they were clearing the minefield, he had felt 'a bit queer'. He was all right again now, but he felt funny. When the infantry finally assaulted the pillbox they found the surviving Germans hidden shivering, clutched together in a cupboard. But up to then the Germans had fought hard.

Sprawled among the seaweed at the foot of the lea wall there were four of the men who had been killed in trying to make a frontal assault on the pillbox, while others went in behind. The Germans had lobbed hand grenades over the walls. They could hardly miss. It hadn't been possible to bury them yet because the burial ground for the beach was still under enemy fire.

AA guns had now arrived on the beach. I sat down for the first time since breakfast and ate some chocolate and biscuits from my 24-hour ration pack.

An RE officer told me that in some places his men had been clearing mines at the rate of seventeen mines in about 10 yards. Most of them had been hurriedly laid. The grass was still dead over them.

The beach dressing stations kept up a constant series of jeep patrols looking for casualties along the beaches. One dressing station had had about sixty casualties during the day, roughly divided into twelve fractures, twelve head wounds, one or two perforating wounds of chest or stomach, and the rest mostly arm and leg wounds.

This beach dressing station was a tent in which eight stretchers had been made up, each with a hot-water bottle. While I was talking to the young doctor in charge a man came running in to report that a CMP had had his foot blown off by a mine. The RE had warned people to take cover while they exploded a mine and this man had jumped on to another one. The jeep went down and evacuated him back to the field dressing station in the village in a matter of minutes. They worked there all night, in the Mairie.[65] Simultaneously they were building a tented Field Dressing Station in a neighbouring field. I went up there that evening.

D-Day ended for me, trying to sleep in a field, with a frighteningly noisy but quite ineffectual air raid around midnight.

_____

65   Local mayor's office.

On D+8 I went back to the beach. The under-water obstacles had been cleared away. D-Day debris of drowned and blown-up vehicles had gone, towed into the minefields, now looking like a long strip of junkyard. The beach staff were living in dugouts along the front – the same dugouts they had scratched in the sand on D-Day, but expanded and developed with packing cases and tarpaulins. The beach dressing stations were packing up. Lately their only casualties had been from AA shrapnel.

It was now a settled organisation ready to work smoothly for months, if necessary.

WITH THE SHERWOOD
RANGERS IN NORMANDY

A s was seen in the previous chapter, Anthony planned to join up with 8th Armoured Brigade once they were all in Normandy. The D-Day plan for the Brigade was that they were to support the 50th (Northumberland) Division in the assault on Arromanches, part of the Gold Beach landing. Sherman tanks with Duplex Drive would be used, but when D-Day came there were severe problems with landing the tanks due to the rough seas. However, the Sherwood Rangers Yeomanry, the unit of the 8th Armoured Brigade with which Anthony would travel, managed to get onto their sector of shore successfully.[1] They would then move inland with great rapidity before encountering extremely tough opposition. Two commanders were lost within a matter of days, Lieutenant-Colonel John Anderson who was badly wounded, and Major Michael Laycock who was killed.[2] Major Stanley Christopherson would then take over, the commander under whom Anthony would spend most of his time in Normandy.[3]

Anthony did not actually manage to join up with his particular Sherwood Rangers tank crew until 8 June, two days after D-Day. The plan had been that he would meet them on the evening of D-Day, but due to battle confusion their precise whereabouts, and that of the Sherwood Rangers main force, was unknown. When he finally found his tank crew, Anthony learned that they had not got ashore until the day after D-Day, 7 June.

Anthony's Normandy papers fall into four parts: meeting up with the tank crew; the full-scale battle of Fontenay-le-Pesnel (usually referred to by Anthony just as Fontenay); his brief time with a specialised unit which recovered and repaired damaged tanks; and his attendance at a medical operation upon a young German soldier. Chronologically speaking, the first part runs from 7 until 9 June; the Fontenay battle was from Saturday

---

1   The Sherwood Rangers Yeomanry was usually known simply as the Sherwood Rangers.

2   Laycock was killed by a direct shell hit on the regimental HQ. There is now a memorial to him and the other officers who were killed with him at Tilly-sur-Seulles.

3   Chapter IV, 'D-Day to the Island', *A Short History of the 8th Armoured Brigade*, foreword by Lieutenant-General B.G. Horrocks, 30 Corps, March 1946, Warlinks website: http://www.warlinks.com/armour/8th_armoured/index.php (last accessed 30 December 2012).

24 June to Sunday 25 June, with overspill onto Monday 26 as the British pushed on towards Rauray; Anthony was with the tank repair and recovery men just after Fontenay; and the operation on the German soldier was probably around 28 June. Shortly after witnessing the operation, Anthony returned to England. His colleague Ernest Watkins records him as arriving back at the end of June just in time for Watkins' own departure for France.

Anthony's Normandy papers contain various drafts at various stages. Although he worked up the Fontenay-le-Pesnel battle into a two-issue article for *WAR*, none of the other papers were completed before his departure for 1 Parachute Division on 1 September.[4] Consequently there are a number of inconsistencies, blank spaces, and places where individual soldiers are hard to follow. For example, the commander of Anthony's tank crew is variously referred to as corporal, lance-corporal, tank commander, or Cook, whilst the tank's gunner is sometimes called Jack and sometimes called Collin. In order to make reading easier, I have used proper names wherever possible, and have assumed that the gunner was called Jack Collin.

It may be useful to briefly summarise who the tank crew were. Lance Corporal Cook, the tank commander, was only nineteen years of age. Anthony would develop a great respect for this 'dark, vivacious, always smiling young man with a very conspicuous trait of self-reliance'. Then there was Hogg, the operator, and Cherry, the driver, a cheerful young man who had earned his nickname because of his flaming red cheeks.[5] Like their commander, Hogg and Cherry were less than twenty years of age. The fourth man, Jack Collin, the gunner, was older and had been with the 8th Army in North Africa. He tended to be rather grumpy, doubtless because he had a great deal to put up with from the three youngsters. Veterans were constantly baited and teased because of their tendency to reminisce at great length about their previous glorious campaigns. Anthony made up the fifth member of the crew, being what he called in one draft a 'guest gunner'. As Cook's tank was in the reserves, it was carrying a crew of four instead of the usual five and thus had one spare seat, usually the co-driver's.

Anthony was clearly planning to write a book on the liberation of Europe, of which these papers would have formed an important part. Even in their incomplete state, they give an entirely fascinating and unique view of the Normandy campaign.

---

4 'Tiger, Tiger, Burning Bright', *WAR*, issues 76 and 77, 19 August and 2 September 1944.

5 'Hogg, the operator' – this is how Anthony always refers to him. He was responsible for ammunition and possibly operating the wireless/RT set.

With the Tank Crew

Anthony now sets off to try to find the 8th Armoured Brigade and his tank crew.

WEDNESDAY, 7 JUNE

The problem now was to catch up with and join the Armoured Brigade. I hopped on an ammunition lorry which took me no more than a few hundred yards before turning off into a field, in which was encamped some sort of rear echelon of the Armoured Brigade.

My next venture was rather more profitable. I got on the back of an RAF lorry, carrying men on their way to service planes as soon as strips had been put down on which they could land. They had come straight from the beach, and were still virginally surprised by everything they saw.

'Look, there's a donkey. Over in that field,' said one of them 'Wonder they haven't eaten it.'

We passed a soldier leaning domestically in his shirt sleeves from the upper window of a house. 'Looks at home doesn't he?' said one man. 'Going to the dance tonight?' he shouted to the soldier.

'No fucking dance here,' shouted the soldier.

We were in a long procession of traffic passing along a hedgeless road with some sort of green crops on either side. We advanced cautiously, and presently stopped. There was a constant rumble of gunfire ahead of us. We regarded the surrounding countryside with marked suspicion, expecting shots to ring out at any time. In the field near where our lorry had stopped there were three dead Germans. The RAF men were seeing this for the first time and their reactions were mixed. Some got out to look. 'Hope you all come back,' said one non-looker.

The first German was a big lumpy youth who had been killed by something which had blown away part of his face. He lay there with a grenade which he had been about to throw, just fallen out of his hand. A few yards away two more were lying face down. One of them had had the side of his body blown away. Their kit had been looted and the remainder of their belongings lay scattered about them. 'Buggers are well clothed, say what you like,' said one of the RAF men.

There were two more lying in the young crops. One had had his head blown in and his face had been crushed into his upturned helmet as though someone had systematically kicked it into pulp. The fifth man had been pepper-potted with bullets and lay with his head in a cluster of wild flowers. Their faces were all a mixture of death-house grey and fruit-juice purple. The RAF men were sickened by the cold and final brutality of what they saw. A few minutes before they had been gaily, adventurously going off to war. The landing, which no doubt they had envisaged for months as unlimited carnage, had temporarily seemed comfortably romantic and pleasantly safe, though spiced with a satisfying sense of potential danger. The bodies made them realise that they hadn't seen anything yet.

'Photograph there you know. Probably of his mother,' said one man.

'Well, it's the only way to win the war isn't it – killing them,' said another.

'It's like a piece of raw meat,' said a third man staring at the most pulped of the bodies.

'What do you think did it?'

'Reckon someone bashed his head in with a rifle.'

'See that photograph of his wife there?'

The procession showed signs of moving on and we hurried back into the lorry. Of course we knew nothing about the general progress of the beach-head and everyone was asking everyone else if they knew any news. The most persistent, and at that point inaccurate, rumour was that there had been a landing at Marseilles. Our progress was a very halting affair; about every 100 yards there was a long wait.

We finally arrived at the small town of Crépon. The streets were in a state of total traffic jam. I recognised some of the assault infantry from the LSI but nowhere could I find any vehicle with the fox's head against a red and yellow background which was the sign of the 8th Armoured Brigade. I decided to carry on with the RAF lorry and trust to chance. We turned to the left and started going backwards, then curved round and presently stopped in the middle of a big space of open land dotted with anti-airlanding poles. A squadron of tanks of the mine-clearing flail-type were scattered over the ground, and thinking they were at least in the same line of business as the 8th Armoured Brigade, I took my sleeping roll off the RAF lorry and introduced myself.

The Major in command of the Squadron had been slightly wounded and was trying with much gallantry, but not much success, to pretend that he hadn't been. The Second-in-Command told me what had been going on.

These flail tanks are fitted with revolving chains and are used to clear mine fields. After coming in on the initial assault they had been hurried up to Creully to be used as ordinary tanks in an anticipated counter-attack by Tigers.[6] But there had been no need for them to go into action and they had lingered on this stretch of open ground. At first light this morning, when they were changing from the close-box formation used by tanks at night to the open position which is safer in day time, they were opened up on by a German 100 millimetre infantry gun. Though the crews were mostly dismounted, they had knocked out the gun with three shots in about two minutes. Five people had been wounded.

---

6   Tigers – the Tiger was the much-feared German tank which was superior in almost every way to the Allied tanks. Anthony's tank was a Sherman, as indeed were most of the Allied tanks in Normandy. The Shermans were comparatively agile and manoeuvrable, but neither they nor the other Allied tanks could match the heavy German equivalents, especially the huge and frighteningly fortress-like Tiger. Although German tanks were clumsy because of the weight of their armour, they were perfectly suited to defence. In a straight contest, they would win every time, having a much longer range than the Allied tanks.

They immediately improvised a party of three flail tanks, two flame-throwing croco-diles, and fifteen gunners acting as infantry, to investigate the position. The two crocodiles squirted a pillbox on the left of the guns in flame, and without much trouble they bagged about a hundred Germans in a trench behind. They also found an 88 millimetre gun and four 75 millimetre guns, which hadn't opened up at all. This particular piece of country had been certified as clear by the spear-head infantry, but of course everyone makes mistakes,

We were standing just by a small copse in which a medical aid post had been estab-lished. The doctor came out to say that one of the Germans whom he was treating had said that there was a wounded Englishman in a shot-up truck some way down the road. The German also said that there were another twenty of his colleagues waiting to be mopped up. Two German prisoners came out of the cottage where they had been having their wounds dressed. One was very young and ingratiating. He had an air of total lack of political conviction or interest. He was an undefendable scallywag in any language. He had a wound in his arm. The other man was an officer, a surly, obstinate, stocky, red-headed man of about thirty, with medals indicating that he had fought on the eastern front and in Africa. He didn't look anybody's friend.

They were being looked after by a tall lanky sergeant who was obviously much enjoying his baptism of action. He wore his overalls and black beret with cowboy rak-ishness and juggled his revolver about with menacing fatalness, 'Why take them to the beach? Why not do them in now?' he asked with slightly self-conscious ferocity.

He went on to talk about what he might well do on the way down to the beach, making blood-thirstily facetious remarks about saving petrol, and coining the happy phrase that the only good German was a dead one. Two minutes later he spoiled the effect by giving the prisoners each a cigarette and a piece of chocolate.

Another more seriously wounded German was brought out on a stretcher when the lorry appeared to take them back to the beach. The German prisoners helped to lift their comrade on board. He was in considerable pain, and the stretcher bearers were by no means experts. He winced and moaned as they unsteadily lifted the stretcher and bumped him against the tailboard of the lorry. At that moment a medical orderly came running out and shouted 'Chuck it, Charlie, we need the stretchers'. The poor devil had to be taken off the rudimentary comfort of the stretcher and stretched on the floor of the truck.[7] However, the lorry driver came round and unrolled his own palliasse for the German to lie on, a ges-ture which was made more generous by the blood-soaked condition of the German, The latter was in considerable pain, accentuated by the fact wherein transferring him from the stretcher they had turned him over the wrong way. He was slowly and painfully turned over.

A shot rang out near us, 'There he is again, that bloody sniper,' said the Sergeant.[8]

---

7   There is a horrible echo here of what happened to Anthony and the other British wounded in Brum-men less than three months later on 23 September. They were all dumped on the floor of a basic army truck and transported many miles without any thought for their condition.

8   German snipers were rapidly proving to be an absolute menace. They appeared even in areas which were thought to have been cleared.

It was now 10.30 p.m. so as soon as the lorry had gone, I made ready to settle down for the night with the flail tanks, which on the approach of darkness came together in a soap-box formation, with their soft-skinned supply vehicles sheltered inside. They want a lot of sleep. It took them hours to settle down for the night. By the time they had manoeuvred their nine tanks into a triangular formation, had picked the guard, held an administrative conference, and settled down for the night, the air-raids started over the beach-head. The noise from there was accentuated by a troop of Bofors sited 100 yards from us.[9] I had pitched my sleeping bag in the dusk under the tailboard of one of the two soft-skinned two-ton lorries in the middle of the blockade. The Sergeant-Major was sleeping on the tailboard above me. He had a strangely persistent tenor snore. The newly arrived airfield construction group kept shouting at each other all through the night. Of course it was reassuring to hear them so anxious to build their airfield, but I couldn't help feeling that perhaps tomorrow would do. Added to all this the guards kept changing rather argumentatively. So sleep was rather patchy and ended altogether with a stand-to at 5 a.m.

THURSDAY, 8 JUNE

At 5.30 a.m. the tanks had to burst out from their harbour – as I believe the term is – because daylight had set in again. About 6 a.m. the neighbouring Ack-Ack opened up on a solitary aircraft. We could see the black puffs tailing it. It was followed by several others and hundreds more black puffs with corresponding noise. I ate some chocolate and sweets from my 24-hour ration pack for breakfast.

The tanks moved off at 6.30 a.m. I sat in the back of one of the three-tonners.

Our progress was marked by a thick cloud of yellow dust, blown off the winding trail of road by the tanks. There were very few signs of battle, except when an occasional group of buildings had been felled. Telegraph wires tended to be down. We passed little knots of dead bodies, sometimes a single one, more often in twos and threes.

'I don't mind seeing these German buggers, but it's seeing one of our own unburied that I don't like,' said someone in the truck. But in fact the bodies were usually German ones. The advancing English had naturally used what little time they had to bury their own comrades first. The bodies had usually been looted, with the valueless contents of their pockets strewn around them. This wasn't always so, it just happened to be so in this particular area.

Our column was stopped by a tank which got caught on a corner. Another tank knocked over a telegraph pole, and the tank coming just behind us knocked a bit off the corner of a house. Local inhabitants watched our passage through the narrow lane by their houses with horrified apprehension. One lady came out to watch us in her dressing gown. This seemed rather eccentric attire, until I realised that it was only 7 a.m.

During one of the waits another tank came up a side road, commanded by a man I had met on the steamer coming over. He was also trying to reach the 8th Armoured

---

9   Bofors – a type of anti-aircraft gun.

Brigade, so I transferred my kit and climbed on board, sitting up behind the turret among a miscellany of water-cans, tins, compo boxes, and a Number 18 wireless set.[10]

It was my first ride on a tank. No doubt about it, this form of progress has its compensations, like being King. Everyone stares impressed. Many of them wave. The essential belligerence of a tank makes its every journey a stirring affair. It may only be going to collect the mail, but it always looks as if it is being thrown in to stem a tide or launch a spear-head.

After about two minutes steady progress we were stopped by a line of traffic. Having crushed a hedge, pushed a lorry a little to one side, and ruined a section of the road, we marked our way round the obstacle and got moving again. We made our way with many uncertain detours to Brigade Headquarters. This was in a newly ruined field of young crops. Tanks and other vehicles were on three sides of a rectangle along the hedges. I found Lance Corporal Cook and his tank, which I had been supposed to join on the evening of D-Day. They hadn't got ashore until late the following day.[11]

Cook was a dark, vivacious, always smiling young man with a very conspicuous trait of self-reliance. He loaded my kit on to the back of the hull with the others, and showed

---

10   Compo box – Composite Rations pack.

11   Anthony adds question marks at this point in the text, though it is not clear whether he is questioning the statement about Cook's tank being delayed or marking some other matter he wants to check. Cook's tank may have arrived late in France because it was one of the reserves.

The 8th Armoured Brigade had had considerable success since the landing. In an untitled fragment of typescript, Anthony summarises this as follows:

'The Brigade landed on D-Day, with two of its regiments supporting two of the assault Infantry Brigades of the 50th Division.

By H+5 hours they were 3,000 yards inland.

By the evening of D-Day they had crossed the River Seulles and were about 6,000 yards inland. They had gone through three villages on the left and four villages on the right, and were on to the heights overlooking Bayeux. (The two regiments were now supporting two different infantry brigades, which had leapfrogged through the assault brigades at H+3 hours.)

By the evening of D+1, Bayeux had been taken on the right.

The Bayeux-Caen road had been cut and we were in touch with the Canadians on the left: this was about 8,000 yards inland.

D+2 was devoted to consolidation. The tanks supported various mopping-up operations; and escorted the infantry into good defensive positions. In the evening the Brigade concentrated just north of the Bayeux-Caen road.

Next morning, D+3, parcels of tanks were still helping the infantry in mopping-up operations. The country was full of enemy parties fighting awkwardly hard.

In the afternoon the Brigade formed up for an attack on Point 103 which was about three miles ahead and overlooked Tilly-sur-Seulles. Under command of the Brigade were an infantry battalion, a field regiment, a recce regiment, an anti-tank battery, and odd parties of Royal Engineers.

Detachments from the recce regiment and one of the armed regiments, sent out ahead to recce, bumped into some enemy which should have been cleared up but weren't. The barrage and the advance had to be held up for the best part of two hours. After that the Brigade pushed right through on to Point 103.

At this point the Brigade had penetrated furthest of any troops into France, and cut a very favourable figure on the map. We were about 1,000 yards from Tilly. The rest of D+3 was spent in consolidating.

This was the picture of the days' activities which I subsequently secured from the brigade intelligence officer. But living as I was in the co-driver's seat of one of the tanks in the protective troop attached to TAC HQ, my picture of current events was not so clear.'

me into the co-driver's seat where I would be riding. He told me to keep my head down when we moved, as many had been blown off by enemy snipers. I had a fairly comfortable cushioned seat, like the high stools at a cocktail bar; it could be raised and lowered like a barber's chair. Immediately in front of me there was a .30 inch Browning machine-gun; on my right there was a wireless set; on my left sat the driver. We were separated by a big crank casing.

You enter the tank through a very heavy metal trap-door. If you feel either safe or bold you ride along with your head sticking up out of the tank. Or probably you ride with it sticking up just far enough to let you see what is going on. Alternatively you can close the trap door and observe matters through a periscope, which affords a pretty fair but not entirely satisfactory field of vision.

I had arrived just in time, because presently came the order to move.

'OK, start-up, Cherry,' said Cook to the driver, a young man who was so named presumably because of his very red cheeks. The noise of starting-up was a cross between a ship's engine and an aircraft.

'OK, move forward slowly. Right. Steady now. Hold it. OK, take her away kid,' said Cook, who, as tank commander, stood looking out of the turret, giving orders through his microphone into the earphones which we all wore. 'Have you got one up the spout?' he asked. I fed the belt of ammunition, which lay stored in a tin box at my feet, into the Browning.

I resolved to borrow at the earliest possible moment some form of goggles, to cope with the cloud of dust thrown up by the vehicles in front. We rumbled along for about half an hour. It was by no means very uncomfortable. The noise quickly faded in one's consciousness, and there was no particular bumping about or vibration.

We turned up into a field, already sign-posted as the Brigade; we were tick-tacked by a captain into a corner at the far end. We stopped under a tree and a shower of blossom fell into my lap.

Cook brought out a big tin of orange juice given by the American crew of the ship in which they had crossed. It went down very well.

'Could do with that fig juice we gave away,' said Cherry.

'That woman needed it much more than we did,' said Cook self-righteously.

They discussed the dead Germans whom they had seen along the route.

'War is a dirty business,' said one. They had all been years in the Army without appreciating this elementary fact. There is nothing like your first view of mangled corpses to set you thinking.

'Any idea where we are, Cookie?' asked Hogg.

'Yes I'll give you a map reference. You're 876778.'

Cook was out of the tank and speculation arose as to the chances of him being sniped. Someone said that there would be one or two things on the body which might come in handy, particularly his watch.

'I'll haunt you forever if you pinch my watch,' said Cook. 'With my dying breath I'm going to spit on my cigarettes, eat my money, tear up my watch. You won't get nothing.'

I should have mentioned earlier on that the reason for sending Cook on the patrol was that he spoke French.

'How about a brew-up? How about a dabble?' asked Cook.

'Want me to get out and be sniped I suppose,' said Cherry.

'Man, there's no bloody snipers. I've had my head out the last half hour,' said Cook.

We got out and made tea. We watched some SP guns firing from the edge of a pub about 300 yards behind us.[12] I should add that this firing had been a constant feature of the afternoon. It is surprising how quickly you get used to detonations in your ears. The guns were at intervals along the copse of about, I should say, 50 yards.

The crew talked about mail. They would like to be able to send some even if they couldn't receive it. Of course so far there was no opportunity to do either. They disclosed the whereabouts of the enemy, and displayed remarkable ignorance of enemy potentials, and also of how much country was needed to destroy a Panzer division. Then came the question of how we were doing on other sectors; or for that matter, on our own sector. A battered-looking corporal from the neighbouring tank said, 'It's always the bloody same. Right up in the front and don't know what the hell's happening. Some day the war will be over and we'll go on.'

'Yeah, waiting for some sucker to turn up and tell us where to go,' said someone.[13]

At 7 p.m. we were still there, unmoved. A lot of planes had gone overhead and a lot of guns had been fired in the neighbourhood. At the moment there was an intensification of the firing, much of it near enough to produce a detonating shake in the tank. Perhaps that is a shade inaccurate. They didn't shake the tank, but they made the loose fittings jingle. Some detonated overhead, others seemed to be directing a pressure and sound wave through the tank to the ground.

We had a very good supper at 7.30 p.m. – stew and sultana pudding, tea and biscuits. There was great shelling going on nearly all the time, then at 8.05 p.m. we suddenly moved.

But not very far … We went through a village, and then turned off into a field where a lot of the Brigade stocked in transport and some tanks were harboured for the night.

Our tank came to rest close in to a hedge about three-quarters of the way down the sloping field. The other hedges of the field were similarly lined with trucks and tanks.

---

12   SP guns – self-propelling guns, i.e. mobile.

13   Under command of the Brigade at this stage (according to Anthony's notes on the Brigade) were an infantry battalion, a field regiment, a reconnaissance regiment, an anti-tank battery, and odd parties of Royal Engineers. Coordinating everyone, whilst supporting the infantry and dealing with a very determined and proficient enemy who was taking maximum advantage of the terrain, was an almost impossible job.

Kit was unhitched from all the odd crannies where it was carried. Big camouflage nets were thrown over the tanks, and a lean-to shelter was erected along one side of it. Some saplings were cut to support it. The more hygienically inclined had a rough wash. All round the field men were sitting in little groups, mostly brewing up tea or cooking a meal. The current tag when anyone got over-authoritative was 'Garn, he hasn't even seen a dead Jerry yet'.

There was a donkey in the field which made awful sounds as of human agony. Cook was eventually jeered into mounting the moke and riding it round in a circle with one of the local funnymen, a Welsh boy called Freeman, running backwards in front of him holding a pin-up girl's picture in front of the moke's nose.

'What are you doing tonight – going to the dance?' I heard someone say.

'No, invited to a whist drive; cleared my mail special,' said the other man.

There was a raid over the beach. The crazy fountains of red tracer looked very lovely against a romantically clear blue sky. I went with Cook to look at a German truck which had been knocked out in the middle of the field. There was a litter of hand grenades, odd-looking bottles, combs, and personal kit on the ground about the lorry which was half over on its side.

It must have been about 11 p.m. before we pulled out our sleeping rolls, and retired under our lean-to for the night. There was a lot of alarming talk about moving at 5 a.m.

FRIDAY, 9 JUNE

But we didn't get up, into pouring rain, until 7.45 a.m. We moved at 8 a.m. back to the same field as yesterday. Where the guns were still firing. Emboldened possibly by our return they started desultory shelling.

Our Troop Commander was Lieutenant Smith, M.F., a very charming but hard-bitten looking man in his thirties.[14] He presently called all crews over to him and said that we were moving up with the guns to protect them. For this we would be divided into two troops of two tanks each. 'Moving tactically. Remember you're moving tactically, so don't just swan about anywhere. I think there's time for a brew-up but be ready to move any time. Have as little as possible off the tank.'

After breakfast and some rudimentary maintenance, we set off at 10 a.m., ran several hundred yards, and stopped. We were told that a Panzer division was advancing up the road towards Bayeux. We were advancing down another road vaguely converging on them, so that contact might be expected. The enemy was counter-attacking but the expected arrival of the 27th Armoured Division was supposed to crush this counter-attack.

---

14 It is not clear whether Anthony was giving Smith's initials (which would have been very unusual in his writings) or there had been a mistyping of MC for Military Cross.

At the moment we were passing through an area heavily infested with snipers, who had already done very well at the expense of tank personnel who showed their heads.

At least the rain had helped to lay the dust. There was no need to wear goggles. We went on about half a mile, and then stopped on the side of an unhedged road. A lot of infantry were lying in the soaking wet grass. There is a lot to be said for having a tank to work from. It may not be as waterproof as it looks – rain comes pouring in through the most waterproof-looking points – but it is many jumps ahead of lying in the grass.[15]

A mysteriously produced mug of tea was handed round for a mouthful. Gunfire opened up alarmingly near and a lot of aircraft flew overhead. Some of our own guns were operating in the next field.

Presently Cook was sent for by the Captain and came back in a dramatic mood, having been told to take two men and reconnoitre an 88 millimetre gun, which had been reported by local inhabitants. Cook was boyishly anxious to go. The rest of the crew maintained a rather more realistic attitude towards such goings on. There was no enthusiasm to go looking for German 88 millimetre guns. But he took two of them, and they went off. While they were gone the fourth man in the crew started brewing up some tea on a petrol cooker, as the crews of the two neighbouring tanks were doing.

There was a lot of shooting going on in connection, I gathered, with clearing our staff line. The Colonel conducting these operations – the CO of the field regiment attached to the 8th Armoured Brigade – had his tank next to ours. He was bald and worldly, not unlike Nat Gubbins, though he looked more capable of writing a comic column.[16] He stood leaning on his tank, studying his map, and talking into his microphone. 'Why don't they engage them? What are we waiting for?' he said plaintively.

A message was given to him that three German 88 millimetre guns were reported to be withdrawing south of Coulombs.

'Ask him how the devil he gets that information. I'm standing south of Coulombs myself,' said the Colonel indignantly.

'Who is J with?'

'He's with friends from the north. Is that clear?'

'Is he with one of three figures or two figures?'

'Three figures. Over.'

'Thank you.'

A little later I overheard a snatch of dialogue with considerable implications.

'They're Canadian tanks in there in the woods, sir.'

'Stop the guns at once,' said the Colonel.

---

15   Anthony would have been remembering his own days as an infantry platoon commander and thanking his lucky stars that he was no longer in that role.

16   Nathaniel Gubbins, humourist and columnist on the *Sunday Express*; Anthony would have known him from the Express building in Fleet Street, and apparently did not think much of his skill as a humorist.

I began reading *Captain Blood* by Rafael Sabatini, which I had found in the tank.[17]

A voice over the radio said 'Our tanks are engaging enemy tanks half a mile south-west of Secqueville, figures 9274.'[18]

'Hallo I'm very glad to hear your voice again. Are you all right?'

'Yes, the thirty German tanks are south-west of Secqueville. I'm watching them now.'

'Grand, give me a running commentary if you can. Our people don't know what's happening.' said the Colonel who was talking presumably to one of his Observation Post officers.

After being away for about two hours Cook and his two men came back having found the 88 millimetre blown up, with only the boots and – of the Germans left.[19] They were in the usual condition of being half glad, half sorry not to have had more exciting times. However, they were flushed with cider, and had mysteriously managed to buy a packet of French cigarettes, without any particular trouble. This seemed much more remarkable afterwards than it did at the time, when we hadn't met enough Frenchmen begging for cigarettes to realise how totally scarce they were.

We settled down to lunch off tinned sausage, tinned biscuits, tinned butter, and tinned tea. In the middle of the meal Cook was called away and came back to say that we were on a job of protecting an SP gun regiment on its way to some high ground. I took a little rapid tuition in how to work my Browning machine-gun. It seemed an idyllically elementary form of gunnery, its lack of precision admirably suited to my own. The gun had a limited field of traverse and elevation. Any target would have to be either crossing the path or suicidally advancing on us. It was then simply a question of hose-piping the target with bullets, starting on the ground in front of the target and working upwards.

There was a cable drum at my feet.

'Will that be enough wire, sir?' asked Cook. Having no intention of using any wire at all, I said that it seemed admirable. It turned out that he thought I was an Observation Post officer, and that I was to jump out of the tank when it couldn't advance any further without being seen by the enemy, and establish an Observation Post for artillery. I quickly disillusioned him.

We set out at 2.40 p.m., and ten minutes later drew up in a field of crops.

The SP guns, mounted on Sherman tank chassis, were deployed all over the field. Our tank and three others with the same job were lined up on the right flank, looking across a field filled with some extraordinary vegetable plant or tree about six feet high. We got out to look round and a shot was fired apparently at us. We had no sooner bolted back into the tank than another one came. There were evidently snipers. The order came to stay in the tank all the time and keep our eyes skinned for shots.

---

17 *Captain Blood* by Rafael Sabatini – escapist adventure story set in the seventeenth century.

18 Secqueville-en-Bassin.

19 'only the boots and –', there is a blank in the typescript here.

'We're at 892733. The enemy are in the corner of that wood over there,' said Cook.

'I hope they can't see us,' said someone else.

'Hallo Cooky, good news,' said Hogg. 'That wood's clear of the enemy, but there's snipers.'

'Snipers.'

'I say again, keep your head down,' said Cook.

'Not arf I won't,' said Cherry.

The SP guns, which were parked all round us, shelled over the woods in front of us. We were turned off the road between St Léger and Sainte-Croix-Grand-Tonne. The land on either side off which we were turned was very flat, but it dipped down towards the woods over which the guns were firing. After two hours we decided to brew up. But as the cooking was starting the order came 'prepare to move.' The infantry prepared to follow us in to clear snipers out of the area. During the morning they had killed or rounded up about forty, but there were still plenty more in the immediate neighbourhood.

The column of SP guns moved laboriously across the fields and along some tracks. We were supposed to be covering them. Indeed I suppose we were covering them, but the only sign of the enemy was one little shot.

'Corporal Cook, are we supposed to be covering the right flank?' asked Hogg the operator.

'Why?'

'Because we can't at the moment.'

'Nothing on the right flank at the moment,' said Cook.

'All right, stand at ease,' said Hogg.

The country opened out a good deal on the other side of the wood. There was an irregular shallow basin, across the bottom of which we went, leading up to a feature called Point 103. We turned off to the left just before approaching this and parked along the hedges of a field, while the SP guns started shelling a pass. Those SP guns were always shelling someone or something.

Corporal Cook went off to look around a bit and came back having found a comfortable-looking farm about a hundred yards away. He was an ingenious young man and it didn't take him long to persuade – that it would be a shrewd tactical move to have our tank cover the area of this farmhouse.[20] So presently we moved across an orchard through two hedges onto a patch of grass outside the farm, where we prepared for a comfortably secluded afternoon.

There were in fact two farms. The one outside which we were parked seemed to be empty, but Cook and I found the family at home in the adjoining farm. There were an old man, an even older and much more quavering woman, a little boy, and the little

---

20 'Didn't take him long to persuade –', there is a blank in the typescript here.

boy's mother who was obviously the administrative brains of the place. They sat round their kitchen table listening in varying degrees of apprehension from the shivering terror of the old woman to the – excitement of the little boy, while the shells poured overhead in both directions.[21] They said that they hadn't slept for the past four nights because of the bombardment. So far they had escaped substantial damage although the buildings were chewed-up in places. They said that the Germans had been very correct up to the moment of departure, when they stole some bread and anything else they could find. The theft of the bread was much more serious than it might seem because of the shortage of it.

They gave us each a glass of some very rough, sour local cider. We watched them eat their meal, which looked about as disastrously unappetising as other people's meals usually do. They were very anxious to know how the battle was going, which of course we didn't know ourselves. I said that the Germans were being forced back quickly, because obviously that was the only thing they could stand hearing at the moment. Meanwhile the Germans busily shelled and mortared the neighbourhood. I got tired of trying to talk French after a bit and went back to the tank, where I ate some more of our endless supplies of sweets and chocolate.

Things quietened down except for occasional mysterious bursts of automatic fire. Then alarmingly, two pistol shots were fired a few yards away. Cherry, the driver, fired his Sten gun at a tree which he declared was moving. I took another man and cautiously edged along into the farmyard where we found that Cook had shot a wounded calf at the request of the farmer.

The farmer and his family set about the business of butchering the carcass though shells were whistling overhead in both directions. The French achieve a remarkable degree of detachment. When everyone else is crouching and doubling, the Frenchman walks calmly up the road, sublimely confident of immunity.

About teatime a full scale battle started up some hundreds of yards away. Terrific machine-gun fire and mortar fire, and heavy shelling. Shrapnel started showering in our garden. A trickle of miserable-looking French people came walking back.

With much crouching and doubling across gaps, Cook and I made our way along a lane in the direction of the firing. We reached a farmhouse overlooking the arena and searched it for a suitable window. We couldn't find one which showed us a thing. There was however, a mirror in which I caught sight of myself advancing, pistol in hand and ferocious in mien. Adapting the words of, I believe, the Duke of Wellington, I might not have frightened the enemy but I damned well frightened myself.

The farmhouse was abandoned while the battle went on, so I took the liberty of looking around. They seemed surprisingly well-off for nearly everything. On the

---

21 'To the – excitement of the little boy', there is a blank in the typescript here.

food side of course this wasn't surprising on a farm, but they had plenty of all kinds of manufactured stuff – matches, cigars, wines. There was an undramatic normality about the apparent standard of living. The women's hats and clothes, the patent medicines, the fancy notepaper, the children's schoolbooks, were all very comfortable. More than could be said for the uncarpeted stone floors of the bedrooms and the uncurvingly right-angled chairs. The only living occupants were a turkey and young in the scullery.

I stood and watched the infantry going down to the battle. They looked pathetically unanxious to get there, and certainly the busy and delighted sounding rat-a-tat-tat of the machine-guns was not inviting.

I followed them down the lane through a system of orchards and meadows to a gateway from which there was a pretty fair view of the battle. The infantry, who had had sharp losses during the day, were digging in for the night. Some were lying in the ditch cooking food. It made our life in the tank seem unfairly sybaritic.

Over in the next field a German Tiger tank was burning, its exploding ammunition making a gruesome display.

The Battle of Fontenay-le-Pesnel

The diary now gives way to a more formal account of the Fontenay-le-Pesnel battle, beginning on Saturday, 24 June, some two weeks after the previous diary entry. Anthony's experiences of the campaign to date are clearly reflected in the opening paragraphs.

★★★

The taking of Fontenay was typical of the early stages of the Normandy campaign. It is told here from the point of view of the tanks, in one of which I was travelling as a guest gunner.

It wasn't a popular kind of warfare with the tank crews who, from their point of view, had known better days in Africa.

These tanks belonged to the famous Armoured Brigade which led the 8th Army nearly all the way from Alamein to Tunis. Here in Normandy they found themselves slowed down a bit. The country was just one large defensive position, hedgerow after hedgerow, behind which the defending German tanks could hide and make every advance either very difficult or very costly.

Everything had to be done from hedge to hedge. The infantry would look through the first hedge and see if there were any obvious anti-tank positions in the next one. If there weren't, the tanks would poke their noses through and shoot up the next hedge before moving across the intervening field with the infantry, and starting the process all over again. The Germans held successive hedgerows all the way back and the expenditure of machine-gun ammunition in precautionary hosepiping was something sensational. The regiments were using more than four times as much .30 calibre ammunition as they had budgeted for. In one spell of five days the Brigade had used nearly a million rounds of it.

An armoured brigade consists of three regiments, each with about sixty tanks, and a Brigade Headquarters with about twelve tanks. This was an independent brigade. It had its own motor battalion, field regiment, signal squadron, Royal Army Medical Corps company, light field ambulance, REME workshop, and ordnance field park. It was like a young Division.

It was now D+18 and the Brigade had been in action all that time and they had suffered many casualties. In less than three weeks they had suffered considerably more than half the casualties which they had had in three months from Alamein to Tripoli, during most of which they were leading the 8th Army.

So far the Brigade had been working with the veteran 50th Division. For this new attack they came under command of the so far largely unblooded 49th Division.[22]

The position was that the enemy was holding the road which ran through Juvigny and Fontenay to Caen. The Division, supported by the Armoured Brigade, had first to clear the enemy from Fontenay and ultimately establish a line running from Vendes to Rauray.

The plan was that the two forward Infantry Brigades of the 49th Division were to advance to the Juvigny-Fontenay road. That would be the first phase.

In the second phase the right-hand Infantry Brigade would get onto the high ground in the neighbourhood known as Tessel Wood. Then in the third phase the left-hand Infantry Brigade would go on to capture Rauray.

The tank in which I was travelling was attached to 'B' Squadron of the Armoured Regiment supporting the left-hand Infantry Brigade.[23]

The CO of the regiment explained the situation to me from his maps which were set up on some ammunition boxes in the 3-ton lorry he was using as an office. He was a creditably bemedalled young man with a twinkling personality and an attractive air of unassuming expertness. The expertness was not surprising because this regiment had been pretty constantly in action for several years, and the atmosphere of professionalism extended through all ranks. Colonel Christopherson was, however, new to his job.[24]

---

22 49th Division – this was the old division of Ernest Watkins, Anthony's colleague at *WAR*, who had been with them in Iceland. Because of their insignia of a polar bear and their supposed cruelty in Normandy, Lord Haw-Haw used to refer to the 49th Division in his radio broadcasts as the 'polar bear butchers'.

23 The regiment was the Sherwood Rangers.

24 Anthony always refers to Major Stanley Christopherson as the colonel; this may be because Christopherson had by now a temporary acting rank as lieutenant-colonel. I have left Anthony's use of 'Colonel' as it stands.

The regiment had already lost two COs in Normandy, one wounded, one killed.[25]

Colonel Christopherson explained that three squadrons were being used in the operation. 'B' Squadron, to which my tank would be attached, had to advance at 4.15 a.m. under a creeping barrage in support of the battalion which was to capture Fontenay. This done, another battalion of the Brigade supported by 'C' Squadron would come down and form up for Phase 3, the final advance to the line Vendes–Rauray. Meanwhile 'A' Squadron would sit in an anti-tank role to meet any threat from the east, particularly enemy tanks counter-attacking across the open ground south-east of Cristot.

The wood north of Fontenay, Le Parc du Bois Londes, was patrolled by both sides. The ground between it and Fontenay was a minefield. In Fontenay itself, and on our particular front, there were various machine-gun positions, and a company plus of infantry. In the ground behind them there were an artillery battery, heavy mortars and an unknown number of tanks. I left the Colonel and made for the far corner of the corn field in which most of the regiment was harboured.

The 'B' Squadron Commander was holding a conference on the ground outside his tank. There were ten officers and NCOs.

'I thought we'd get there about 5.30 and I take you down for a last talk with the Colonel,' he was saying as I arrived. 'I am not sure you and I shouldn't go out tonight in the scout car and leave little Willie to bring the Squadron out. The only thing is, Willie, for God's sake, don't get into every fight you find.'

Major Lawton did not approve of the minefield, particularly as not one of the mine-clearing devices which he had asked for was available. Therefore, only one troop was to be sent ahead with the infantry with the morbidly interesting role of testing the strength of the minefield.

Of course, it was no use risking the whole Squadron.

The Troop Commander of this troop was naturally the pivotal figure of the conference.

'When I move out onto that flank, will it be first light?' he asked.

'Be about 4.30. I'll tell the wretched Sergeant you'll be there,' said Lawton.

'That's the field we linger in, isn't it sir?' said the Troop Commander pointing to the map.

Lawton explained that he had to risk the first troop on the mines to makes the holes in the hedge for the infantry to get through.

'There are German OPs in the churches, so we'll have to knock the church towers to pieces. There are three of them. It's not a nice thing to have to do, but there you are.

'Things may be pretty hot so we shall have to sleep in the tanks. I wonder if we want a piquet. I don't think so. There's nothing a piquet can do. It so easily gets scattered, and

---

25   Lieutenant-Colonel John Anderson was the CO who was badly wounded, and Major Michael Laycock the CO who was killed. Laycock was killed by a direct shell hit on the regimental HQ. There is now a memorial to him and the other officers who were killed with him at Tilly-sur-Seulles.

we shall have the other boys very close at hand. I might ask the Colonel if he can smoke the line of that road for us.

'OK, boys, I think the whole thing's a piece of cake. The only thing is you mustn't get demobilised by a mine, so look out for that. Now do remember we've got a new Infantry Division here, and it's most important for the whole thing to be a success. OK, boys, let's get cracking at 8.30.'

The conference broke up. Lawton told me that the enemy were the 25th Panzer Grenadiers. We were given our frequency and call sign. Our tank would be operating on frequency 6722. The code sign was Yoke tonight and it would be X-ray tomorrow. 'Make yourself X-ray twelve if you want to ask anything. But we don't want to use the air at all until H-hour, except the forward troops.'

The tanks were parked at intervals all over the cornfield. It hadn't done the corn much good.

We had a hurried snack of biscuits, jam and tea. The neighbours came over to watch it, and to exchange fervent wishes that we were back home. Cherry, our driver, recalled that at this time on a Saturday evening he would be out on his old bike. 'Ah,' said everybody, 'just the job.'

Our Sherman had a crew of four, with myself observing matters from the co-driver's seat. Three of them, including the tank commander, were under 20. The fourth was an 8th Army veteran.

Lance Corporal Cook, the tank commander, drew me aside: 'Did you ask for us to go on this?' he asked. I made a non-committal answer.

'Just the chance I've been waiting for,' said Cook who was always ready with the right emotion. This may sound rather unkind, so let me hasten to add that he had also shown himself to be ready with the right action when necessary.

The order to move came at 8.30 p.m. The nineteen tanks of the Squadron, the two medical half-track vehicles, and the Squadron Commander's scout car moved in open order across two fields, and then went into line ahead on a track running along a hedge.

The way was lined with little groups of infantry digging in, standing about, or cooking on pathetically little fires. At 8.50 p.m. we passed a notice: 'No vehicles to pass this point'. We went on some little way further and halted.

Three graves had been dug near the hedge. 'See where that Captain's been buried there, Cook,' said Cherry, 'The little white one next to the hedge.'

'Killed 16.6.44,' said Cook, reading out the dead man's name and regiment.

The graves vary in condition but usually they all look as if some effort has been made to make them look more attractive, but the workmanship and available materials vary. These three were particularly attractive, small white crosses about eighteen inches high with the dead man's name, rank, unit, and date of death stated in black. There were bowls of roses at the foot of each grave, the bowls being army ration tins.

The isolation and simplicity of graves like these is sometimes more readily suggestive of the horror of it all than the mass mournfulness of a cemetery. It was a lyrically lovely evening, mellow and radiant. We were in a field, and the graves were the only sign that a few hours ago men had lost their lives to take it all to pieces. The grass just went on growing. Nature did not mourn the battle.

Then passing on a bit we came to some shepherds' cottages. They were all shattered with shell holes and coated thick with yellow dust thrown up by the passage of tanks. Nearby there were some burnt-out tanks, two British and one German.

The buildings had all been shattered, but the countryside at first glance was quite untouched.

The evening which had been very quiet was now disturbed by shells rushing overhead; 25-pounders were being fired in the next field. We passed more groups of infantry standing about in casually normal attitudes, but with strained tired faces. Some shelling started.

'See that load of shit going up in front there,' said Cherry.

'Think how much better we are off than that bloke in front in the scout car. Ain't we lucky,' said Cook reassuringly.

Some stray tracer was drifting up, and a sinisterly static figure-of-eight cloud of mauve smoke rose slowly just above the trees before us. It was 9 p.m. and we had been stationery for some minutes, spread out in single file along a right-angled hedge.

We stayed there for a quarter of an hour and then moved down into a lane. Infantry signallers were working on a cable along the lane. A man was climbing a broken telegraph pole. We went up the lane and turned left at the end into a field; this was our destination for the night.

On turning into the field we turned out and took up positions with our guns pointing effectively through the hedges. We came to a halt straddled across a shallow ditch, just next to a burnt-out German armoured car number 934966. The ditch around it was littered with bits of British and German uniforms, empty cigarette packets, grenades, rounds of ammunition, and a letter addressed to SS Mann Alfred Arndt; it had been posted in a place called Hirschberg on the 19th of June.

It was 9.30 p.m. Just ahead of us was the little wood where, some 400 yards away, the German minefields began.

'Funny to think there might be enemy patrols looking at us now,' said someone.

'Which is the way back to the beach?' asked Cherry.

Three German aircraft flew across, machine-gunning us from about 200 feet. The tanks were parked unobtrusively around the field but the two ambulance vehicles attached to the Squadron with their glaring Red Crosses effectively expelled unobtrusiveness. One tank had slipped a track and was being repaired in mid-field.

Cook shouted over to the next tank, 'Are you going to have a meal?'

'Don't know yet.'

But presently everyone started. We made a new desert cooker. This is simply a large biscuit tin neatly filled with earth or sand soaked in petrol. Light the petrol and stand well clear. It heats water much better than the petrol cookers which the tanks carry, though these are themselves extremely useful and necessary.[26]

Half a dozen British aircraft went over, viciously pursued by barraging enemy flak. The evening sky was now reddening to darkness. 'Look at that sky,' said Cook, 'the life blood of the soldiers, reflected in the sky.'

'When I was in the desert, we had a sky like that every night,' said Cherry. He hadn't been in the desert, but this was the current joke among the non-8th Army men, to defend themselves against the too easily provoked reminiscences of the desert warriors.

Hogg who was listening in on the set put his head out of the tank and said, 'Hey, Cooky, you must have two men in the tank ready to make it go. That's what he's telling the others.'

The neighbours called over, 'Hallo, there. What are you then? Tough men, eh?'

We stood there in the gloaming, pondering on the way tea which for minutes has been much too hot suddenly becomes much too cold.

At 11 p.m. a signal came: 'All form a tight box in mid-field.' We backed with the others into a closely packed blockade with guns facing outwards in all directions. The two soft-skinned ambulance vehicles were protected inside the blockade.

Night was just about falling and the sky was a colder blue. Cherry and I sat on our small seats. The others sprawled themselves sardine-fashion over the floor of the turret.

'Funny how all these rumours get round isn't it?' said Hogg. 'I heard when we were with the Lancers that we were going to attack Fontenay. Funny isn't it?'

It was now 11.15 p.m. but I didn't feel tired. One's whole body was alerted. At 11.45 we were summoned to a conference of two commanders. We stood around Major Lawton in one corner of the blockade.

'Look, gentlemen. Everyone stay in their tank. Keep the usual watch – someone awake in each tank all night. If there's any trouble use the Sten gun, not the Browning. Remember in a few hours there will be hundreds of infantry everywhere. They will be forming up in the field just behind. There's already a company out cleaning up as far as the minefields. So for God's sake be careful who you're shooting.'

A sergeant interrupted him to say that he had heard that last night the Germans had come up to the left-hand pen and branched off at the infantry, presumably to make them give away their positions. The infantry had made no reply. Were we to do the same thing?

'Exactly the same,' said the Major. 'For God's sake remember we are not here to drive the Germans out of the county until tomorrow. Don't open up unless they are definitely attacking us. It doesn't matter about walking around the field. All that matters is just to defend the blockade.'

---

26   The petrol cookers were Tommy Cookers. With macabre humour, the Germans called the Sherman tanks Tommy Cookers because they so frequently incinerated the crews inside.

Another sergeant reported the discovery of a mine in the field. 'Right, I'll roll it out,' said the Major, 'Now you know the alternative plan. If Two Troop do all right, follow through. If not, go down to cover the village and do anything we can to help the infantry. Now remember it's important for everything to go perfectly.'

I followed Major Lawton across the field to investigate the alleged mine. On the way he came across a suspicious object in the ground. He followed it rigidly with his foot and sent me to borrow the Doctor's torch. But the Doctor hadn't got a torch, so the Major decided it wasn't a mine. And came to a similar decision about the other one.

'Now, no one ought to leave camp. Get back in the tanks!' he shouted at some shadowy figures gossiping together in the darkness.

Our tank wasn't much good as a bedroom. Cook, Jack, and Hogg packed themselves in a sardine formation on the floor of the turret. Cherry and I had to sleep on our seats. The seat is about the same size as the high stool of a cocktail bar. It is built for the driver to sit upright, and therefore is not ideal for trying to recline. There was no support for the head at the back, nor to the left. If lolled to the right it fell among the complications of the wireless. It was impossible to sit facing forward with head in hands because of the guarding machine-guns. I achieved a fair state of equilibrium, with my feet shot in the small space above the tank shaft, and my head nestling against a piece of steel framework. On the other hand, Cherry, whose amenities were no more receptive, dropped off to sleep straight away. Personally I found it difficult. The one thing to be said for the arrangement was that the tank was quite warm.

Hogg, the operator, who was on guard, was singing 'Only for ever' followed by 'It's foolish but it's fun'. Jack, the desert warrior, started a dissertation on how something obviously sounds different in the desert.

'Tell us about the desert, Jack,' said Cook unkindly. 'Tell us what it was like in the 8th Army.'

The desert warrior maintained a disgusted silence.

'Tell him about the time you joined the Army, Cherry,' said Hogg. 'Tell the desert warrior.'

'You blokes want to watch yourselves and all,' said the desert warrior.

'Why?'

'The way you're going on you'll have no mucking rations left.'

'Liable to get pneumonia,' said Cherry. 'I'll tell you when I first slept like this in a tank in a minute.'

'All right you mark my words,' said the desert warrior.

'I'd like to redesign this tank without the diff so I could stretch my legs out,' said Cherry.

They began to settle down to sleep. There was complete silence outside. Broken about every ten minutes by mortar and gun fire.

I didn't seem to sleep much but I must have dozed some of the time. I did my turn of guard duty from 3.30 a.m. to 4.30 a.m. I opened up the hatch above my head, which incidentally takes some lifting, and watched the ground immediately in front of us. How difficult it is to keep a satisfactory watch on the smallest piece of ground in the half light before the dawn. It made one realise what an excellent chance there is of approaching unobserved.

The barrage began 4.15 a.m. I never heard such a noise. Not just one noise but noise in several moods, some shattering, some whining, some staccato, from vicious whine to tube train roar. Tracer started flying to and fro on the left. Verey lights were going up over the German lines. Concentrations were being fired on all known enemy localities.

At 4.50 a.m. with the noise still going on, we turned out again to the same position in the hedges as the night before. A red glow of fire had started half-left behind the trees. It occurred to me that it was Sunday morning. The rushing tearing noises overhead, though friendly, made one feel very unprotected. I was grateful for the covering shells provided by the tanks, which were now vibrating with the roar of the guns.

The Huns seem to enjoy an inhuman feed of replenishment. They seemed definitely to throw more and more shells quicker and quicker.

The radio war was now in full swing. I put on my earphones and started listening in.

The Squadron Commander was urging, in strongly urgent language, that the infantry should keep near their set.

'X-ray nine for Christ's sake keep near your set. I've been trying to get you for fifteen very vital minutes.' Then he said to someone else, 'It's the same old story. Infantry Sunray just gone off.'[27]

A new kind of heavy banging started going overhead, each one shaking the tank.

The forward troop indignantly reported that there was still no sign of any guide from the infantry.

'Hallo X-ray two, still no sign of any guide. Try and get that message through.'

'Hallo Baker three, where the flaming hell are you?'

'I'm coming up,' said Baker three.

'You ought to have been there hours ago.'

The barrage and machine-gun fire continued. At 5.10 a.m:

'Hallo X-ray eleven, we are all behind you now. Stick it, old man, stick it. You are doing damn well. I'm still trying to get through on the other line.'

'This bloody smoke. I'm in a pretty thick fog. I've lost touch with everyone. I don't know how long it will last. Over.'

'Hallo X-ray nine, same old story. Communications collapsed completely. The only thing is to prepare to stay there.'

---

27   Sunray was the code name for the Infantry.

'Hallo X-ray, position is that smoke has been put down, probably by the enemy.'

'Hallo X-ray, smoke is bloody awful. Never seen anything like it.'

'Hallo X-ray two, yes I understand. The only thing is to hang on.'

'Hallo X-ray, useless unless they send a guide.'

'I want you to work your way forward to the left-hand corner as far as you can. I don't want to – without results but I would like to work my way forward.'[28]

The forward troop had got caught in a tremendous smoke screen, equivalent to a thick London fog, and found it impossible to establish contact with the Infantry Battalion in any co-ordinated way. The Infantry CO had lost touch with three of his companies, and altogether it was an interesting object lesson in what can be done with smoke.

The Squadron Commander spoke:

'Hallo X-ray two, how now?'

'Hallo X-ray, thick as ever. I can see one of our friends. I am going to chuck a head-set over the side and see what the position is. He is not a Sunray.'

Another voice broke in: 'Can you see where that bloody gunfire was coming from?'

Then the leader of the forward troop came back on the air:

'Hallo X-ray two, the friend I had at my side has vanished and I can't see him any more.'[29]

The Squadron Commander summarised the situation to his CO: 'Hallo X-ray, this is the forward element, have lost touch. We are under heavy mortar fire. Some units can't see a thing owing to smoke.' A little bit later he reported: 'X-ray two has been talking to a Sunray on my level. He is exceedingly confused. And we all are.'

About 6 a.m. our tanks began to be shaken by a series of explosions perilously near overhead. They were near enough so that it was necessary to hold yourself straight to avoid being crushed against the side of the tank. At 6.45 a.m. the forward troop was being told to get into a static position and dig in. The CO of the Infantry Battalion was out of wireless touch, and his Second-in-Command was on his way to the Brigadier of the Infantry Brigade for orders. The CO had ordered one sub-unit to dig in and had lost contact with the three other companies. The enemy infantry were reported to be massing for a possible counterattack.

At 6.50 a.m., for no apparent reason, things were said to be improving a bit. We were then lined up against a hedge and had just been warned to watch right. The guns covered to the right. Heavy machine-gun fire was reported from our left flank 8869.

'Hallo X-ray, Sunray here wants to know what you have available.'

'Hallo X-ray nine, has he applied?'

'Hallo X-ray, he is making one. That is why he wants to know what you have.'

At 7.30 a.m. we moved through the hedge across a corn field. I leaned forward on the

---

28 'I don't want to –', there is a blank in the typescript here.

29 'The friend' – meaning the infantry.

Browning and took a nap. Meanwhile the infantry and a considerable part of its casualties were making their way down to the village.

At 8.15 a.m. we moved round east of the wood into a field overlooking the village, which was completely obscured by a misty pall of smoke. We paused and then moved another 300 yards down a gentle slope towards the village. Our tank halted beneath an apple tree. The village began to take shape through the smoke, illuminated by the sunshine of a perfect summer Sunday morning.

Over the air they were talking about which gaps in the hedge it was possible to put the infantry through with the least cost in casualties. Someone said: 'We are overlooking a small place that had a lot of punishment. But still standing. Would you like us to give more punishment?'

The Squadron Commander reported to the Colonel that we were in a good position to observe enemy activity. He said that there were a lot of Observation Posts in the village, and he was going to get permission to blast these out.

The barrage had stopped and the infantry were creeping up. The tank standing next to us had been ordered to fire at one of the three church steeples in the village. These were being used for German Observation Posts. He fired about a dozen 17-pounder shells, and finally hit the steeple several times.

At 8.50 a.m. we were ordered to fire at the left-hand church steeple. Cook said: 'Load H.E. Electric pylon, one o'clock. Steeple with smoke coming from it. Quick, chaps, get your do on it before it's covered in smoke.'

'Fifteen hundred,' said Jack, the gunner.

'Better make it two thousand.'

The tank's 75mm gun fired. The noise was terrific, but not unbearable. The tank is jerked backwards and forwards like a chair with the devil at the helm.

'You missed it, cock,' said Cook. 'Load H.E.'

'Too much range,' said Jack.

'Down to fifteen hundred,' said Cook.

There was a smell of cordite as the shell case fell with a rattle onto the floor of the turret. They fired another H.E. 'Wait a minute. I think it's gone all right. All right, have a dabble. No, wait a minute, it hasn't gone. Cover nest again.'

A voice interrupted on the wireless: 'Infantry situation is going well.'

'Very glad to hear it.'

Cook continued: 'Bring him down again. Another two hundred.' The tank shook with another explosion: 'That was right. You want to come left a bit.'

'No more H.E. left in the turret,' said Hogg.

'OK, could you whip the reserves up, Major?' said Cook to me. Behind my feet there was a rack of 75mm shells. It was a considerable undertaking to prize them out of their pigeon holes. They were not only clipped in, but stuck fast.

'See if the Browning works,' said Cook, referring to the .50 calibre machine-gun mounted on the turret. It started firing just over my head, and its repercussions hurt my ears much more than the big 75mm gun. It was a diabolical noise, which no amount of cotton wool, which I hate to be plugged in my ears, could effectively muffle.

An enemy tank was reported among the trees to the left of the village. Looking hard, I just caught a glimpse of something which might have been it. An indignant voice said over the air: 'Baker, where the hell have you been? There's a bloody Hornet here. Why the hell don't you keep your men on the set?'

Orders were given for the tanks in our troop to attack the enemy tank. We all fired at it. 'Just a bit minus, cock. Up a bit, Jack, up,' said Cook.

I just saw the head of it by drawing in with my Browning machine-gun. The hunted enemy bolted, hugging the trees and making for cover. From where we were, unable to appreciate its particular limitations of manoeuvre, it seemed suicidally unresourceful. We were all flaming away at it, and presently it blew up. We all machine-gunned the spot; my Browning kept jamming.

The tank burned steadily for a little while, and then its ammunition started exploding, and it sent up a steady column of flame to a tree-top height. We went on handing up more ammunition from the rack just behind me.

Over the air a voice said: 'Our friends (meaning the infantry) don't want any more fire. Our friends are getting into the buildings and they report some white flags waving.'

One of our own tanks was reported as hit in the carriage and immobilised. The Squadron Leader said: 'I think they can well afford to get down in the ditch where they are.' The CO of the regiment asked who had got the tank. Apparently it had been hit from a rather unsuspected direction.

'Larwood did it with a very fast one,' said the Squadron Commander, I think rather mysteriously.

'OK, we'll get down to recover it. We ought to get on to who did it. Any idea who did it? Tank or gun?'

Presently the commander of the knocked-out tank was brought to the microphone and said: 'I'm dead sure it was H.E. from the shit all over the place.'

'Get that big boy of yours and blow him up.'

'We fired. Others fired. The tank blew up. We all machine-gunned the spot.'

There were slightly involved claims as to who had done it. 'Well done,' said the Squadron Commander.

A German Tiger was reported in the middle of the village, and the Squadron Commander said, 'If we could find out where the infantry are, it would be a good thing to stonk the square near the church'. This was presently done.

At this time there was a running current of shell and mortar and machine-gun fire being exchanged in and around the village. Sometimes a crop of shells would burst near enough overhead to shake the tank and sometimes tracer would drift in our direction, but considering our exposed position we enjoyed a remarkable immunity from enemy attention, which was, of course, well-occupied all round.

About 10 a.m. there was an interval in the battle. The smoke had cleared away and left the battered little village exposed in the brilliant morning sunlight. Over to the left, the tank, now identified as an SP gun which our united efforts had knocked out, was still burning. Isolated shots from snipers whistled about at intervals. In some ways isolated shots are more alarming than a big volume of fire. As it whistles by you, you feel that careful thought, pepped up with spite and malice, has been put into aiming it.

At 11 a.m. I climbed out of the tank and went across to see the Major. With some alarm I watched a number of shell-bursts, just overhead. Each produced a belch of blue-black smoke. A sergeant was standing near me with binoculars. 'I can't see where that one is, can you?' he said. On my way back I was knocked off my feet by the blast from a 17-pounder gun which unexpectedly fired as I passed by. It hurt my ear drums in no mean fashion. They were now firing at the target which had been reported in the village.

'I shall want a running feed,' said one of the tanks.

'Something to eat or drink?' asked the Squadron Commander.

'It's these things we've been flinging about all morning. We've lost plenty of them,' replied the tank.

Coming as a complete stranger to this form of double talk, it didn't take long to realise that they were talking about ammunition and petrol. I shouldn't think it would take any English-speaking Germans long either. This particular conversation continued:

'I have the soft balls that X-ray would like and I could bring them to his last night's bedroom if that would suit him,' said the man whose business it was to run the forward supply echelon. Arrangements were then made for individual tanks to return to last night's harbour and replenish their ammunition.

Our next door neighbour asked: 'Can you see those people walking about at figures 50 yards left to the wood?'

'Not yet.'

'There's two buggers there.'

'I think it's two French people. They're not doing anything active.'

'Yes, I think that's about what it is,' said the Squadron Commander. 'So be very careful not to do anything there.'

Our tank then reported having seen a tank left of the burning wreck. The Squadron Commander asked everyone to report if they thought it was a tank. Someone said it wasn't, at which Corporal Cook indignantly maintained that he had seen two men get out of it.

'I believe you're right. All stations train on it,' said the Squadron Commander.

We all started firing again. But no gratifying enemy brew-up resulted.

'Hallo X-ray twelve, if that's the position you mentioned, it looks like a false alarm,' said the Squadron Commander.

'I don't think it is. I bet he'll move in a few minutes,' said Cook.

'OK, give it a few more,' said the Squadron Commander, and we started firing again.

Someone reported some Germans walking about in the foreground and asked if it was worth getting artillery onto them. 'I don't think we dare, without knowing more about the position of our own infantry,' said the Squadron Commander.

'Hallo X-ray one, there's a hell of a scrap going down in the village. Is it theirs or ours?'

'Ours.'

'Going very near our own positions.'

Cherry, who slept very well last night, was asleep again. 'I'd like a nice sultana pudding,' said Jack.

The Squadron Commander reported that the Brigadier of the Infantry Brigade was 'absolutely screaming for knowledge of what's going on in the village'.

'OK. I'll go down and have a look on foot,' said the Troop Commander.

'Hallo X-ray nine, don't take any risks, but if you could get some information it would be invaluable,' said the Squadron Commander.

Just after 12.30 a terrific machine-gun duel started between guns firing from the village and guns firing a few yards away from us. Our own machine-guns were firing with distressing effects on one's ears. We were being fired on from the woods to the left of the village. And were trying to pin-point the flash of the H.E. which was thunder-clapping at us. We fired at a point where I thought I detected it. But the firing at us went on for some time. Over on the right we could see a Sherman which had been blown up, presumably by the same 88. Presently the firing became too hot and we were backed away from our exposed position into shelter behind a hedge.

I forgot to mention that a little earlier on we machine-gunned a party of about fifty German infantry who very ill-advisedly started moving across our front in the corn field. The party seemed very unresourceful about avoiding our machine-gun fire. Some went to ground in the corn, others plodded on. I operated my Browning with no real feeling, until they started firing back, at which my feelings underwent a sudden development.

A little later on I discovered that we had withdrawn because Tigers or Panzers had been reported as approaching.

We were next to a cow, one of the thousands whose swollen bodies were strewn about the Normandy fields. Like all the others, its legs stuck up in a horribly girlish high kick. There was a filthy smell of decay. So outstandingly filthy that presently we moved. We moved some 50 yards, but found that it wasn't enough to get out of range of the unfortunate animal. We found ourselves next to two dead Tommies, from whom we took a Bren gun. It was just a pleasant Sunday morning, shooting at church steeples and replenishing deficiencies from the dead.

To my despondency I found that it was only 1.52 p.m. The day seemed to have gone on much longer. I started tidying up the heap of cartridge cases in the well of the tank under my feet.

A tank commander called the Squadron Commander in a very agitated voice to say that he was being fired on by 88s from the village. And got the answer that the Squadron Commander was out of the tank at the moment 'but I'll give him your message on his return'.

One tank had been sent ahead into the village and now reported that he had gone too far and wasn't quite sure where he was. He sounded a bit flustered. It was then necessary for the Squadron Commander to tell him where to go and what to do without telling the enemy where he was and what he was doing. A lot of double-talk went on about being 'a little too far north-west of where we hoped to go yesterday'.

When the tank had finally orientated itself, the Squadron Commander said: 'OK, X-ray five, carry out instructions. Blast off at the house. Then carry on down the road and try to patrol it.'

Someone else reported: 'We have just been fired on by 88s.'

'Ah, I've just got a dose of the same myself,' said the Squadron Commander. 'Just keep your head down.'

'Are those people French, walking out there in front?'

'They are definitely Jerry, I am sure of it. They are definitely German infantry where that dirt was.'

We all started firing at some dots in the cornfield. H.E. started coming over and bursting overhead. A near one shook the tank so that you had to brace yourself to prevent your head being knocked against the side. A little bit later the tank in the village reported again: 'I have just been doing the job I was told to do, blasting the house, and it turned out fairly successful.' The shelling went on and someone reported, 'At 903655 I have seen something which may be responsible for flinging this dirt down on us.'

Meanwhile the Squadron Commander had gone down to hold a conference with the forward troops. The meeting had been mortared and two officers wounded. He came up on the air, talking to the Doctor: 'I've got a couple of casualties down at the bottom corner of the wood, Jimmy and Colin. Can you send down a half-track? Over.'

At 2.30 p.m. the Colonel enquired: 'Hallo X-ray, I am right in saying we are not on the south road yet?'

'Hallo, X-ray, Yes'.

A little later the Squadron Commander asked: 'Hallo X-ray four, have you seen anything of those people who came on their feet?'

'No.'

'Keep a look out.'

Miscellaneous instructions and adulations continued to be exchanged.

'Hello X-ray five, well done. But don't go charging ahead south of the southern road.'

'Hallo X-ray two, for God's sake get a move on. You're being bloody slow.'

The tank in the village was interrogated again: 'Hallo X-ray five, are you still on the road or south of it?'

'Hallo, X-ray, I am still on the road and shooting up what I was told to.'

'Did you see enemy infantry moving about?'

'Yes, that is what I have been doing. Blasting them up. They are still north of the southern road.'

'OK. Well done.'

Somebody's CO was anxious to know how near the tank in the village had got to Point 96.

At 3.15 p.m. we came out from behind the hedge on to the open ground facing the village, went down a track, and turned right up a hedge lined with infantry vehicles and men cautiously advancing into the village. Our job was to support X-ray five in supporting the clearing of the village. Just on our left a jeep was blown up by H.E. We made faltering progress, under heavy H.E. and mortar fire. The trees of the neighbourhood had all been shattered by H.E. Two stretcher bearers walked worriedly by, one holding a Red Cross flag aloft, the other spectacles.

We started moving up the track, but then decided that it looked even more mined than the others, and turned round to follow a parallel track at the other side of the hedge. I warned Cook to stay strictly in the track of the tank immediately ahead of us and to leave it to do the minefield pioneering. 'Don't look as if he's too bloody eager,' said Cook. Indeed the tank in front was feeling its way with due gingerness.

We moved along to the end of the hedge where some infantry were digging themselves in. To the right there was a burning British tank and a brewed-up German Mark 4. The British tank was burning slowly and peacefully.

The village with its three churches was in a basin equally lined with houses and trees. It must have been an attractive place a few days before – they build delightful houses in these parts. Solid, neat, happy and durable. But all the houses we could see had been shelled or set on fire. Over the road infantry were going through a house on the lookout for snipers. A little further down, the house with the German soldiers inside it which the advance tank had burned up was blazing like a great torch. The enemy were mortaring our area with considerable enthusiasm. It was now 4.30 p.m. on a Sunday afternoon.

'Funny where all the civilians get to in these places,' said Jack.

Wherever they had got to, they had gone. There wasn't a civilian soul in sight. Whenever the noises of battle stopped for a few minutes, the place was ghostly still. Like an abandoned town. The desertedness was accentuated by a white rabbit which kept running in and out of the houses. They keep a lot of rabbits in these parts. The mortality among cows continued to be sensational. Wherever you looked there were cows, distressing in death, lying on their sides, with two legs kicked up at unsuitably jaunty angles.

'I'll finish this book yet,' said Cherry.

'Haven't you yet?'

'I start and then muck starts flying about and I can't concentrate.'

'The muck's flying around here all right,' said Jack.

'These mortars are deadly,' said someone, 'I wish they'd get 'em knocked out.'

We hadn't been there very long when the Squadron Commander called up the various troop commanders to ask how they felt about staying in the village with the infantry.

'Our flat-footed friends, of course, will watch you with a strained air until next Christmas. We want to help them but we must give ourselves enough time to get a meal and refit for tomorrow.'

But the troop commanders expressed a modified contentment with their situation and elected to stay. We got out and made tea. We had some biscuits and jam. It was our first organised meal of the day.

Very soon afterwards we were recalled to replenish fuel and ammunition. We made our way back down the track and lane along which we had come forward, and found the Squadron, some in a single line along a bank in which a lot of infantry positions had been excavated. The others were parked in an orchard. We filled up with water, petrol and ammunition.[30]

While the crew brewed up a meal, I went to the Squadron Commander's conference of tank commanders. The Squadron had lost two tanks during the day so that one of its troops (each of three tanks) was written off and the remaining tanks merged with another troop. The Squadron Commander told them that they had half an hour to replenish before moving off. They would not be going into action again tonight, but would be held in immediate readiness to do so.

However, this did not apply to our tank. We were to transfer to 'C' Squadron, which was supporting an imminent infantry attack on the part of the village still in German hands.

We made our way down towards the village again, in search of the Squadron which we were to join. Down in the village things didn't seem to have changed much. Another house was in flames. The infantry were still digging in. Some of them were manhandling an anti-tank gun into position. They said that enemy tanks were said to be forming up. We let them fill their water bottles from the water cans which we carried roped to our hull. They looked dreadfully tired and grimy, their clothes and features caked with light-brown dust. They had been in action for a fortnight. There were about forty of them, dug into a series of weapon pits on a slope facing the main body of the village. They said that they were all that was left of their battalion. But, of course, that is a very frequent delusion of small isolated bodies of men. Casualty estimates are always wildly high.

---

30 'We filled up with water, petrol and ammunition'. In one of the Normandy papers, Anthony gives the following details: 'Tank units have a considerable appetite for petrol and ammunition. The ammunition required for an armoured brigade is comparable with the supply for two infantry divisions. After a very heavy day's fighting an armoured brigade may need nine 3-ton loads of ammunition. Each 3-tonner carrying 288 rounds of H.E.'s. On this particular Sunday the brigade required two loads of H.E.'s, four loads of H.E., and two loads of 17-pounder ammunition.

The day's requirement of petrol for the regiment was about 700 gallons, which is about one 3-tonner load. Also half that amount of diesel fuel.'

People are very free with talk of regiments and battalions wiped out, decimated and utterly destroyed. Their worst experience had been a solid half hour of rocket shelling which really made them feel that their number was up.

In order to advance further into the village, we had to turn round the corner of a house to the right, following a lane which, the infantry warned us, exposed us to Spandau fire.[31]

We now started running through the enemy-held part of the village as I had read the map upside down. Not so much as a single shot was fired at us, although a few hours later a full-scale attack had to be mounted to clear the Germans out of exactly the same area. Perhaps the small groups of enemy scattered about the village thought there was something fishy in this apparently pointless excursion by a solitary Sherman.

The situation in the village was very confused. There was no saying who was behind and who was in front. Everything was very quiet. There wasn't a shell to be seen.

Coming up a narrow strip of road we came on a small detachment of English infantry with an anti-tank gun. How they got there and what they were doing there was not particularly obvious. The sight of them was extraordinarily heartening. It made our apprehensive alertness seem rather stupid.

But after all it wasn't so stupid. The infantry men pointed out, through a gap in a hedge, a German Tiger tank engaged in towing a fellow Tiger which had been knocked out.

The infantry had been trying unsuccessfully to manoeuvre their anti-tank gun into position from which they could get a shot at it. By some fortunate miracle the Tiger's guns were traversed so that they pointed in the opposite direction. We backed our tank a few yards down the hedge to a point there so that the Tigers were sideways on to us. She was a sitting target. We fired a shot and seemed to hit it in the suspension. We hastily fired another and definitely hit it.

With the felicitations of the infantry in our ears, we started off up the road at considerable speed. We travelled as far as the end of the village, then turned back across and came back by the other road.

Eventually we found 'C' Squadron and attached ourselves to them. We formed up without any particular attempt at concealment on the ground in front of the village. The infantry started working their way up between us. It was raining hard and generally speaking a filthy night. Even with its hatches down, the tank was not as waterproof as it looked. Besides which the rain made it impossible to see through the periscope, so that it was as well to keep the lid open and take the rain.

Of course the unfortunate infantry had no choice but to take it. They were crawling up through the corn or long grass, and digging in. Placed behind the steel walls of our tank, we all felt terrific sympathy and admiration for them. Inside a tank you can at least carry a certain amount of personal kit. You have something to hide behind, a firm

---

31   Spandau – British name for a particularly lethal type of German machine-gun.

base to operate from, reassuringly formidable equipment. The accommodation may be cramped but you get used to that. At least you don't have to carry everything on your back. At least the tank can put you where you have to go. Compared with the infantry, life in a tank seems an unfairly sybaritic existence.

These emotions were intensified when enemy machine-guns started opening up from the village. Machine-gun bullets simply bounce off a tank. All that happens is a noise like metal rain. But they don't bounce off a human being. The firing went on for a long time. The infantry made their way forward in bounds, without seeming to take any real precautions. They moved with a horrifying slowness. Just as the tracer fire directed against them also moved with horrifying slowness. Tracer really is the most deceptive stuff. It has a hypnotic effect. You watch it gradually being directed more and more in your direction, but it comes in such slow arcs, when fired from any distance, that it hardly seems worthwhile taking cover. Even when at pretty close range it doesn't look to be beyond human power to dodge out of its way at the last minute. But, of course, it would be the last minute and no fooling. On another occasion, not this one, I watched tracer hitting the wall of our tank just in front of where I was sitting, watching through the periscope. I found that this induced a sensation of light-headed relief.

We started up engines at 10.25 p.m. and advanced slowly into the village. There was a great deal of machine-gun and mortar fire coming and going in all directions. Our .50 calibre machine-gun kept firing in its ear-splitting way, but I couldn't traverse my Browning sufficiently in the right direction to join in. They were firing at houses and hedges from which tracer was coming.

We clambered through a hedge, which, like all the local hedges, was built on a bank. The Sherman drove up the bank as if it was going on up into the air, and then overbalanced down the other side. We went across a field, unavoidably squelching over a dead cow, and turned left into a lane, which was already crowded with military traffic. It was getting dark now and it was difficult to see the long line of infantry who had dropped down in the ditches on either side of the road. We stopped at a corner in which stood a crucifix.

The tank ahead of us went over a mine. There was a lightning-white flash which momentarily enveloped the tank with flame. The tank hesitated in its tracks, but then rolled on and went several yards before stopping.

Treading with careful strictness in its tracks, I went up and asked them if they had been in any way disabled by the mine. They said that apart from having been jerked in their seats they had felt nothing and there didn't seem to be anything the matter with the tank.

There was now a considerable traffic jam up the lane, and I walked up to see what was the matter. I met the rather harassed CO of the battalion concerned, who said he had, roughly speaking, lost his battalion.

'It's impossible country to fight in,' he said, 'they march up, they lie down, and you've lost them.' As if in illustration of his complaint, a section came up the lane, got into the ditch, and were lost to sight. Indeed, in this country of high lanes and many hedges, corn fields and ill-defined front lines, it was almost impossibly difficult to maintain coherent formations. Especially when, most of the time, even the officers have precious little idea what is going on. They know what ought to be going on, but that is a very different matter, even when things are going quite well. It is very easy to say that the Colonel ought to know where his men are, but men can be very elusive.

One of the Colonel's companies was engaged in clearing an objective just ahead of us. A lot of smoke was being put down and gave the wet and murky darkness the effect of a foggy night in London. It was obviously getting too late, i.e. too dark, for the tanks to do anything effective. A lot of tracer was flying about. Someone started mortaring us. And about a hundred yards away two houses were burning.

It must have been about 1 a.m. when the line of tanks turned round and withdrew a little from the village into harbour for the night. I hadn't been able to sleep very satisfactorily the previous night, but I found no difficulty now. With the wireless set for a pillow, and with most of my body suspended in the air, I went straight off into a dreamless sleep.[32]

Life began again about 5 a.m. Our tank was behind a hedge, looking across at the north-east corner of the village. Along the hedges of the field in which we had slept the night were the other tanks of the Squadron and some carriers belonging to the Brigade motor battalion.

There were also infantry dug in along the hedges.

---

32 Anthony gave two summaries of the Fontenay battle. The first was in his unpublished article beginning 'I was only in one real battle'. Here he wrote: 'The battle went on all day; hard and shapeless and difficult to describe. The Germans didn't go willingly, they kept coming back, but they were gradually forced back all the time. On a newspaper map set in the official communiqués which I saw subsequently, the advance looked pretty quick and coherent. It didn't seem quite so easy at the time.'

In the *WAR* article on Fontenay ('Tiger, Tiger, Burning Bright') he gave a much more official-sounding version. 'Summarising the day: in the original dawn attack the enemy smoke had given rise to a lot of stragglers and confusion among the assaulting infantry. At one time there were only about sixty men taking any organised part in attacking the village. By the end of the afternoon there had been about 300 holding a tight perimeter around the crucifix in the north end of the village, with the right-hand Infantry Brigade fairly well on in the Caude Rue part of the village.

The plan was that as soon as Fontenay had been cleared, another battalion, supported by the squadron to which we had been transferred, would go right through Fontenay and capture the crossroads about 500 yards short of Rauray. But the original assaulting battalion couldn't quite clear the village, so at 9 p.m. the other battalion was put in to attack through them. They got through quite easily, through the orchard on to the Fontenay-Juvigny road. They met nothing but odd snipers and machine-gun fire, and sent through their success signal at 9.45 p.m. They just missed a lot of Germans who were getting away in trucks.

This was the process which we had been supporting, and which could be said to complete the taking of Fontenay.'

For breakfast we had tinned pork stew. Although we hadn't had a meal for some time I found it a little bit sickly at that time of day. I ate most of the pork, but I couldn't take much interest in the vegetables. The thing one really wanted was a cup of tea. When we had finished we gave a cup to the unfortunate infantry who, we had become suddenly aware, were enviously watching our picnic party.

We went into the village again.

'D'y'see what we went over then?' said Cherry.

'Yes, here's another one,' said Cook. We had run over a couple of dead bodies.

Three prisoners came down the road with their hands up and two escorts. The prisoners were young, beardless and very weary. Their pink lips were illuminated against the dust and grime which marked their faces.

We were now in a country road with buildings on each side of us. The open country started about 200 yards up the road. The infantry were forming up. I got out to ask the infantry CO what was going on. He was standing by a low stone wall talking to the artillery OP officer. Apparently there was only one objective left in the village, and it was now being attacked. At this point the conference was interrupted by mortar fire. It was right on us. We all ducked against the wall.

'I reckon they are the people at the farm and I can't get on to the FOO,' said the artillery officer.[33] There were many more explosions about our heads. 'That's the boy, that's the bugger,' said the artillery officer.

'He's getting conscious of us,' said the Colonel.

A white rabbit rushed round the corner and hared off up the road. It looked like the same one we saw yesterday. I wonder if it got any sleep.

All this time the voices on the air were continuing, they never seemed to stop. They seemed to be tireless. Nothing puts them out, nothing unduly elates them. Through all the coming and going, the disasters and the successes, their monotone continues unchanged. Sometimes they unbend to say 'Well done' to someone who had done wonderfully. But sudden reverse or the probability of death normally causes no modulation.

One of the voices was now saying: 'We must all realise that our friends are forming up along the track eastwards. I wonder if your boys could move forward south of the orchard and engage the Tiger in our friends' report. The Tiger is reported at 873660.'

This kind of unceasing dialogue has a fascination of its own from the fact that you never know what will turn up next. But even the tank crews find after a few days of it that the earphones are boring into their heads and that the onset of insanity cannot be long delayed.

The white rabbit continued to run about. We followed some other tanks a little way up the road, but then came under heavy mortar fire again and reversed back down the road into a bit of shelter.

33 FOO – Forward Observation Officer.

We stood at a crossroad and watched the infantry forming up. They crossed the road in a nervous crouching run, carrying spades, rifles, mortars or Brens, and looking oddly unorganised. Section by section they crouched into the ditch, then turned through the hedge to a small field, advanced across the 80 yards or so of grass, and then cautiously made their way along the wall of a shell-battered building. A tank interrupted the flow and went across the road. Another infantry section ran across into the ditch. They looked so young and so unfairly weighted with worry.

We had temporarily attached ourselves to the artillery Major, whose tank was dodging about the road, just ahead of us, with a certain degree of uncertainty.

'I wonder if that Major in front knows what he is doing,' said Cook.

'I think so, he is doing all the talking on the air,' said someone.

'That means everything does it?' said Cherry cynically.

The infantry started creeping further along the ditch. A tall infantry major carrying a rifle stopped to talk to the artillery tank in front. A 17-pounder tank passed across the crossroads immediately in front of us and was waved to by the artillery Major. Half a tree fell down rather mysteriously in our immediate neighbourhood. A sniper's bullet spat against the wall nearby. We moved slowly up the road towards the beginning of an avenue of trees.

Six tanks had moved up in front of us. Arrived under the avenue, we all turned to the right and backed into a ditch. Immediately in front of us there was a corn field about 500 yards wide, at the other side of which there was a wood held by the enemy. Our job was to support the infantry taking this wood, from which machine-gun fire now started coming. Sitting there in the tank one didn't half feel a target. Enemy machine-gun fire, or enemy fire of any kind, always seems so much more vehemently determined than the fire put down by your own side. The artillery Major announced over the air that the machine-gun east of the orchard from which most of the fire was coming was going to be dealt with. Our own tank started firing into the hedges to our right. The infantry started putting up a smoke screen, and we edged forward across the road into the ditch on the opposite side.

On the way we passed a haystack which was on fire and burning steadily with a lot of flame and smoke. As a voice announced that one of our tanks had been knocked out, three tanks ahead of us turned off into the corn field and swung across it in support of the infantry, whose heads kept bobbing up in the corn.

'Can you see the infantry crawling across the field?' said Cherry.

'Must be bloody awful in that wet grass,' said Cook.

Six German aircraft came over us at fifty feet.

'I should hate to upset them,' said Cook.

'I don't think they like us much,' said Hogg.

'Corporal Cook, would you mind very much if I had a nap?' said Cherry, and proceeded to do so. The degree of detachment which men achieve in the sight of other men going into action is extraordinary. Here a few yards ahead of us, a company of men were going through machine-gun fire to storm a copse on the other side of the field, and this man was not interested enough to keep awake and watch it. On another similar occasion I had seen him reading a book by Sidney —.[34] Astonishing really when you come to think of it, for after all you can't have a much more fundamental show than a company of infantry going into the attack a few yards away. The idea that Mr — is more engrossing is a little on the whimsical side.

The copse at the other side of the field was getting more and more smoke-infested. The three Shermans were advancing towards it with about 50 yards' gap in between them. It was more difficult to follow the progress of the infantry whom they were supporting. Presently the Sherman on the right was hit, and started to burn. We heard on the air that one of the crew had been badly burned. But the others had apparently got away all right. At first there was simply a thick column of smoke, but then the ammunition started blowing up.

The Tigers which had knocked out the Sherman now turned their attention to us. There was a terrific explosion immediately overhead, knocking my head against the hull. We withdrew some 5 yards into the alleged shelter of a tree. Over in the copse two giant torches of black smoke and flame were burning about 8 yards apart. The Tigers were reported to be in the next field and they were now firing at us hard. We moved back into the road and went back along it.

It seemed appallingly callous to leave the infantry crouching there among the corn, pinned down by mortar and machine-gun fire, threatened by Tigers, and anyway soaked by rain. But, of course, in fact they weren't being left. It was impossible for the Shermans to tackle the Tigers by sitting and waiting for them. It was necessary to approach them from the flank. By a fortunate dispensation of providence we were not sent to do this. We moved back to a small orchard, following the artillery Major. We passed a man wounded in the neck, he was being helped along by two stretcher bearers and seemed to be walking quite casually but every few steps he stumbled and winced.

We had been in the orchard before going up the road to watch the attack. It hadn't changed much, except that the house on the corner was now on fire. It was now 11 a.m. Six more German aircraft flew over the orchard and Cook fired a few rounds at them. 'The trigger tank, that's what we are,' he said.

Up the other end of the orchard there were infantry dug in on three sides along the hedges in the ditches. As always, it was difficult at first to see what relation the people dug in here were to the infantry we had just watched advancing across the corn field. They were in fact the company on the right flank and their advance had been temporarily delayed by the same enemy fire which had destroyed the right-hand Sherman. The left-hand company had gone into the copse but were pinned down there. They were reporting heavy casualties and the air was busy with the reports of the activities of the Tiger tanks.

---

34   Anthony left a blank here for the author's name to be filled in later.

At 11.15 a.m., rather hesitatingly, the sun came out. The enemy were counter-attack-ing with Tigers and Panthers. It was also said that he had captured some Shermans and was using them. The infantry Company Commander at the other end of the orchard told me that one of his patrols had killed twenty-two Germans and taken four prisoners, another had killed eight.

For a while the orchard was fairly peaceful. I ate some biscuits and jam. But at 12.15 p.m. the peace was disturbed by terrific banging from SP guns, which were gun-ning for us in the orchard. For some little time it seemed that the end of the world had come but then it stopped.

At 12.50 p.m. Cook called me up to see a Tiger tank. There was a little square yellow box of turret showing just to the right of a pylon. Evidently it was firing the other way, presumably at 'C' Company of the infantry battalion which we had watched advancing across the field and which was now stuck in the copse. The infantry Company Commander was superintending the proceedings. An anti-tank sergeant was brought up to see what he could do with the target. He was a whiskered young man with a shaven rivulet down the centre of his face. He said he thought he could hit it. Then at this point someone remembered that we had a 17-pounder down at the other end of the orchard. A stray sergeant-major went off to bring it up quietly. We all moved very quietly. A little group of us stood intensely watching what we could see of the turret of the Tiger. It was about 300 yards away and mostly hidden behind the hedge. Meantime, Corporal Cook, the personality kid, jock-eyed our tank up into position alongside the newly and quietly arrived 17-pounder Sherman. The rest of the crew regarded this as a piece of gratuitous exposure to the Tiger's expected reply. It was all very well to do what you were told but don't go asking for it, was their point of view.

'It's either him or us now,' said Cook with his usual gift for the dramatic.

We moved up the hedge, and then backed a bit, until Jack the gunner was satisfied with the view. The infantry withdrew a few yards to watch the impending duel.

'Traverse the gun a bit,' said Cook. 'Can you see the target?'

'Right on that bushy tree isn't it?' said Jack with what seemed deplorable vagueness.

'Let's see through your periscope,' said Cook. He leant over in front of the gunner. 'No, that's not it. Driver, come back. No, go forward a bit.'

'Wouldn't like me to go sideways?' enquired Cherry.

'Now can you see it?' said Cook.

'There's a twig in the middle but I can see it all right,' said Jack.

'Wait till that 17-pounder fires first. What do you make the range?'

'Five hundred, no, four hundred,' said Jack.

'Four hundred from here,' said Hogg.

'Get ready to put another H.E. in as soon as it's fired, gunner,' said Cook.

It was now 1.30 p.m.

'Fire when you're ready,' said Cook. By this time I was quite used to the gun's reper-cussions in the tank. The gun fired.

'That went right,' said Cook. 'A wee bit left, Jack.' It fired again: 'It's going all right I think – bring it left and fire.'

'Plus wasn't it?' said Jack.

'Right and plus,' said Cook.

'Long way plus,' said Hogg.

'Bring it down,' said Cook.

Into the midst of all this excitement came another voice over the air. It mentioned a man by name and said 'Please inform him that he takes over the duties of Post Corporal as from now. He is to collect what mail he can and go back down the line.'

Hard on that whimsically refreshing change of subject came an announcement from someone called Easy Four, who said that he had knocked out two tanks and was fresh out of ammunition.

'Go to the north-east corner of the wood where you will find a vehicle similar to yours. Replenish and get back. You're doing very well. Being very useful,' said another voice.

Meanwhile our own duel, after starting so promisingly, had come to a dreary anti-cli-max, as the decision ripened that we had been attacking an already dead German tank. Otherwise why didn't it do something? Even if only go away. Presently Corporal Cook made a reconnaissance down the hedge and reported that it was indeed a knocked-out tank. So we had a cup of tea instead.

All this time the company whose attack we had watched in the morning was pinned down in the wood. Presently we joined a column of tanks which was going up to relieve them. This process took up most of the afternoon. It hadn't got properly started when the time came for our particular tank to return to Brigade Headquarters.

'Down by the Beaches Where the Minefields Lay ...'

Down by the beaches where the minefields lay, the most likely disaster for a tank was to have its trap knocked off by mines. When they advance further inland past the coastal belt of minefields, shells and mortars begin to cause the damage. The mortars were get-ting a lot of effective hits on tank turrets.

Of course a tank is built to stand a good deal of punishment. Small arms fire and indi-rect shell-hits simply bounce off after making some sort of dent in the armour.

But one direct hit may do the miserable trick. One armour-piercing shell may smash up the steering, the gear box, and the instrument-panel, by ricocheting off one onto the other. If it hits the gear box, the tank will almost certainly 'brew up' (tank man's term for explosively burning out); most tanks do brew up when knocked out.

During the last few days there had been a lot of mortar hits on tank turrets. The mortality amongst tank commanders had been very high, because of the necessity to expose themselves in order to find out what was going on – a particularly dangerous necessity in this closely wooded and sniper-infested country.

Each squadron of tanks has its armoured recovery vehicle, which is simply a Sherman tank without a turret, fitted with apparatus for towing back damaged tanks or for repairing them on the spot. The ARV is armed with a .30 inch Browning machine-gun, two Brens and two Stens.[35] It carries oxy-acetylene welding and cutting plant, a jib for lifting tank engines etc., a 100-foot wire tow rope, five 20-foot hawsers, two towing triangles, lifting jacks, and sets of wooden planks for crossing ditches.

The crew of each ARV consists of a sergeant and a craftsman who belonged to the REME and two drivers who belong to the Tank Regiment itself.

Say that a Sherman tank weighs 30 tons – i. e. you need to exert a dead pull of 30 tons to get it moving. The ARVs are often used in pairs. By an arrangement of wires and snatch blocks they can together exert a 5 to 1 pull. So taking it that one ARV will pull 15 tons, which is not wildly inaccurate, two of them can pull 50 tons, in other words they can pull a Sherman out of some extraordinary situation.

One ARV can tow, from a firm base, any tank. But tanks get stuck in all kinds of positions and in all kinds of ground.

The Technical Adjutant of the regiment was in charge of recovery. His name was Captain Douglas Collins, and before the war he had been an agricultural auctioneer in the West Country. He was a vivacious individual with a local reputation for taking all sorts of chances in recovering tanks.

His sub-unit was camped in a field some little way behind the front line. Their job was to keep the tanks in action. There were eleven fitters per squadron whose job was to do all repairs which weren't serious enough to have to be sent back to the workshop.

On this particular evening there were five Sherman tanks to be reconnoitred and if possible recovered. It was reported that in one of the tanks there were three bodies.

'Want us to dig three graves then, sir?' asked the Technical Sergeant-Major.

'Yes and get some disinfectant, some of them are very bad. They'll fall to pieces when you get them out.'

Collins and I were travelling in his scout car. He told the ARV crews where to meet us. 'By the monument on the corner where they are digging holes to bury the chaps.'

We set off along the lane and presently came to the open field immediately behind the front line. A message came through on the radio that a tank had broken down. We left the road and travelled across an extremely bumpy cornfield, trying unsuccessfully to find where it was. We passed through a field in which tanks withdrawn from the

---

35 ARV – Armoured Recovery Vehicle.

battle were resting, and approached Fontenay from the north-west. On another road we could see our three ARVs on their way to the rendezvous.

A message came over the air from one of the squadron commanders telling Collins to collect his ARVs and put them under cover. The enemy were approaching in an unexpected manner. The ARVs were making for trouble. Collins tried to warn his ARVs over the air but it was too full of battle conversation. We set off at high speed, but by the time we got to them the alarm seemed to have passed over.

We came on one of the tanks which we were supposed to recover. It was completely burnt out and unrecoverable. It had been hit by an 88 through the engine. We left it and made for the next.

This was the tank in which the bodies had been reported. There were two shell holes in the hull. Inside the turret there was a pathetic shambles of – and roasted human flesh.[36] It was a filthy sight. Standing next to it was another tank with its trap shot away.

'Come up in the morning if the place is clear and put on new suspension and trap,' said Collins. 'Hurry up Sergeant Parker.'

Collins and I made our way down the hedge towards another Sherman. A passer-by explained to us what had happened. This Sherman had been knocked out by a German Tiger. Whereupon two other Shermans had knocked out the Tiger, but had themselves been knocked out by a second Tiger which they had not seen in time as it crept up the hedge towards them.

We went forward down another hedge towards one of the Shermans. A man called out to us to hurry up.

'What's the matter? asked Collins.

'There's no one in front of us, buddy,' said the man.

'How far's the enemy?' asked Collins.

'About 800 yards,' said the man.

In illustration of his point came a series of discouraging explosions just over the hedge. We duly retired.

There were two 17-pounders burnt out. In one of them there was an identifiable body but it was very badly burnt and fell in pieces every time they tried to get him out. They left him for the burial party which would come up later.

'Get the Padre and the disinfectant when we get back,' said Collins.

About 40 yards away there was a Sherman caught in an American long-topped shell-hole. The tank was all right but it would need two ARVs and a wedge to get it out.

We started driving back. All this time Collins was controlling the driver's every movement, 'Hold it, Peake. Advance slowly, left,' etc.

It was reported over the air that strong pockets of enemy infantry and tanks were infiltrating on the right flank. German patrols were coming through where we had

---

36 'Pathetic shambles of —', there is a blank in the typescript here.

just been. We came up to some light reconnaissance tanks sitting in hull-down positions overlooking the valley from which the enemy was supposed to be advancing. Above the trees we could see the dust of the enemy tanks and a minute later this was reported on the radio. We passed some assault sappers preparing a demolition in the road. An assault RE would lie in the ditch and press the button as a German tank went over it.

An American two-star general and a brigadier general went by in a scout car, followed by a jeep marked C of E – a chaplain was burying the dead.

Collins complained that there was no definite thrusts. There was mortar fire on the left so we turned right up a lane and advanced into the wedge which our forces had driven into enemy territory. The situation was a bit obscure on the left.

We came on a tank with engine trouble and Collins directed it to be shackled up with two ropes and towed straight back. It was one of the new 17-pounder tanks and must get back into the battle as quickly as possible.

We went up into a field where our tanks were in defensive position behind the hedges with a screen of anti-tank guns. The neighbourhood was being shelled. 'Glad you joined?' the driver asked me. He was reading a detective story.

'When does death laugh at the best laid plans of mice and men? And what happened to a homicide case when a tough detective lieutenant goes all-out soft on a blonde and gorgeous torch singer – whose husband lies cooling in the morgue?'

The story started with dash: '"Listen mug," a voice said coldly. "Lay off the dame, see? She didn't do it. I did."'

I read this while Peake went to look at a dead German officer whose – and swollen body was crumpled in the bottom of a weapon pit.[37] This unpleasant sight emphasised the relations between a weapon pit and a grave.

Some troops were disposing of a sniper, one of several who had been operating in the branches of some tall trees. I stood beneath one tree and took several minutes to identify the sniper's body, so well had he camouflaged himself. I could just see a boot hanging down and the outline of the helmet. There were four of these on various trees in this field. And it required a considerable expenditure of time and ammunition to locate and kill them. They sold themselves dearly. They did not give up when they were wounded. They shot it out to the end.

We learned that where the man had warned us not to waste time there had been four German Tigers lying in the orchard all afternoon. But like the snipers, these Tigers did not waste their concealment on unpromising targets.

Collins stopped a passing ambulance to speak to the Regimental Padre who was travelling on it. He was a mild young man with spectacles, in the ambulance he had the Second-in-Command of 'A' Squadron who was wounded but not badly and two other wounded men. The other two members of the crew had been killed.

---

37 'A dead German officer whose —', there is a blank in the typescript here.

'A little job for you, Padre, on Point 103 tonight. OK?' said Collins.

We drove on. We passed a shapeless bit of high ground – not even outstandingly high – which had claimed most of an infantry battalion and six tanks to date.

We called on the forward supply echelon commander to tell him what was going on and to give him some orders. It was now 9.30 p.m. The forward supply echelon commander would come up forward with a light ammunition vehicle (a captured German one) with enough ammunition to help out a squadron in need. About a mile behind would be waiting a complete load of petrol, diesel oil, ammunition, food, and water.

We drove back to the field in which we had started out. Collins ordered a rum issue for the men who had pulled the bodies out of the tank and buried them. His batman had been particularly upset. It was the first time he had seen anyone he knew in that peculiarly horrible state of death. The boy was sitting apart from the others, and had been crying a little. It was the first time he had seen any of his friends dead. For that matter everyone felt pretty sick.

'All because some fucker wants to make some fucking money, that's all it is, fucking greed of money,' said the Sergeant-Major.

'Ask the REME to get the tank with all the blood on it out of the way. Doesn't do any good to have people seeing them,' said Collins.

'I'll have to get on to the hygiene people for the disinfectant,' said the Sergeant-Major.

'Yes, do that,' said Collins.

'The REME from the Lancers came to natter because we were taking the suspension off one of his tanks. I told him if he can do anything with that tank again, he's a fucking good man,' said the Sergeant-Major.

'You're sure that tank is definitely no good again?' said Collins.

'I told him if he can do anything with that tank he's a good man,' repeated the Sergeant-Major.

'Well, don't take any notice of him,' said Collins.

'I didn't,' said the Sergeant-Major.

During the evening we had wreckaged six knocked-out tanks, of which one had been recovered, one would be recovered tomorrow, and four had been written off as not worth recovering though they would be collected by REME in about a month's time. Their location had been noted and reported to Brigade. The War Office would be notified that the Brigade was so many tanks short of their establishment, and would duly send replacement tanks.

All the crews who had been saved would walk back to the forward echelon. They would be sent back to the relative comfort and security of the Brigade rear echelon, fed, clothed, and then sent to the forward delivery squadron to become the crew of a new tank. The time which normally elapsed between being shot out of one tank and starting again in a new one was twenty-four to seventy-two hours.

The recovered tanks are worked on by teams of fitters who have the mechanical experts' devotion to their job. On this particular day one team of four, which had been out tonight, had worked during the day, worked all the previous night, all yesterday, and all the night before that. They do some prolonged spells, e.g. seventy-two hours' continuous work with only two hours sleep. But of course, except in exceptional circumstances, it doesn't really pay. They begin to imagine that things are wrong which aren't really wrong.

During this particular day the achievements were as follows.

They had recovered a Sherman which Collins had originally wreckaged three days before but which had until today been unapproachable because of the enemy. They had mended one of the tank's tracks on site. The radiator had been holed and the carburettor shot away which meant lifting the engine and it was a workshop job. Therefore, it was handed to the ARV which would evacuate the tank to the Brigade workshop.

A 17-pounder Sherman had been towed in with engine trouble. The petrol filters were choked with dust, and the ignition was faulty. This was fixed in two hours by one fitter working with the tank's crew, and was sent back to the battle.

Another Sherman had been brought back, suffering from engines which wouldn't start and wireless which wouldn't work. New batteries and new automatic voltage control were fitted, a job which took two men five hours.

The Sherman in which the dead men had been found had to be disinfected and then evacuated to Brigade workshop to be fitted with a new turret. It would be gone for about a week.

Another Sherman was suffering from sluggish pulling and wouldn't drive out of second gear. Presumably it had injector trouble. It was being handed to the ARV for vetting, This would be done by a Staff Sergeant, REME, and would possibly be a twenty-four-hour job. Finally there was a Sherman with its suspension and one track blown off. The necessary part had been cannibalised from an unrepairable tank, ready for fitting in the morning. Then it would be refitted and sent back to its squadron. This would be probably a fifteen-hour job putting the suspension on and would employ the ARV crew of five plus three fitters.

Towards midnight, Collins took a small convoy up to the regiment which was harboured just to the rear of the front line. There was some work for the fitters to do with the forward squadron which was covering the infantry over night. But the Colonel wouldn't allow them to go up because of the noise they would make, so at about 1 a.m. we returned. Collins was going to be up again at 5 a.m.

'An Operation was Performed'

This article was in early draft and there are a number of blanks in the text, either because Anthony needed to remember, or to look up, a word, or because his typist could not understand his dictation.

★★★

SS Panzer Grenadier Thielemann was eighteen years old. He had been wounded three days before, probably by H.E. shrapnel. None of us spoke German so we couldn't ask him. If he had been English, the Sergeant said he would have guessed it to be due to mortar fire, the chances of any British casualty being due to German mortar fire were always high. But the card round Thielemann's neck was not very definite. He had been wounded three days before and was now awaiting evacuation to Great Britain. His wound was in the buttocks and it was getting gas gangrene, so he had to be operated on before leaving for England.[38]

He had had three medications outside in the tented resuscitation ward. He had had an injection of morphia to allay his anxiety and another one of atropine to stop his secretion. If you give ether without atropine, the patient may be nearly drowned by bubbling secretions in his lungs. The other patients did not take much notice of Panzer Grenadier Thielemann. Mostly they were not in very good shape themselves. Otherwise they would not have been in the resuscitation ward. They weren't necessarily on the danger list, but they weren't at their best.

About an hour later Thielemann was taken on a stretcher through the door of the stone barn (the tented resuscitation ward was pitched before this as an outhouse). The barn was high, wide, and musty. There were two operating tables. And a great deal of surgical apparatus partly arranged on the basket lids of the medical carriers. About a dozen pairs of surgical rubber gloves were hanging out to dry on a line rigged up across the barn.

The surgeon, a slim pale Major of 35, put on a rubber apron, a white hat and a surgical overall, washed himself very thoroughly and put on rubber gloves. Captain Thlm, the anaesthetist, made an incision in Thielemann's left arm which was bound down onto a splint.[39] He started injecting pentothal. He injected fairly quickly, paused, and then gave some more. Thielemann went out in under a minute. The anaesthetist kneaded the flesh on his face, opened the unconscious eyes, and said, 'He's ready'.

Thielemann was lying on his side. He was wearing his army shirt, and was covered in army blankets except his leg.

---

38   Gas gangrene – a very dangerous necrotic infection which destroys muscle tissue.

39   Captain Thlm – so his name appears in the typescript which seems to be an error but there is no way of checking.

The wound in his buttock was not a very impressive affair. Major Clark, the surgeon, opened it up swiftly. He probed inside the wound with his hand and there was a squelch of blood. He started cleaning out the wound with strips of lint. There was a good deal of evil-smelling diseased flesh, discoloured by the gas gangrene.

Once he had cleaned this out the wound seemed a clean and not a very frightening affair. This unfortunate young German had had a big slice cut out of his right buttock, but it didn't look at all irreparable. The idea that it might be responsible for his death seemed rather far-fetched. The whole thing seemed to be well under human control.

But unfortunately Clark, in the course of his probing, discovered that the hole went into Thielemann's bowel thus it was, therefore, necessary to take a piece of bowel out and drain it.[40] The operation thereupon became a serious one, and the prospect of Thielemann's survival was greatly reduced.

The Major sprinkled penicillin powder in the wound.[41] Sprinkling penicillin powder is a strangely unsurgical looking process. It doesn't seem probable that it could possibly have life-saving effects. It was the least scientific process of all, less impressive than the nurse sprinkling the baby with talcum powder.

The sheet below Thielemann was now swamped with blood. The Major plugged the wound with lint, and covered it with a big wad of cotton wool, held in place with sticking plaster. He explained to me that to try to prevent the whole body being infected with the gas gangrene he would have to drain Thielemann's bowel above the site of the injury, and make an incision in the intestine through which the motions would come instead of going down into the affected part, which would not have a chance to repair itself. He changed his gloves and the operating overall. Apart from the anaesthetist he had two RAMC operating room assistants, a Corporal Ashwell and Private Sherry. There was also a French nurse called Mademoiselle Madeleine José, who had volunteered her services on D-Day and had been working with the unit ever since.

The anaesthetist put the syringe in place, still injected into Thielemann's arm, strapping it to the arm with sticking plaster before beginning to inject blood through it. The blood came from a bottle suspended over Thielemann's head on a metal stand, and connected to the syringe by a rubber tube in the course of which there were transparent sections through which the blood could be seen dripping.

'He's coming round. Get the other needle and do something about that,' said one of the operating room assistants. Some more pentothal was injected.

Thielemann's feet were filthy. His face was fevered-looking with many days' growth of rather precociously vigorous beard. He was not a bad-looking boy, and it was easy to imagine him not being unpleasantly aggressive in battle. Corporal Ashwell and Private

---

40 Anthony or his typist puts a question mark after 'Thielemann's bowel'.

41 Penicillin was the new wonder drug, and had only become widely available for the treatment of injured Allied servicemen in 1943–44.

Sherry, helped by the anaesthetist and the French nurse, now moved him over onto his back. He moaned, though not particularly in pain. It was the kind of moan associated with the expression of emotional rather than physical pain.

They pulled the blanket away and lifted his shirt to disclose his stomach. It looked so healthy and normal that it seemed a sin and shame to cut it open. Mademoiselle started shaving the hair off his stomach. Someone had given her a safety razor but she couldn't get on with it at all and presently substituted a cut-throat.

The Major explained to me that he was going to cut into Thielemann's abdomen, bring out a loop of the large bowel and make a hole in it through which the motions could pass. This would give the wound in the buttocks a chance to heal up, though the process would take several weeks. A little crop-headed French priest with an orien-tally – face appeared in the doorway of the barn and stood watching us benevolently.[42] The Major said that on D-Day the Curé had arrived with a bottle of excellent cham-pagne which a patient just operated on joined them in drinking.

The anaesthetist started injecting more pentothal, while the operating room assistant rubbed Thielemann's belly with slavime, which is an antiseptic.[43]

The operation area was now framed with white sheets clipped to each other and to the blankets. Thielemann who had been rather restless was now quiet.

'Let me know just before you're ready to cut,' said the anaesthetist.

'We're ready to go now,' said the surgeon.

'When you say,' said the anaesthetist.

The Major's knives had very small blades, like razor blades with the corners rounded off. As he cut the skin of the stomach, Thielemann writhed. The anaesthetist opened the patient's eyes, but they showed no signs of consciousness.

'Scissors please.' The Major started fixing on the scissor-like artery clip which shut off the bleeding point. He pointed out to me the layers of the human body; the skin, then a layer of fat, then the layers of muscle. 'That's the —. This fellow's going to have a very sticky passage.'[44]

He now had six artery clips fixed to various bleeding points. He probed in the wound with his fingers, put a swab in and when it came out clean said 'OK, no contamina-tion,' i.e. the gangrene had not spread. He pulled a half loop of the bowel out of the wound and supported it by threading a glass rod underneath it. Then he began to stitch the stomach lining to the bowel to make a watertight junction. He stitched with a curved needle. Methodically and undramatically. When you come down to it surgery is a remarkably simple business. In appearance.

---

42 'With an orientally —', there is a blank in the typescript here.

43 'Slavime' may be a misspelling or mistyping; possibly Anthony meant one of the sulphonamide group of antiseptic drugs.

44 'That's the —', there is a blank in the typescript here.

Along one side of the wall there was a bench on which the anaesthetist had hung up his equipment. There was a hole in the wall just above it, in which a rat presently appeared and watched us.

'Hey, see that rat,' said the anaesthetist, hearing which the rat prudently withdrew.

'Now you mention it, there are mighty few rats,' said the surgeon continuing to stitch Thielemann's stomach lining.

'Yes, I should have thought this being an old barn would have been full of rats,' said the anaesthetist.

The Major pointed out to me that he was sewing the stomach lining onto little bits of fat attached to the intestines. In twelve hours nature would make good the junction.

Thielemann started giving a series of groans. The anaesthetist was holding his jaw up so that the tongue would be held forward and not interfere with his breathing. The crimson blood continued to drop from a bottle through the two little – into Thielemann's arm.[45]

Another doctor came into the barn and took a professional look at the case.

'Got a hole in his rectum,' said the Major.

'Ugh,' nodded the doctor.

'Suggested it didn't it?' said the Major.

'Blood in the stools did,' agreed the newcomer. 'Would you like to share a room with me in the chateau?' he said to the anaesthetist, who said that he would like this very much.

Private Sherry held the syringe in place against Thielemann's arm while the anaesthetist tested his blood pressure with one of those concoctions they strap round your arm and which are called, he told me, sphygmomanometers.

'The scissors, Mademoiselle, please,' said the surgeon to the French nurse.

'Oui,' said the French nurse.

'Blood pressure's OK, 120,' said the anaesthetist. The surgeon fitted a small kidney-shaped contraption of rubber tube and glass tube in such a way that it helped to keep a small semicircle of bowel out of the main cavity of the stomach. They started dressing the artificial wound with a layer of gauze impregnated with Vaseline, then they put more gauze on top, and finally bandages that passed under the body and secured with a safety pin.

It all seemed so natural, so straight-forward, and so matter-of-fact that I was surprised when the Major told me that Thielemann was in a very poor condition and his prospects of survival were not good. Things were always very difficult once gas gangrene set in. It wasn't so bad in the case of a foot or leg. If you cut them off early enough there was nothing to worry about but you couldn't do that when part of the trunk was involved. Of course the penicillin was capable of wonders in combating gas gangrene.

---

45 'Through the two little —', there is a blank in the typescript here.

The wound had been powdered with it and he would have injections every few hours for several days, and also an anti-gas gangrene serum on leaving the theatre.

The operation was finished at 1.10 p.m. It was the 114th which Major Clark had performed in some three weeks. His next case was being prepared on the other operating table. It was to clean up and sprinkle sulphonamide paste on a burnt hand. It was a petrol burn caused in lighting a petrol stove. Before going on to it he had to write up his report on Thielemann. He wrote 'wound right buttock involving rectum', and described what he had done to it.

In the meantime the anaesthetist was having some difficulty with Thielemann who was restless. 'Sie still, sie still,' he shouted.[46] Though of course Thielemann was still unconscious. Being battle-tired he would sleep comfortably for at least three or four hours without feeling any pain. When he awoke and if he complained of pain, he would be given morphia.

This Field Surgical Unit consisted of the surgeon, the anaesthetist, the two operating room assistants, three drivers, three nursing orderlies, and a batman or general duties orderly. They were carried in two 3-tonners and one Humber seven-seater. They could pack up in two hours and on arrival somewhere else set up in two hours. Their equipment included a generating set to give them their own electric light and about sixty pairs of rubber gloves.

The new patient was not enjoying himself much.

'Oh, oh, my Christ.'

'All right Jimmy, it's all finished,' said the orderly soothingly.

'Please Christ. Wait till I'm well away for gosh sake. Put the bloody stuff in.'

'All right, Jimmy, you won't know anything about this afterwards,' said the nursing orderly.

Up at the other end of the barn the German was moving a bit. His face wore an expression of strained distaste. He was whimpering a bit. They were bandaging the injection hole in the vein of his left arm, and covering him with blankets. Then they carried him back into the tented resuscitation ward outside. Many men were wounded in the morning, operated on two hours later, and despatched to England in the evening. Thielemann couldn't be moved for at least ten days.

---

46 'Sie still' – 'Shut up' in German.

WITH 1ST PARACHUTE BRIGADE

Anthony returned from Normandy thoroughly determined to get back to front-line reporting as soon as possible. On his return to the *WAR* office, he told Watkins that his next excursion would be a parachute drop with 1st Airborne Division, wherever and whenever that would be. There is no information on how he had made contact with someone influential enough within the Division to give him permission for this attachment, which began two months later.

The unit to which Anthony was attached was 1 Parachute Brigade HQ. The command centre of 1 Parachute Brigade, Brigade HQ coordinated the activities of its 1st, 2nd and 3rd Battalions, commanded respectively by Lieutenant-Colonels Dobie, Frost and Fitch. It was the same John Frost who had been on the Bruneval raid which Anthony had covered in *WAR* in November 1942, which had quickened his interest in the airborne forces.

Anthony arrived at Brigade HQ, based near Grantham, on Friday evening, 1 September, He was expecting to join them in a drop, code-named LINNET, on Belgium, near Brussels, on the Sunday. However, Allied victories were now coming thick and fast. Paris had been liberated on 25 August, and such was the speed of the Allied advance that LINNET would swiftly be cancelled with Brussels being liberated by the ground forces on 3 September.

Uniquely amongst Anthony's work for *WAR*, there survives a part-pencil, part-typescript draft of his time at 1 Parachute Brigade HQ, which he entitled 'Jumping to a Conclusion: Part One'. He began it on the Friday of his arrival, evidently intending to write Part Two once they had landed in Belgium. 'Jumping to a Conclusion' was a typical Anthony play on words, referring to the end of the war which he and the Brigade would reach by parachute jump. Before the end of the month, this little joke would take on a horribly macabre twist. Understandably, Watkins did not use 'Jumping to a Conclusion' as the title of the article which was printed in *WAR* on 14 October. There is a possibility, however, that Anthony himself had changed the title before he left for Arnhem on 17 September: the title which was printed, 'Airborne Worries: Waiting to be Scrubbed', has his characteristic touch.

'Jumping to a Conclusion' included many operational details about LINNET. Once LINNET was cancelled, these became redundant, but Anthony retained much of his initial work because it vividly set the atmosphere at Brigade HQ. Other operations succeeded LINNET over the next few days, and were also cancelled. Eventually, the operation on which Anthony would fly with 1 Parachute Brigade HQ was MARKET GARDEN, the highly ambitious plan to capture key Dutch bridges, including the road bridge at Arnhem.

On Friday 15 September, Anthony met up briefly with Watkins in London and gave him the text of his article. Watkins would later recall:

> Anthony and I had dinner together at the Connaught Hotel on the Friday before the Sunday assault. I don't know how much he knew then of the plans for that operation; he would never have broken security by telling me anything, however much he knew. He hadn't escaped the strain of waiting, although he could conceal most of it. And I had no premonition that he was so close to the moment of actual departure. He was a little distrait, which I could understand. We separated about 9.30 and that was the last I saw of him.[1]

Not having time to make contact with his brother, Anthony scribbled a postcard to Geoffrey which simply read: 'We are jumping to a conclusion.' He knew that Geoffrey would immediately understand the tiny coded message. He also wrote to Robert Graves about a literary matter. Once again he did not say where he was going, but Graves would have drawn the obvious inference from Anthony's closing words:

> I am going away for a few days and hope to see Jenny who seems to be having a marvellous time, which I suppose you have heard about, and wrote to me last from Brussels.[2]

Jenny Nicholson, Graves' daughter and Anthony's girlfriend, had arrived in Brussels with an elite group of war correspondents for the liberation. Jennie was a PR officer in the WAAF, and her article on the liberation of Brussels would be published in *WAR* that November.[3]

The tone of Anthony's article on 1 Parachute Brigade HQ is very cheerful and, in the event, distressingly hubristic. Like just about everyone else at Brigade HQ, in 1st Airborne Division, and Montgomery's 21st Army Group, he expected the operation to be an outstanding success, much on the lines of D-Day. So confident were the authorities that all would go to plan that a complete PR team would accompany the airborne operation when it finally left England.

---

1   Ernest Watkins, 'It is Dangerous to Lean Out', p.248.

2   Anthony Cotterell to Robert Graves, letter, undated but clearly after the liberation of Brussels on 3 September and before 17 September. Robert Graves archive, The Library, St John's College, and St John's College Robert Graves Trust.

3   Jenny Nicholson, 'Fair Women and Brave Men', *WAR*, issue 82, 25 November 1944.

The text of the *WAR* article is full of military acronyms which make it somewhat hard reading seventy years later. For this reason, names had been substituted wherever known. This is especially important because all the men whom Anthony mentions would be key figures at the subsequent battle at Arnhem bridge and its terrible aftermath. Here follows a very brief summary of who these men were and what happened to them at Arnhem.

The Brigadier of 1st Parachute Brigade was Gerald Lathbury, a personal friend and the acknowledged deputy of the Commander of 1st Airborne Division, Major-General Roy Urquhart. Seriously wounded and captured during the battle, Lathbury later escaped back to British lines with the aid of the Dutch resistance.

The Brigade Major was Tony Hibbert. Hibbert took Anthony under his personal care after the battle ended, and they tried to escape together. They were captured and held by the Germans for two days. Hibbert was on the truck at Brummen, and his escape from the truck precipitated the fatal shooting. Hibbert escaped back to British lines in late October with the aid of the Dutch resistance. Once back in England, his account of what had happened at Brummen was the first detailed news that Anthony's family received of what had happened to Anthony.

The following officers were also on the truck at Brummen; none were injured and all spent the rest of the war in German captivity: Bernard Briggs, the Staff Captain; Douglas Mortlock, the Brigade Royal Army Signal Corps Officer; Bill Marquand, the Signals Officer; Cecil Byng-Maddick, the Deputy Assistant Adjutant Quartermaster.

The Medical Officer was David Wright, who with Jimmy Logan, another Medical Officer, established an Advanced Dressing Station in the cellars of HQ at Arnhem bridge. He went into captivity with the wounded.

'Airborne Worries: Waiting to be Scrubbed'

The use of airborne troops to exploit opportunities as they occur is a fine idea, but a little wearing on the nerves.

I reached the Parachute Brigade HQ on Friday evening, the jump being planned for Sunday morning. The Brigade staff was in a state of considerable apprehension; not that the operation would take place, but that it wouldn't. This was the third time they had been alerted since D-Day, and they found each stand-down more progressively discouraging.[4] As Major Hibbert, the Brigade Major, talking on the telephone to someone at Division, said, 'The only thing that gives us slight sickness is every time we turn on the wireless, hearing the news.'

---

4   Anthony was incorrect about the number of stand-downs. In fact it had already reached fourteen.

No doubt about it, the news was depressingly good, the BBC announcers tediously smug, the arrows on the newspaper map moved nearer to Germany almost as you looked at them.

About the operation itself there was not a great deal of evident excitement, no doubt because this was the oldest and most seasoned Parachute Brigade. There was nothing experimental or uncertain in their approach, apart from the inevitable personal uncertainties of anyone approaching an operational jump.

'What are you going to do, hook up when you take off?'[5]

'No, when I pass the coast.'

'I'm going to hook up everyone on the ground.'

'Oh, I don't know. People want to go and be sick or move around.'

The conversation was shot with these technicalities.

I spent the evening reading the operation orders and in having the plan explained by Major Hibbert in the briefing hut. Next day I went ten miles to hear the briefing of B Company of one of the battalions, which I was to join after dropping.

The company had been brought in to the Intelligence Battalion HQ, the oak-panelled drawing-room of a country house. They stood or sat round a large square model of the piece of country involved, and listened to their company commander, a Major with the MC.[6]

'The general form of the operation is to cut off the German retreat,' he began. It would be idle to pretend that this stirring announcement caused any evident flutter. The riveting fascination of the pre-D-Day briefings had flown.[7]

The battle began to unfold itself in anticipation.

'Phase 2 will be to move to the railway station and establish a firm base until we know if there is anyone in the town. If there is, we'll have to deal with them. Number 6 Platoon' (who were leading the line of march) 'will adopt battle formation in taking the station, in case of accidents. Number 4 Platoon will cover the east and south-east approaches to the station, Number 5 Platoon the west and south-west approaches.'

'In Phase 3 the company less one platoon will move to this position here,' and he pointed on the map to a position near the rest of the battalion. 'Number 5 Platoon with two PIATs and a mobile MG will block the eastern approaches to the town.[8] Any questions?'

---

5   The term 'hook up' described the method in which the airborne soldiers used a kind of rigging which would automatically trigger the opening of their parachutes when they jumped from the aircraft in quick succession.

6   Major Douglas Edward Crawley, who had already won the Military Cross and would win a second one at Arnhem.

7   In the original draft, Anthony adds the following information about Crawley's briefing on LINNET: 'He went on to say that the latest available information was that the 21st Army Group had reached Arras, and the Americans were pushing up into Belgium. The enemy were thought to be pretty well non-existent about the dropping area, and to be confined to low-grade troops in the neighbouring towns. But there was always the possibility of colliding with a division in transit, apart of course from the people whom we were supposed to cut off.'

8   'Mobile MG' – probably, in fact, a Medium Machine Gun. The PIAT was a shoulder-fired gun which fired an armour-piercing shell and was at its most effective against lightly armoured vehicles.

'How long are we holding, sir?'

'Depends. If the enemy don't attack us we'll have to go and find them.'

'When does this drop come off, sir?'

'Sunday morning, about nine-thirty.'

'How far to march, sir?'

'From the RV to this position is about five miles. B Company have, unfortunately, got further to go, around the eastern edge of the town.'

'What's the DZ like, sir?'[9]

'Rough.'

Platoon commanders then took over their platoons, some to study air photographs and maps, others to another model which showed the DZ. I followed Lieutenant Levene's platoon.[10]

'As you can see, the DZ is fairly flat, but there are a lot of houses and trees breaking it up ... RV at this place, and get the pronunciations right, in case you have to ask. But you shouldn't need to ask. You can tell it by the church. There are three churches, but ours is the only one with a tower. The others have spires. Now you want to memorise this map. What is this place?' He pointed to one rather absent-looking member of the audience.

'I've forgotten, sir,' said the man, smartly and in a soldierly fashion.

The briefing continued.

Chutes were drawn and fitted after lunch, to the invariable accompaniment of depressing jokes: 'You've got a blanket in there, not a chute,' or 'Looks like it's full of dirty washing.'

Meteorologically, the day had been disastrous. An almost continuous downpour, while, so we heard, there was a fifty-mile-an-hour gale in the Channel. And, by way of lending an extra fillip, it was announced that, owing to rerouteing, an earlier start must be made, and reveille would be at 0300 hours. It was, therefore, in no mood of facile optimism that we retired to bed, soon after the time laid down – 2000 hours.

There is nothing like wet weather and the apparent likelihood of frustration to deflate nervous excitement and to induce that, in some ways, advantageous mood of not caring much what happens – not really expecting anything to happen, either.[11]

Nonetheless, I began to think of tomorrow's jump as an ordeal. Not that I really

---

9   DZ – Dropping Zone.

10   Actually, Lieutenant Hugh Levien. When the battalion finally parachuted into Holland rather than Belgium, Levien's platoon would be ambushed on the way to Arnhem – several would be killed and the remainder taken prisoner. Anthony was not amongst them, either because he had been assigned to another group, or more likely because he had reassigned himself as he often did at D-Day and in Normandy.

11   In the original manuscript, Anthony wrote that whilst he was typing up this last paragraph, Brigadier Gerald Lathbury came into his room and confirmed the rumour that Allied tanks were already at the drop zone. Lathbury told him that 'the main remains of the German Army were still back somewhere in the neighbourhood of the Somme'. Anthony added this information as a postscript, which he crossed out once LINNET was cancelled.

believed that the parachute wouldn't open or that I should be injured in landing. The apprehension was all connected with the test of will-power involved in jumping out of the aircraft. Also, I was jumping last, which increased the chances of having to watch some demoralising hesitation or technical hitch. Of course, there shouldn't be either, but there might be. And how doubly maddening to break your back or be sniped in the air at this stage of the war.

Such notions made recurrent darts across my mind. The prospect of doing something horribly unnatural in the morning produced a tendency to linger over the normal routine of going to bed, so that the intervening hours would last as long as possible, so that the inevitable despairs of the early morning could be postponed and camouflaged.

All of which led up to a knock on the door shortly after 11 p.m. and the Corporal storeman bending down by my sleeping bag to say that the operation had been postponed thirty-six hours. I was not really surprised. I was not really anything.

There was another plan the next day, another briefing, then a final scrubbing of that particular interlude. There was no doubt about it – we were doing far too well in France and Belgium.

Monday was declared a holiday, or shall we say a half-holiday because no one was particularly festive. At about 11 a.m. the BBC programme was interrupted with an announcement that Brussels had fallen. Brigade prayers for the temporary recovery of the German Army continued. After lunch we went to the movies, came back and listened to records of Frank Sinatra, who enjoyed a considerable following among the Brigade staff. Some went off to town, others fell asleep with the unhealthy fatigue of Boxing Day.

Nothing happened on Tuesday. After lunch we went to the movies again, this constituting the first time the Brigadier had been to the pictures two days running. Conversation at teatime was depressed. Tomorrow it would be three months since D-Day. Self-pity reigned. Most people had seen all the movies. They didn't want to read, get drunk, write letters or play bridge. They had packed and unpacked their kit, cleaned their weapons, and even slept too often to want to do so any more.

However, the six o'clock news did say that the German resistance was stiffening. The firmer resistance of the Germans was repeated at nine o'clock and a wave of enthusiasm swept over the Mess. As an expression of rising morale, most of them joined in a thunderflash battle in the garden.

The days passed. The operation was postponed, modified, amended and postponed again. The field cashier brought us French francs, Belgian francs, Dutch guilders and finally German marks. Friday came and we drew our chutes again in the afternoon. It had been an unpromising morning, raining hard, and with a culminating signal from Command that all previous correspondence from Command in connection with the Command Athletic Championships was now cancelled.

At tea the weather cleared a bit. The gentleman on the wireless said that if we were to visit a Northumbrian barn dance we should be astonished at the gaiety of it all. The operation was still uncertain, but the Brigadier said that he felt we were going and others expressed a hunch to the same effect. Practical details came in.

'Twenty minutes warning, four minutes red and then off,' was agreed.

'When are you jumping, Bernard?'

'Number one.'

'Difficulty with number one is to know whether to jump or not when you're on the wrong DZ.'

'You jump on the green light,' said the Brigadier firmly.

It began to look as if we were indeed going to jump on the green light. The discontents and frustrations were subtly replaced by the apprehensions of anticipation. Dinner was at 7 p.m. and most people went to bed immediately afterwards. We were told that in the event of a cancellation we should know by midnight. The authorities were better than their word. It was 11.30 p.m. when I was woken to be told that bad weather had caused a 24-hour postponement.

I had now been exactly a week with the Brigade. The seventh day we rested, but feeling progressively more nervy. Towards evening on the eighth day, by one of those odd twists of the human nerve barometer, everyone was unusually gay and almost foolishly confident.

The weather was good and the news gave no signs that advances on the ground would make our landing superfluous. The job itself was attractively spectacular.[12] 'Nothing can save us now,' said the Brigadier, and everyone laughed excitedly.

All the same it wasn't long after dinner when the telephone rang to announce a 24 hour, or perhaps a 48 hour, postponement. For a novel reason, however: not because the ground forces were advancing too fast. This time they were not advancing fast enough.

'Another day or two, and we'll all be bats,' said the Brigadier, on edge with frustration.

'There's a hoodoo on this Brigade, you know,' said Marquand.

'You're absolutely right,' said Byng-Maddick furiously.

They settled down to play bridge and their irritability was further fed by discovering that the mess staff had been playing with the cards and had made them filthy in the process.

'I wish to God we could ring up home,' said Briggs.

'What is it today?'

'Frankly, I've lost count.'

'I'd have bet anything this was the day,' said Byng-Maddick.

'Good thing we didn't go last night. With this counter-attack we'd have had it properly,' said the Brigadier.

'We'll have to unload the gliders,' said the Intelligence Officer. 'They've been loaded

---

12 'Attractively spectacular' – this was OPERATION COMET, which involved the capture of the road bridge at Arnhem but none of the other ambitious objectives of MARKET GARDEN.

a week. They'll fall apart.'

'Thank God I haven't shaved.'

'My laundry won't stand it,' said Byng-Maddick (nearly all their kit had been sent overseas in advance). 'You know what we'll have next. People coming up from 6th Div. giving us lectures on how to do it.'[13] He picked up a chair, which promptly fell apart.

'Even the bottom falls out of the bloody chair. Next thing'll be route marches again.'

'Send them on a route march tomorrow,' said the Brigadier, coming back into the room. 'Oh no, I suppose we can't.'

'Trouble is these 24 hour postponements. Never time to do anything' said Hibbert.

On Saturday morning the Brigadier took me for a long walk in the grounds of the local big house. I asked him whether he didn't find the prospect of responsibility for the lives of his Brigade in battle a horrifying one.

He said he was still appalled by the thought of having to make quick decisions in battle, but he wasn't worried when it came to the actual making of them. He also suffered from a sense of oppression and 'Oh-my-God' when summoned to Divisional HQ and told to plan an operation in a few hours. I asked just how much of the plan he had to make himself. He said that in this case the General had given him the Brigade role and left the rest to him.[14] Then the General had flown up the next day to ask him what he meant to do. He, in his turn, had given the three battalion commanders their general roles and not bothered them with guidance which they were all too experienced to need.[15]

All he had done in the way of criticism had been to point out a minor road from an airfield which one of the COs had ignored and suggest that they put an outpost on it. He threw a passing bouquet to his Brigade staff who reduced his work a tremendous amount, he said, by not being afraid to take decisions, and also by being experienced enough to make the right ones.

The cancellation for that day was unique in that it came in the early evening.

'It really is purgatory, this hanging about,' said Byng-Maddick.

'You realise that we've been on thirty-six hours' notice for getting on for a month?' asked Hibbert.

'Signal exercise, that'll be the next thing,' said Byng-Maddick.

'That's the 19th time we've been within hours of getting on the planes,' Hibbert went on bitterly. 'You realise that no one's the slightest sympathy with us. You get no marks for

---

13   '6th Div.' – meaning 6th Airborne Division, who had landed in France on D-Day.

14   The General – Major-General Roy Urquhart.

15   'The three battalion commanders' – Lieutenant-Colonels Dobie, Frost and Fitch. John Frost of 2nd Battalion would be the commanding officer at Arnhem bridge.

mental strain.'

'You got any aspirins, David?' Hibbert asked the doctor.[16]

'Hundreds of them, in serried rows.'

'Bloody awful, trying to kill time,' said Hibbert.

That was Saturday, 9 September. Actually we took off on 17 September, the DZ being in Southern Holland.

NOTE BY ERNEST WATKINS

This article was completed by Major Cotterell during his attachment to 1 Airborne Division and while waiting for the start of the operation. The operation turned out to be the Battle of Arnhem. No news has been received of Major Cotterell since 17 Sept 1944.

---

16   The doctor was the Medical Officer David Wright.

APPENDIX

Military Abbreviations

AA – Anti-aircraft

Ack-Ack – wartime name for the AA

ARV – Armoured Recovery Vehicle

ATS – Auxiliary Territorial Service, the women's branch of the British Army

BEF – British Expeditionary Force

CMP – Corps of Military Police

CO – Commanding Officer

H.E. – High Explosive

CSM – Company Sergeant-Major

LAV – Landing Armoured Vehicle

LCA – Landing Craft Assault

LCM – Landing Craft Mechanised

LCT – Landing Craft Tank

LSI – Landing Ship Infantry

MO – Medical Officer

NCO – non-commissioned officer

OC – Officer Commanding

OR – Other Ranks

RAMC – Royal Army Medical Corps

RASC – Royal Army Service Corps

RE – Royal Engineers

REME – Royal Electrical and Mechanical Engineers

RNVR – Royal Naval Volunteer Reserve

SP – Self-propelled

TAC HQ – Tactical Headquarters

WAAF – Women's Auxiliary Air Force

WVS – Women's Voluntary Service

Anthony Cotterell Works Used in the Book

BOOKS

An Apple for the Sergeant (Hutchinson and Co., London, 1944).

Oh! It's Nice to Be in the Army! (Victor Gollancz, London, 1941).

RAMC, An authoritative account prepared with the assistance of the Army Medical Department of the War Office and the RAMC (Hutchinson, London, 1943).

What! No Morning Tea? (Victor Gollanz, London, 1941).

MISCELLANEOUS ARTICLES OR FICTION

'And What Did They See?', *WAR*, issue 36, 23 January 1943.

'The Sergeant's High Jump', *OFF PARADE*, 15 January 1944.

D-DAY - TYPESCRIPTS AND ARTICLES

Diary typescript, no title, unnumbered pages, running from 20 May to 5 June 1944.

'Sitting on the Fence', *WAR*, issue 73, 24 June 1944. Material overlaps with the diary, but gives more detailed account of the marshalling camp and briefings.

'Is This the Way to the Second Front?', typescript, unnumbered pages. Longer version of 'Sitting on the Fence'.

'On a Steamer Going Over', begins 1 June and ends at 10 in the evening on 5 June. Based on diary with additional technical and briefing info. All capital letters typed on Naval Message paper. Abbreviated version appeared in Part 1 of *WAR* article below.

'A Day at the Seaside', *WAR*, issue 74, 8 July 1944:

Part 1: 'Going on Board' (based on diary and 'On a Steamer Going Over').

Part 2: 'Going on Shore' (original notes no longer extant).

NORMANDY - TYPESCRIPTS AND ARTICLES

With the tank crew:

Various typescript papers, without titles or numbers:-

Pages beginning: 'The Brigade landed on D-Day, with two of its Regiments supporting two of the assault infantry brigades of the 50th Division.'

Pages beginning: 'The problem now was to catch up with and join the Armoured Brigade.'

Pages beginning: 'Our progress was marked by a thick cloud of yellow dust.'

Pages beginning: 'I resolved to borrow at the earliest possible moment some form of goggles.'

Details of Sherman tank.

Pages beginning: 'The driver pointed to one of three graves by the side of a hedge.'

Pages beginning: 'I was only in one real battle.' Version of the Fontenay battle.

Pages beginning: 'The taking of Fontenay was typical of the early stages of the Normandy campaign.' Used as basis for *WAR* article below.

WAR Article, 'Tiger, Tiger, Burning Bright', issues 76 and 77, 19 August and 2 September 1944.

8 Armoured Brigade Group Operation Order No. 26, 24 June 1944 (Copy number 19, Anthony Cotterell code letter 'I').

ASSOCIATED PAPERS, FORMING INDIVIDUAL ESSAYS OR ARTICLES

Normandy typescript, unnumbered pages beginning: 'Down by the beaches where the minefields lay'.

Normandy typescript, unnumbered pages but with a title: 'An Operation was Performed'.

OTHER MANUSCRIPTS, TYPESCRIPTS AND ARTICLES

1941 Diary, typescript. (This includes the 'Defending the Realm' and Motor Contact Officer course, and other papers.)

1944, With 1st Parachute Brigade:

'Jumping to a Conclusion', handwritten and typed manuscript;

'Airborne Worries: Waiting to Be Scrubbed', *WAR*, issue 79, 14 October 1944.

BIBLIOGRAPHY

ABCA, WAR, & ERNEST WATKINS

Adam, Sir Ronald, 'A Farewell Message from the Adjutant-General', *WAR*, issue 97, 14 June 1945.

Army Film Unit, *The Story of the Army Bureau of Current Affairs*, black and white film (Ministry of Information, 1943), Imperial War Museum, London, ref: MGH.

Flavell, E.W.C., 'British Parachutists', *WAR*, issue 7, 13 December 1944.

Nicholson, Jenny, 'Fair Women and Brave Men', *WAR*, issue 82, 25 November 1944.

The ABCA Handbook, A Manual designed for the guidance of all officers in the conduct of talks and discussions on Current Affairs, Preface by the Secretary of State for War (ABCA, The War Office, August 1942).

The ABCA Song Book (ABCA, The War Office, 1944).

Ernest Watkins Papers, Special Collections, University Of Calgary, Accession Number: 469/90.9:

'ABCA I, Inception', file 6.1.

'It Is Dangerous to Lean Out' (incomplete draft), file 5.1–5.2.

'Out of My Wits', files 6.3.1–7.1.2.

Fragment inside novel *Irregardless*, file 3.4.

ARCHIVAL SOURCES

33 Netherlands War Crimes Commission papers, Dutch National Archives, The Hague, Netherlands.

Airborne Museum, Oosterbeek, Netherlands.

Army Personnel Centre, Historical Disclosures Section, Glasgow.

Commonwealth War Graves Commission.

National Archives, 619 Squadron Operations Record Book, AIR27/2131.

Robert Graves archive, The Library, St John's College, and St John's College Robert Graves Trust.

Robert Graves archive, the Poetry Collection, University at Buffalo, the State University of New York.

COTTERELL FAMILY ARCHIVES – ANTHONY COTTERELL

See also 'Anthony Cotterell Works Used in this Book'.
1941 Diary, handwritten.
1941 Diary, typescript.
1943 Parachute course, typescript.
Personal correspondence.
Normandy and D-Day papers.

COTTERELL, ANTHONY – PUBLISHED WRITINGS

Main Articles
'A Day at the Seaside: Going on Shore', *WAR*, issue 74, 8 July 1944.
'And What Did They See?', *WAR*, issue 36, 23 January 1943.
'A Sergeant in Tow', *WAR*, issue 72, 10 June 1944.
'Airborne Worries: Waiting to be Scrubbed', *WAR*, issue 79, 14 October 1944.
'Completely in the Air', *Horizon*, June 1944.
'Daylight Bombing', *WAR*, issue 54, 2 October 1943.
'Sitting on the Fence', *WAR*, issue 73, 24 June 1944.
'The Airborne Forces', *WAR*, issue 32, 28 November 1944.
'Tiger, Tiger, Burning Bright', *WAR*, issues 76 and 77, 19 August and 2 September 1944.
'The Sergeant's High Jump', *OFF PARADE*, 15 January 1944.

Books
An Apple for the Sergeant (Hutchinson and Co., London, 1944).
Oh! It's Nice to Be in the Army! (Victor Gollancz, London, 1941).
RAMC, An authoritative account prepared with the assistance of the Army Medical Department of the War Office and the RAMC (Hutchinson, London, 1943).
Roof Over Britain: the Official Story of the A.A. Defences, 1939–42 (The Ministry of Information, HM Stationery Office, London, 1943).
She Walks In Battledress (Christophers, London, 1942).
The Expert Way of Getting Married (T. Werner Laurie, London, 1939).
What! No Morning Tea? (Victor Gollancz, London, 1941).

INTERNET

Horrocks, Lieutenant-General B.G., *A Short History of the 8th Armoured Brigade*, foreword by Lieutenant-General B.G. Horrocks, 30 Corps, March 1946, Warlinks website: http://www.warlinks.com/armour/8th_armoured/index.php (last accessed 30 December 2012).
384th Bomb Group website: www.384thBombGroup.com/ (last accessed 30 December 2012).

NEWSPAPERS AND PERIODICALS

Mackenzie, S.P., 'Vox Populi: British Army Newspapers in the Second World War', *Journal of Contemporary History*, Vol. 24, No. 4 (Sage Publications Ltd, October 1989).
Redford, Duncan, 'The March 1943 Crisis in the Battle of the Atlantic: Myth and Reality', *History*, Vol. 92, No. 305 (2007).

OTHER SOURCES

Alanbrooke, Field Marshal Lord, *War Diaries, 1939–45* (Weidenfeld and Nicolson, London, 2001).

Allen, R., with co-operation from Frost, John, *Voice of Britain, The Inside Story of the Daily Express* (Patrick Stephens, Cambridge, 1983).

Anon, *Instructions for British Servicemen in France 1944* (Bodleian Library, University of Oxford, 2005).

Carstairs, John Paddy, *Hadn't We the Gaiety?* (Hurst and Blackett, 1945).

Chorley, W.R., *Royal Air Force Bomber Command Losses of the Second World War*, Vol. 4: *1943* (Midland Publishing, Hinckley, 2007).

Christiansen, Arthur, *Headlines All my Life* (Heinemann, London, 1961).

Crang, Jeremy A., *The British Army and the People's War, 1939–1945* (Manchester University Press, 2000).

Deane-Drummond, Anthony, *Return Ticket* (Collins, London, 1953).

Grant, Ian, *Cameramen at War*, (Patrick Stephens, Cambridge, 1980).

Gray, Jennie, *Fire By Night, The Dramatic Story of One Pathfinder Crew and Black Thursday, 16/17 December 1943* (Grub Street, London, 2011).

——, *Major Cotterell and Arnhem: a War Crime and a Mystery* (Spellmount, Stroud, 2012).

Grove, Eric J., *The Royal Navy since 1815* (Palgrave Macmillan, London, 2005).

Harrison, Mark, *Medicine and Victory: British Military Medicine in the Second World War* (Oxford University Press, Oxford, 2004).

Hawking, Desmond (ed.), *War Report, D-Day to VE-Day, Dispatches by the BBC's War Correspondents with the Allied Expeditionary Force 6 June 1944–5 May 1945* (BBC, London, 1985).

Hawkins, T.H., and Brimble, L.J.F., *Adult Education, The Record of the British Army* (Macmillan and Co, London, 1947).

Horne, Alistair, with Montgomery, David, *The Lonely Leader: Montgomery 1944–45* (Pan Books, London, 1995).

Latawski, Paul, *Battle Zone Normandy: Falaise Pocket* (Sutton Publishing, Stroud, 2004).

MacKenzie, S.P., *Politics and Military Morale* (Oxford University Press, 1992).

Middlebrook, Martin, and Everitt, Chris (eds.), *The Bomber Command War Diaries* (Penguin, London, 1990).

Moorehead, Alan, *A Late Education, Episodes in a Life* (Hamish Hamilton, London, 1970).

Rose, Norman, *Vansittart, Study of a Diplomat* (Heinemann, London, 1978).

Vansittart, Lord Robert, *Black Record: Germans Past and Present* (Hamish Hamilton, London, 1941).

——*Lessons of My Life* (Hutchinson & Co,. London, 1943).

Watts, Stephen, *Moonlight on a Lake in Bond Street* (The Bodley Head, London, 1961).

Wilson, Alyson, *St Michael's, Chester Square*, Church History and Guide.

ACKNOWLEDGEMENTS

This book is the twin, so to speak, of my 2012 biography of Anthony, *Major Cotterell at Arnhem, a War Crime and a Mystery*. The research for the biography provided the framework for this edited edition of Anthony's writings, and the full acknowledgements, bibliography and sources for both volumes can be found in *Major Cotterell at Arnhem*.

I would like, however, to acknowledge here the additional help given by Anthony's cousins Rosemary McGrath and Robert Crews in the attempt to positively identify Anthony as being the man standing to the right of Stanley Maxted in the AFPU footage taken immediately prior to Arnhem (see photographic section). Although no documentary evidence has been found, it is extremely likely that this was indeed Anthony. His presence in the AFPU footage was first spotted by Andrew Reeds in his own research on the Arnhem PR coverage, and I thank Andrew for generously sharing his observation.

INDEX